Eroticizing Aesthetics

Global Aesthetic Research

Series Editor: Joseph J. Tanke, Associate Professor, Department of Philosophy, University of Hawaii

The Global Aesthetic Research series publishes cutting-edge research in the field of aesthetics. It contains books that explore the principles at work in our encounters with art and nature that interrogate the foundations of artistic, literary and cultural criticism and that articulate the theory of the discipline's central concepts.

Titles in the Series

Early Modern Aesthetics, J. Colin McQuillan
Foucault on the Arts and Letters: Perspectives for the 21st Century, Catherine M. Soussloff
Architectural and Urban Reflections after Deleuze and Guattari, edited by Constantin V. Boundas and Vana Tentokali
Living Off Landscape: Or the Unthought-Of in Reason, Francois Jullien, translated by Pedro Rodriguez
Between Nature and Culture: The Aesthetics of Modified Environments, Emily Brady, Isis Brook and Jonathan Prior
Reviewing the Past: The Presence of Ruins, Zoltán Somhegyi
François Jullien's Unexceptional Thought: A Critical Introduction, Arne De Boever
Figural Space: Semiotics and the Aesthetic Imaginary, William D. Melaney
Eroticizing Aesthetics: In the Real with Bataille and Lacan, Tim Themi

Eroticizing Aesthetics

In the Real with Bataille and Lacan

Tim Themi

ROWMAN & LITTLEFIELD
Lanham • Boulder • New York • London

Published by Rowman & Littlefield
An imprint of The Rowman & Littlefield Publishing Group, Inc.
4501 Forbes Boulevard, Suite 200, Lanham, Maryland 20706
www.rowman.com

6 Tinworth Street, London SE11 5AL, United Kingdom

Selection, Editorial Matter, Introduction, Chapter 3, Chapter 6 and Conclusion Copyright © 2021 by Tim Themi.

This volume contains revised versions of the following publications and are reproduced with permission:
Themi, Tim. "Bataille and the Erotics of the Real." *Parrhesia: A Journal of Critical Philosophy* 24 (2015): 312-35.
Themi, Tim. "Lacan, Barthes, Bataille, and the Meaning of the Eye—or Gaze." *The Undecidable Unconscious: A Journal of Deconstruction and Psychoanalysis* 3 (2016): 93-123. University of Nebraska Press.
Themi, Tim. "Nietzsche's Relation with Psychoanalysis: From Freud to Surrealist Modernism, Bataille and Lacan." In *Understanding Nietzsche, Understanding Modernism*, edited by Brian Pines and Douglas Burnham, 189–207. London: Bloomsbury, 2019.
Themi, Tim. "Bataille, Literature, Happiness, and Evil." *Continental Thought and Theory: A Journal of Intellectual Freedom* 2-3 (2019): 180-201.

All rights reserved. No part of this book may be reproduced in any form or by any electronic or mechanical means, including information storage and retrieval systems, without written permission from the publisher, except by a reviewer who may quote passages in a review.

British Library Cataloguing in Publication Information Available

ISBN: HB 978-1-5381-4782-5

Library of Congress Cataloguing-in-Publication Data

Names: Themi, Tim, 1975-, author.
Title: Eroticizing aesthetics : in the real with Bataille and Lacan / Tim Themi.
Description: Lanham, Maryland : Rowman & Littlefield, [2021] | Series: Global aesthetic research | Includes bibliographical references and index.
Identifiers: LCCN 2021005560 (print) | LCCN 2021005561 (ebook) |
  ISBN 9781538147825 | ISBN 9781538147849 (paperback) |
  ISBN 9781538147832 (epub)
Subjects: LCSH: Love. | Erotica. | Aesthetics. | Bataille, Georges, 1897–1962. | Lacan, Jacques, 1901–1981. | Nietzsche, Friedrich Wilhelm, 1844–1900.
Classification: LCC BH301.L65 T44 2021 (print) | LCC BH301.L65 (ebook) | DDC 111/.85—dc23
LC record available at https://lccn.loc.gov/2021005560
LC ebook record available at https://lccn.loc.gov/2021005561

Dedication

For Laure...

O Persephone, you nourish all,
Always, and kill them, too.

HYMN TO PERSEPHONE

Contents

Acknowledgements ix

Abbreviations xi

Introduction 1

1 Bataille, Nietzsche, Lacan, and the *Real* of Erotics 15
   1.1 Palaeolithic Transition from Animal to Human 16
   1.2 Death of Tragedy from Socrates' Incompetence 20
   1.3 Taboo on Transgression from Yahweh's Ignorance 26
   1.4 Capitalism's Curious Service of Goods 32

2 Metaphorizing the Split Gaze of Bataille's Story of *Eye* 47
   2.1 Surface Formalism: Metonymic Cross-cuts of Metaphoric Chains 48
   2.2 Depth Contents: The Violence of the Eye's Transgression 54
   2.3 Sade's Sovereign Man: The Rape of Priest's Eye by the Gaze 59

3 Bataille, Nietzsche, Lacan, and the *Real* of Aesthetics 75
   3.1 Dissident Surrealism: Bataille's *Documents* Critique of Aesthetics 76
   3.2 Lascaux Caves: Divine Animality as the Originary *Real* of Aesthetics 81
   3.3 The *Accursed* Sovereignty of Art, and Nietzsche 88

4 Nietzsche's Affirming Psychoanalysis in Freud, Surrealist Modernism, Bataille, and Lacan 97
   4.1 Germanophone Context: Nietzsche and Freud 98

	4.2	Francophone Context: Bataille, Surrealism, Modernism, Lacan	106
	4.3	Dionysian Context: Presence of Myth in Absence	113
5		From Dionysos to Devil: Bataille's Evil Happiness of Literature	125
	5.1	Literature's Quest for Happiness of the Erotic	126
	5.2	Literature as Condescension of Desire to Evil	130
	5.3	Poetry's Force of Sovereignty from the Rut of Literature	134
	5.4	Art and Politics: Separate Connection of the Imaginary and Symbolic in the Real	140
6		Eternal Returns: Erotic Politics in Bataille's *Blue of Noon*	149
	6.1	Superficial Socialisms – The Case of Lazare	150
	6.2	Superficial Surrealisms – The Case of Xenie	154
	6.3	Libidinal Demands for Death – The Return of Dirty *Doro-thea*	159
	6.4	Split-Subjects of Political Economy – Left, Right, Left . . .	163

Conclusion   173

Bibliography   187

Index   203

About the Author   217

Acknowledgements

An earlier version of chapter 1 appeared as "Bataille and the Erotics of the Real," *Parrhesia: A Journal of Critical Philosophy* 24 (2015): 312–35; chapter 2 as "Lacan, Barthes, Bataille, and the Meaning of the Eye— or Gaze," *The Undecidable Unconscious: A Journal of Deconstruction and Psychoanalysis* 3 (2016): 93–123 (University of Nebraska Press); chapter 4 as "Nietzsche's Relation with Psychoanalysis: From Freud to Surrealist Modernism, Bataille and Lacan," in *Understanding Nietzsche, Understanding Modernism* (Bloomsbury 2019); and chapter 5 as "Bataille, Literature, Happiness, and Evil," *Continental Thought and Theory: A Journal of Intellectual Freedom* 2–3 (2019): 180–201. These have been further reworked into a sequential whole for the present book, and I would like to thank all the editors and reviewers involved, in particular Jared Russell from the Institute of Psychoanalytic Training and Research, New York. I must also acknowledge Dr Alison Horbury from the School of Culture and Communication at The University of Melbourne.

Abbreviations

The works of Georges Bataille:
Ab = *L'Abbé C*
AN = "Autobiographical Note"
AS = *The Accursed Share*
BN = *Blue of Noon*
CH = *Cradle of Humanity*
E = *Eroticism*
G = *Guilty*
IE = *Inner Experience*
L = *Lascaux; or, the Birth of Art*
LE = *Literature and Evil*
M = *Madame Edwarda*
ON = *On Nietzsche*
SE = *Story of the Eye*
TE = *The Tears of Eros*
TR = *Theory of Religion*
US = *Unfinished System of Non-Knowledge*
VE = *Visions of Excess*
WS = *Writings on Surrealism/The Absence of Myth*

The works of Friedrich Nietzsche:
AC = *The Antichrist*
BGE = *Beyond Good and Evil*
BT = *The Birth of Tragedy*
EH = *Ecce Homo*
GM = *On the Genealogy of Morals*
GS = *The Gay Science*

TI = *Twilight of the Idols*
WP = *The Will to Power*
Z = *Thus Spoke Zarathustra*

The works of Jacques Lacan:
S = *The Seminar of Jacques Lacan*
Éc = *Écrits: The First Complete Edition in English*

The works of Sigmund Freud:
SE = *The Standard Edition of the Complete Psychological Works of Sigmund Freud*

Introduction

In 1957 and nearing the end of his oeuvre, Bataille puts together the book *Eroticism,* alternatively titled *Death and Sensuality: A Study of Eroticism and the Taboo*, which serves nigh as the definitive illumination of his life's philosophical work.[1] All the threads of the past three decades of toil seem to come together here, spun through the portal of the erotic Bataille stakes finally as the 'standpoint that brings out the fundamental unity of the human spirit' (E, 8). Acknowledging in this that he is in a sense 'to follow a path where others have trodden before' (E, 7), a Freudo-Nietzschean trace discerns itself in the stressing of a sexuality linked in a paradoxical erotics with loss, dissolution in a continuity of becoming, and an awareness of death – of proclaiming Nietzsche's 'Yes to life' (TI X, 4; EH III-I, 3), and 'assenting' to it, Bataille exalts, even 'to the point of death' (E, 11). But this is also what Bataille's contemporary in Lacan of the expressly Freudian field would call 'the *jouissance* [enjoyment] of transgression' (SVII, 195), two years later in his 1959–60 *Seminar VII* on *The Ethics of Psychoanalysis*. It constitutes the most *direct* satisfaction of the drives, which, in going beyond our usual pleasure principles – restricted by 'reality' with taboos and prohibitions – hearkens back through Bataille to both the death-drive in Freud and the Dionysian affirmation of Nietzsche that emerged from his study of *pre*-Platonic Greece.[2]

This book positions such work of Lacan with Nietzsche and Freud as a backdrop from which to illuminate Bataille's erotic interventions into the history of Western thought – where by detailing the often strikingly similar insights and concerns these figures share, it will be possible to reflect back on Lacan, Nietzsche, and Freud in a new Bataillean light. What may be new in this is that while it is generally known from Bataille's 1958 'Autobiographical Note' that 1923 was when he experienced Nietzsche as 'decisive' (AN,

106), this was also the year he began reading Freud, which Stuart Kendall records as beginning with the *Introductory Lectures on Psychoanalysis* first 'published in France in the previous year'. Further to this is that after his own analysis with Adrien Borel in 1927, one of the first French analysts and founders of the Freud affiliated Paris Psychoanalytic Society, Bataille read Freud's *Totem and Taboo* 'repeatedly' as key for his bourgeoning interest in 'cultural or anthropological analysis' – while in 1932 he read the *Interpretation of Dreams*, having in 1931 also considered translating Freud's essay on Dostoevsky with André Breton's 'soon-to-be-ex-wife'.[3]

As Bataille himself acknowledges in his 1961 Madeleine Chapsal interview a year before his death, without the analysis with Borel he never would have felt 'viable' enough health wise to actually write, having felt by it 'profoundly moved' and 'completely released'.[4] But despite such clinical significance, Dennis Hollier will also mark Bataille's preference for Freud's texts on 'collective psychology', such as *Group Psychology and the Analysis of the Ego* and *Totem and Taboo*, along with those 'commonly rejected as being speculative' such as *Beyond the Pleasure Principle*, where the death-drive as a traumatic repetition beyond usual pleasures – towards a possible mastery, even in death – was disclosed.[5] Benjamin Noys additionally observes how Lacan's notion of *jouissance*, a 'shattering enjoyment that is "beyond the pleasure principle"', drew on Bataille's connecting of violence with sexuality and even suggests 'Bataille's contribution to Lacan's thought was erased' – a point perhaps echoed by Carolyn Dean who concluded 'Lacan is perhaps closer to Bataille than we realize', and Patrick ffrench who considers Bataille's 'connections' with Lacan to be so 'overwhelming' as to merit 'extensive consideration elsewhere'.[6]

Part of what is new about the present book is that it is this *elsewhere*, in seeking to carefully coordinate such connections between Bataille and Lacan to see how they shed light on each other, corroborate each other, but also address potential lacks and build on each other. This will ultimately draw on the Freud who was Lacan's major reference and the Nietzsche who was not only Bataille's but also anticipated key findings in psychoanalysis, which Freud himself acknowledged was 'in the many instances'.[7] Thus, while in the 2014 *Lacan's Ethics and Nietzsche's Critique of Platonism*, I brought Lacan and Nietzsche into proximity in this way via Freud – and in their shared critique of the Sovereign Good of Christian-Platonic metaphysics so as to *rethink* the foundations of Western Ethics[8] – the present work extends this procedure in a new but cognate direction with the distinctive thought of Bataille.

Bataille was the stellar underground figure of interwar Paris – founder of the initial inspiration of French Nietzscheanism with the secret society and journal of *Acéphale* (headless), while also linked through familial connections to Lacan, the 'French Freud'.[9] Bataille's work can even be viewed as a unique synthesis of the Dionysian wisdom of Nietzsche's philosophy and the growing awareness of the sexual real made possible by the pioneering works of Freud. Elisabeth Roudinesco, for instance, locates Bataille as 'one of the first French Nietzscheans', who, along with being one of the first interwar writers with 'experience of the analyst's couch', was 'a great reader of Freud', of his group psychology, and notion of 'death instinct'. She also marks how Bataille's notion of heterology, as a science of the radically heterogeneous Other, influenced Lacan's notion of *the real* as 'impossible', 'doomed', 'irrecoverable', or 'unassimilable' to consciousness, with psychoanalysis now conceived as a science of such a real. All of this is what occurs, moreover, through a 'long, subterranean friendship' which included Lacan remarrying Bataille's first wife, the actress Sylvia Maklès/Bataille – raising their daughter along with his own who later married the Jacques-Allain Miller that would eventually take the reins of Lacan's Seminar and School.[10]

When it comes to his connection to Nietzsche, Bataille had the sense he was all but sole heir. In his 1945 *On Nietzsche* he cries: 'my company on earth is mostly Nietzsche', 'the only one to support me: he says *we*'; 'there are so few of us!' (ON, 3, 9) – while in his three volumed *The Accursed Share* (1946–53), the second of which is an earlier unpublished version of *Eroticism*, he adds: 'I am the only one who thinks of himself not as a commentator of Nietzsche but as being the same as he', 'placed under the same conditions', 'to rediscover lost sovereignty', 'in which *The Accursed Share* [La Part Maudite] perceives a basis for starting anew' (AS III, 367). Bataille's aim here in invoking Nietzsche will be '*to lift the curse that this title calls into question*' (AS I, 9) – the curse on that *part*-we-share with other mammals in the rest of nature – to overcome the hyper-negation that consigns the original religious eroticism of the Hellenic Dionysos to the Hebraic Christian-Platonic Devil. But this is a burden the present work will show that Freudo-Lacanian analysis can also help to bear.

Upon his death in 1962, the journal *Critique* Bataille founded after the war released a special issue in his honour with articles by those such as Barthes, Sollers, and Foucault. But Bataille had not only influenced such post/structuralist figures – who often used Nietzsche as a referent – he also brought psychoanalysis to bear on the intellectual milieu he shared with Lacan.[11] Thus, when Lacan later complains in 1971 that his 'followers' were reading Bataille so as to claim a 'non-knowledge' at the price, perhaps, of *psychoanalytic* knowledge, it is not the case that this should apply to Bataille himself – which Lacan affirms in saying of Bataille that while 'non-knowledge is perhaps lying around in two or three spots in his writings', 'goodness knows he didn't have a field day with it'.[12] Even Hollier had marked Bataille's use of psychoanalysis to *inveigh* against those who sought escape from 'sexual drives' and 'perverse desire' by some 'idealist plot', or 'disguise of symptomatic transpositions', that are 'occasioned by repression' – especially those *artists* and surrealists 'selling complexes' replete with mystifications while claiming to incorporate psychoanalysis themselves.[13] On the basis of such of Bataille's concerns, then, and considering his many commentaries on works of art, this book will come to explore his interventions into *aesthetics* in particular, and his linking of it – *as an ethics* – to the inscription of an erotics around a psychoanalytic real.

Linkages between an ethics, erotics, aesthetics, *and the real,* can thus be posed here in an introductory way that bears on what Bataille shares with the works of the Nietzsche, Freud, and Lacan that will be brought in to help grasp his thought in key relevant moments. For aesthetics invokes the *bodily* senses, as its etymology implies (αἴσθησις, αἰσθητικός)[14] – which can impact on our sensual or erogenous zones through what Nietzsche saw as our *animal* physiology, and strike us with an erotic hue. This depends on how much of this oft-prohibited realm we can bear to acknowledge in the moment, where the part we typically censor out is the heterogeneous real. Such a real, however, can never be willed away for long, for it is implacably *real* as this term favoured by Lacan and also used by Bataille suggests. Hence it *returns*, after repression, displaced in some kind of imaginarized projection or metaphorizing form – where the privileged place for this is in the realm of aesthetics, where the creative imaginary is celebrated and expressly on show.

To further articulate, then, the significance of such relations between aesthetics, erotics, and the real, this book will introduce Bataille's definitive philosophical texts and examine them alongside his commentaries on various artistic works – including his own – from dissident surrealism to the animal cave paintings of Lascaux. The aim will eventually become to extract a criterion for aesthetics that can serve as an ethics, based on Bataille's many fascinating oeuvres as both a creative artist and a rigorous scholar. But what again may be particularly novel to the reader is how fruitfully Bataille's later genealogy of *Eroticism* of 1957 can frame such of his earlier interventions into aesthetics, across his previous three decades of work – and how Freudo-Nietzsche-Lacanian notions can shine much light on this in a way that even enables Bataille's own distinct findings to reflect back on such of his esteemed predecessors and contemporaries in most revealing ways.

Chapter 1 begins with an exploration of the anthropological taboo–transgression relation meticulously outlined in Bataille's culminating works, where taboos placed on our bodily animal aspect at some point give way to a *transgression* that reunites us erotically with what was lost in the real. It documents our shifting structures of what Lacan calls *jouissance*, the enjoyment of transgression, through four historical epochs: the initial Palaeolithic transition from animal to human; the flourishing of the archaic-classical Greek; and the eventual condescension of the Christian and the Modern. It also enumerates some of the consequences of these mutations for an ethics and aesthetics, and looks at Nietzsche's specific intervention into Greek Tragedy as uncovering a Socratic turning point for the worse.

Primary texts discussed include Bataille's *Theory of Religion* (1948), *The Accursed Share Vols. I & II* (1949–52), *Eroticism* (1957), and *The Tears of Eros* (1961) – along with Nietzsche's *Birth of Tragedy* (1872) and Lacan's seminar on *The Ethics of Psychoanalysis* (1959–60). In this the chapter considers how Bataille's erotics of the real might contribute to both Lacan's ethics of psychoanalysis and the genealogy of morals disclosed by Nietzsche. Combining Bataille's taboo–transgression correlation with Lacan's analytic of the real, symbolic and imaginary, I trace a degenerating loss of the erotic function of religion, ethics, and the aesthetic through the Platonic, Christian, and Modern Science epochs that Nietzsche's revaluations of the Good also centre on. I suggest an ethics of the real – as a sublimated re-knowing of the unconscious desire configuring the underlying perversity of the drives – is best served by restoring something more of a living openness to the originary erotics observable in the culture of pre-Platonic Greeks. This is manifested most famously perhaps in their polymorphous libidinal structures, their stories of the gods *and* goddesses, and the ritual festivals of Dionysos to host the works of the greatest tragic poets.

With a framework of Bataille's thought now established, chapter 2 returns to his initial and most famous literary work: the 1928 erotic novella *Story of the Eye*. This is the text later discussed from a structuralist linguistics perspective by Barthes, but also from a psychoanalytic perspective by Bataille himself, making use of his sessions with the Borel he sought treatment from in the same period, discussing the imagery from his clinical couch. Lacan's own formal linguistic approach to analysis of the 1950s, along with Bataille's later writings on Sade, will also be used to try and frame the metaphorized violence of the text, particularly as it comes to be inflicted on the *eye* itself.

Readings discussed include Bataille's 'W.C. Preface to *Story of the Eye* from *Le Petit* (1943)', and the 'De Sade's Sovereign/Normal Man' chapters from *Eroticism* (1957) – along with Barthes' seminal 'Metaphor of the Eye (1963)' essay on *Story*, Lacan's 'Instance of the Letter in the Unconscious, or Reason Since Freud (1957)' article from the *Écrits*, and the parts on the distinction between 'the eye and the gaze' in Lacan's *Seminar XI* on *The Four Fundamental Concepts of Psychoanalysis* (1964). In this the chapter dissects the eye metaphor in Bataille's *Story* by combining Barthes' formal approach with Lacan's to flesh out the cross-cutting of metaphor and metonymy within. With this formal structure in place, I then wade deeper into the contents side of *Story*, to clarify the dark desire at play *beyond* what Barthes was able to imagine, through further engagement with Lacanian psychoanalysis and Bataille's later philosophical works on the erotic. Finally, I turn to Bataille's treatment of Sade's Sovereign and Normal Man in *Eroticism*, to suggest the violence of the *Eye* metaphorizes as it *argues for* a crossing of the bar of resistance towards the sexed *gaze* – in response to the particularly ossified taboos of Christianity on the fluidity of the *real*.

In terms of how ossification could affect even the psychoanalytic community, Lacan in his 1953 paper, 'The Function and Field of Speech and Language in Psychoanalysis', would bemoan a 'disappointing formalism that discourages initiative by penalizing risk', leading towards a 'docile prudence in which the authenticity of research is blunted even before it finally dries up' (Éc, 198). Shortly after this stunning rebuke, he asks in response to the same problem whether psychoanalysis, as 'a method based on truth and demystification of subjective camouflage', could itself 'apply its principles to its own corporation', so as to question creatively and reconsider the analysts' 'role in relation to the patient, their place in intellectual society, their relations with their peers, and their own educational mission' (Éc, 200). Such moments show how innovatively transgressive Lacan could be, even though, as the psychiatrically qualified clinician and founder of his own school and seminar, he will always seem to bear a more stoic sobriety next to the Bataille who was always more directly engaged with the arts – wherein he would confront the grounds, and *abgrunds*, of creativity itself.[15]

Heading, then, into the turn of the 1930s, chapter 3 explores Bataille's editorship of the art journal *Documents*, which seems to gather all the surrealists with whom surrealist founder Breton had fallen out. It examines Bataille's reputed transformation of the question of aesthetics from this highly polemical period, and seeks to contextualize its critique of the beauty ideal and high-low distinction in terms of his later captivation with the divine animality of Palaeolithic art. It also situates Bataille's critique of aesthetics in light of the earlier intervention into aesthetics made by his most acknowledged precursor in Nietzsche, whose life for Bataille increasingly goes on to attain an accursed sovereignty itself akin to a great work of art. Readings discussed include Bataille's 'Big Toe', 'Formless', 'Rotten Sun', 'Language of Flowers', and 'Base Materialism' articles from *Documents* (1929–31), along with his *On Nietzsche* (1945), *Accursed Share Vol III, Sovereignty* (1953), *Lascaux; or, the Birth of Art* (1955), and the more recent collection of his specialist lectures and articles on the pre-historic, *The Cradle of Humanity: Pre-historic Art and Culture* (2009).

Also discussed will be the 'Will to Power as Art' section of those of Nietzsche's notes posthumously collected in *The Will to Power*, a section which Heidegger devoted the whole first volume of his Nietzsche lectures to in the mid-1930s, thus indicating their importance.[16] Chapter 3 evaluates

Bataille's critique of 'aesthetics', 'beauty', and the boundary between 'high and low' by reference to Nietzsche's famous adsorption of all aesthetic dichotomies to the physiological distinction between *abundance* and *lack*. The aim will then become to incorporate Bataille's later focus on the Palaeolithic *birth* of art, deemed to coincide with the birth of humanity from animality through religious rituals of taboo-and-transgression, so as to clarify the role of aesthetics and erotics in this with kindred Lacanian concepts of sublimation and the real. In terms of raising earthly objects to the dignity of the real-Thing – as Lacan defines sublimation in his *Ethics* (SVII, 112) – finally I turn to Bataille's positioning of Nietzsche as the sovereign man of art to develop a criterion for aesthetics based on a *sovereignty* of the *real*, which I argue can be performed as an ethics of *jouissance* and transgression in a creatively well-guided, analytically attuned and dignified, restructuring manner.

After the war existentialism became Bataille's main object of concern, due to what he perceived was Sartre's reduction of art to a predetermined political purpose, along with his hostile review of Bataille's *Inner Experience* (1943) book during the occupation.[17] At the same time, and not unrelatedly, Bataille suddenly begins to make some positive appraisals about surrealism, which by then was a fading dominance in the wake of existentialism's rise, referring to himself as a kind of supporter as an 'old enemy *from within*' – with Breton in turn reciprocating the rejecting of past polemics for bearing on hasty misrecognition.[18]

Chapter 4, then, examines Bataille's positive reappraisal of surrealism after the war by linking its techniques of free-association both to Freudian psychoanalysis and a reopening primitivism that somehow instantiates the modernist concern for *the new*. But first it will discuss the prior influence of Nietzsche's philosophy on the founders of psychoanalysis themselves, namely Freud and his earliest collaborators east of the Rhine. For based on a crisis of Enlightenment faith in reason, Nietzsche and Freud had both exerted a profound influence on the cultural modernism of which Bataille, surrealism, and Lacan were later part. The aim will thence become to consider how Bataille's more definitive emphasis on Nietzsche's work enables a space for a more affirming psychoanalysis, flowing on to stabilize a more positive criterion for a new aesthetics in line with what Bataille calls being '*beyond but alongside surrealism*'.[19]

Readings discussed include Bataille's postwar articles 'On the Subject of Slumbers (1946)', 'The Absence of Myth (1947)', 'Notes on the Publishing of "Un Cadavre (1947–)"', 'Surrealism (1948)', 'The Surrealist Religion (1948)', 'Surrealism and God (1948)', 'Surrealism and How It Differs from Existentialism (1948)', and 'Surrealism from Day to Day (1951)' – along with Paul-Laurent Assoun's study of *Freud and Nietzsche* (1980). By tracing, then, the initial continuities *and* discontinuities between Nietzsche and

Freud forward to the French Nietzschean and French Freudian we mostly find respectively in Bataille and Lacan, chapter 4 discerns how the Nietzsche–Freud relation impacts the cultural modernism of which surrealism was a part, which Bataille was engaged in as a practitioner and a critic, with Lacan a witness to it all. Lastly I enumerate vis-à-vis the modernist spirit some of the consequences of the restored Nietzsche–Freud relation not just for a new aesthetics, but also for an ethics beneficial for psychoanalysis *and* philosophy – *and the arts* – which I argue can move us towards an ameliorated society built on a 'love of realities' in the sense of recognition *and* affirmation, to better navigate the straights of *jouissance*.

Chapter 5 now continues the exploration of aesthetics as the ethical space for an affirming erotics through Bataille's mature reflections on literature – many of them published in the journal *Critique* he edited after the war until his death. Bataille's final formulation of the taboo–transgression correlation, linked in literature to two very different promises of happiness and a complicity with evil – particularly in poetic literature – will be found here as central to his vision for the arts as a whole. Lacan's triad of the symbolic, imaginary, and the real will also be adopted to structure and clarify Bataille's paradoxical final aim to have art *separately included* in the world somehow as happily *heterogeneous*.

Readings discussed include Bataille articles 'André Masson (1946)', 'From the Stone Age to Jacques Prévert (1946)', 'Happiness, Eroticism, and Literature (1949)', 'René Char and the Force of Poetry (1953)', and the 'Emily Brontë' and 'William Blake' chapters of *Literature and Evil* (1957). Also discussed are Lacan's 1976 seminar *The Sinthome* on James Joyce, and Nietzsche's critique of Kant's notion of aesthetic 'disinterest' from the *Genealogy of Morals* (1887). Chapter 5 examines what programme Bataille's philosophy of art can offer in terms of future writings of artistic works, including the novel which he famously wrote himself. I begin with his 1949 'Happiness, Eroticism, and Literature' which posits literature as a quest for happiness, and compare this with his 1957 *Literature and Evil* which posits it rather as a quest for 'Evil'. Then I explore those of his writings that invoke poetry to break from the rut that befalls prose, so as to reach a more *immediate* experience. Finally, I turn to the need for separation Bataille posits between the poetic and the rational that must also somehow be a path between the two – whereupon I argue that a clarity of consciousness of these two distinct but related realms, which in Lacanian terms correspond to the distinction between the imaginary and the symbolic, can constitute Bataille's directive for future works: to help us *think* within the *real* of their *experience*.

With the increasing importance Bataille attached to the necessity for a separation of art and politics, the question arises as to how one might broach the topic of politics in a work of art, if it all, which Bataille actually did in his 1935 novel *Blue of Noon*. Politics was unavoidable at the time upon collapse of the bourgeois centre, with various forces arriving to secure the vacuum – leading Bataille to send a card to colleagues asking: 'What to do?/About Fascism/Given the insufficiency of Communism'.[20] Bataille's sense was that the Marxist project was foreclosing the very *jouissance*, both erotic and violent – usually the privileged domain of aesthetics – that the rising tide of fascism was able to exploit, rendering opposition impotent. His sustained attempts to mitigate this problem through three decades of work have renewed prescience for our today, with fascism inexplicably on the rise again, but perhaps the best place to begin to grasp this is *Blue of Noon*, which is not at all without an abundance of erotic truths. For as Bataille was to put it in a later 1957 forward, 'everyone depends on *stories*, on *novels*, to discover the manifold truth of life' – namely, those which 'have the power to confront a person with his fate'.[21] Chapter 6, then, will examine the erotic aspect of Bataille's political novel *Blue of Noon*, and treat it as a key locus for concerns about the rise of fascism and insufficiency of attempts to oppose it.

Readings discussed include Bataille's 'The Psychological Structure of Fascism (1933)', and *Vol I, Consumption* (1949) and *Vol III, Sovereignty* (1953) of *The Accursed Share* – along with Freud's 'The Tendency to Debasement in Love (1912)', *Group Psychology and the Analysis of the 'Ego'* (1921), and 'The Resistances to Psychoanalysis (1925)'. Chapter 6 deploys the striking genealogies of Bataille's postwar *Accursed Share* to ground such of his activist works as *Blue of Noon* of the 1930s, which could range from the scholarly and literary to the 'ferociously religious'.[22] I suggest his analysis of how the twin rivals of capitalism and communism both arose from the decline of the Monarchic reveals us caught in the same split-subject as before, in constant misrecognition of the true subjective nature of sovereignty. I argue this aspect of subjectivity is especially pertinent for us to reconsider with the return of fascism of today, which only more analytic consciousness of erotic truth – as manifested by the protagonists Dirty and Troppmann of *Blue of Noon* in their final confrontation with death – could ever help us mitigate in favour of reason.

The overarching goal of this book is to see how Bataille's understanding of a fundamental connection between aesthetics, erotics, and a heterogeneous real both emerges from and may be developed further with the cognate concerns of his principal philosophical reference in Nietzsche, and, more specifically, with the depth psychological elements of Nietzsche's thought extended in the libidinal direction by Freud and Bataille's contemporary Lacan. Its conclusions will suggest both Nietzsche and Lacanian analyses are central to sufficiently grounding Bataille's thought on topics ranging from ethics to erotics and aesthetics – especially on the necessary differences and connections between them and politics. I suggest Bataille's oeuvre itself is a superlative example of how one might conjoin and expand the philosophical and proto-psychoanalytic elements of Nietzsche's primary thought, and the necessities of doing so into the twenty-first century and beyond.

NOTES

1. Michael Richardson suggests *Eroticism* 'is perhaps the summation of his life's work'. Originally published as *L'Erotisme* in 1957 by Les Editions de Minuit (Paris), it was the first English edition that was published under *Death and Sensuality: A Study of Eroticism and the Taboo*, in 1962 by Walker and Company (New York), while the first City Lights edition in 1986 (San Francisco) went for *Erotism: Death and Sensuality*. Richardson, *Georges Bataille* (London: Routledge, 1994), 22.

2. Richard Boothby connects the Freudian death-drive to Nietzsche's Dionysos by reading the latter's twin Apollonian function as linked to the ego-imaginary register of Lacan, in dialectical opposition to the (Dionysian) real. See the 'From Schopenhauer to Nietzsche' section of Boothby, *Death and Desire: Psychoanalytic Theory in Lacan's Return to Freud* (New York: Routledge, 1991), 196–203.

3. Kendall, *Georges Bataille* (London: Reaktion, 2007), 50–1. Freud, *Introductory Lectures on Psychoanalysis* (1915–1917), in SE15 and SE16; *Totem and Taboo: Some Points of Agreement between the Mental Lives of Savages and Neurotics* (1913), in SE13, 1–162; *The Interpretation of Dreams* (1900), in SE4 and SE5; and "Dostoevsky and Parricide (1928)," in SE21, 175–96.

4. Richardson, ed., *George Bataille: Essential Writings* (London: SAGE, 1998), 221.

5. Denis Hollier, *Against Architecture: The Writings of Georges Bataille*, trans. B. Wing (Cambridge, MA: MIT), 108. Freud, *Group Psychology and the Analysis of the Ego* (1921), in SE18, 65–143; and *Beyond the Pleasure Principle* (1920), SE18, 16–7, 35–6, 38.

6. Noys's impression is that such erasure occurs because Lacan aims for a psychoanalytic institution of knowledge, which Bataille as the perennially heterogeneous figure, along with the matter of *jouissance* itself, seems to cut against – as the schisms of analytic schools, including Lacan's own, bear out. The erasure, of course, can cut both ways, where caught in the desire for heterogeneity Bataille scholarship may eschew affiliation with science and psychoanalytic knowledge. A recent collection, for example, features only two references to Lacan in the Index, with a missing third seeming to only touch without acknowledgment how I 'compare' or 'juxtapose' repression's return and taboo's transgression in the 2015 article 'Bataille and the Erotics of the Real', which expounds the genealogical significance and many profound connections in a detailed and substantial way. This article is an early version of what appears here in its definitive form as chapter 1. For a recent collection with no reference at all to Lacan in the Index, see also Mark Hewson and Marcus Coelen, eds., *Georges Bataille: Key Concepts* (London: Routledge, 2015). Noys, *Georges Bataille: A Critical Introduction* (London: Pluto, 2000), 3, 33. Dean, *The Self and Its Pleasures: Bataille, Lacan, and the History of the Decentered Subject*

(Ithaca: Cornell, 1992), 249. Ffrench, *After Bataille: Sacrifice, Exposure, Community* (London: Legenda, 2007), 8–9. Oxana Timofeeva, "'The Only Real Outlaws': Animal Freedom in Bataille," in *Georges Bataille and Contemporary Thought*, ed. W. Stronge (London: Bloomsbury, 2019), 159. Themi, "Bataille and the Erotics of the Real," *Parrhesia: A Journal of Critical Philosophy* 24 (2015): 314.

7. Freud, "On the History of the Psychoanalytic Movement (1914)," in SE14, 16.

8. Themi, *Lacan's Ethics and Nietzsche's Critique of Platonism* (Albany: SUNY Press, 2014).

9. Jared Russell notes how this was initially a pejorative by a populist French nationalist text of 1990, which also dubbed Foucault as 'The French Nietzsche', Derrida as 'The French Heidegger', and Bordieu as 'The French Marx'. See *Psychoanalysis and Deconstruction: Freud's Psychic Apparatus* (London: Routledge, 2020), 2.

10. For further documentation of Bataille's biographical links with Lacan and interwar influence as a reader of Freud with *experience* of the couch, see Roudinesco, *Jacques Lacan: Outline of a Life, History of a System of Thought*, trans. B. Bray (New York: Columbia University Press, 1997), 121, 131, 135–8, 280.

11. Foucault for instance notes: 'What gave me for the first time the desire of doing personal work was reading Nietzsche. I said earlier that I wondered why I had read Nietzsche. But I know very well. I read him because of Bataille'. Richardson, however, suggests Foucault's view of transgression detaches it from taboo and thus from what is *concrete* in 'Bataille's own approach', with those who made Bataille 'patron saint of post-structuralism' tending to follow suit. Hewson and Coelen also mark 'several critical studies' to show post-structuralism to not represent Bataille's 'real concerns', which come to the fore in 'sociology, ethnology, and history of religions'. For a study on the divergences and confluences between Lacan and Foucault, see Nadia Bou Ali, Rohit Goel, eds., *Lacan Contra Foucault: Subjectivity, Sex and Politics* (London: Bloomsbury, 2018). For a review of this that marks the absence of Foucault scholars along with the predominance of Sloveninan School Lacanians, and that 'only half of the chapters bear directly on the complex relationship between Foucault and Lacan', see Alex J. Feldman, *Notre Dame Philosophical Reviews: An Electronic Journal* (2019): (accessed July 14, 2020) https://ndpr.nd.edu/news/lacan-contra-foucault-subjectivity-sex-and-politics/. Foucault, "Structuralism and Post-Structuralism (1983)," trans. J. Harding, in *Aesthetics, Method, and Epistemology, Essential Works of Foucault, 1954–1984, Volume Two*, ed. J. Faubion (London: Penguin, 1998), 449. Richardson, *Georges Bataille*, 6–8, 135. Hewson and Coelen, "Introduction," in *Georges Bataille: Key Concepts*, 5.

12. Chris Vanderwees cites Colette Soler to suggest 'these followers gave privilege to castration' to the extent of 'idealization'; he also notes Lacan's pointing to an 'Aristotelian logic', of 'all that is not black is non-black', here at fault, as if there were not a whole *spectrum* to traverse in between when it comes to analytic discourse on what Lacan calls 'the palpable frontier between truth and knowledge'. This should be used to qualify Noys's claim that it is the privilege to castration that separates Lacan's notion of the real from Bataille's. Lacan, *Talking to Brick Walls: A Series of Presentations in the Chapel at the Sainte-Anne Hospital (1971-1972)*, trans. A.

R. Price (Cambridge: Polity Press, 2017), 9. Vanderwees, "Talking to Brick Walls," *Psychoanalytic Discourse* 4.1 (2019): 105. Soler, *Lacan: The Unconscious Reinvented*, trans. E. Faye, S. Schwartz (London: Karnac, 2014), 96. Noys, *Georges Bataille*, 31–2.

13. Hollier, *Against Architecture*, 108–12.

14. See entry αἰσθάνομαι in Henry G. Liddell and Robert Scott, *A Greek-English Lexicon: With a Revised Supplement* (Oxford: Clarendon Press, 1996), 42; also available at G. R. Crane, ed., *Perseus Digital Library*, (Medford: Tufts University, 2007), accessed April 30, 2020, http://www.perseus.tufts.edu/hopper/morph?l=ai%29sqanomai&la=greek#lexicon.

15. While Bataille's overt penchant for bordellos, group sex and swinging, orgies and intoxication also seems to widen his perceptible differences with Lacan, the latter also came to be known for his polyamory and marital 'infidelities', for leading a 'double life' in initially running two families concurrently, while later making mistresses of some of his 'training analysands or ordinary patients'. Further to this perceptible difference might be what Roudinesco notes is Miller's later interpretation of Lacan in a more formalizing way, perhaps culminating in the parapraxis of the Index Miller drew up for the *Écrits* in 1966 in which 'he left out the name of Georges Bataille, though of course he was mentioned in the text'. This is where Lacan links Schreber's *inner experience* that 'God is a whore' to Bataille's of the prostitute *Madame Edwarda*, suggesting that Bataille 'describes the odd extremity of this experience' (Éc, 485, 488). The omission is since corrected (Éc, 872). Catherine Millot, *Life with Lacan*, trans. A. Brown (Cambridge: Polity Press, 2018), 27–8, 92–3. Roudinesco, *Jacques Lacan*, 79, 180–1, 307, 387. See also Bataille, *Guilty*, 13; and *The Sacred Conspiracy: The Internal Papers of the Secret Society of Acéphale and Lectures to the College of Sociology*, eds., M. Galletti, A. Brotchie (London: Altas Press, 2017), 220, 249, 309, 347, 410.

16. The equiprimordial status of the sensuous and non-sensuous emerging from volume I of these Nietzsche lectures, overcoming both the 'deprecation of the sensuous as well as the extravagant elevation of the supersensuous' that characterized Platonism, is foregrounded in the earth-world dynamic of Heidegger's lecture-essay, 'The Origin of the Work of Art', from the same 1936 period. Heidegger, "Volume I: The Will to Power as Art," in *Nietzsche: Volumes One and Two*, trans. D. F. Krell (New York: HarperCollins, 1991), 209; and "The Origin of the Work of Art," in *Poetry, Language, Thought*, trans. A. Hofstadter (New York: Harper & Row, 1971), 15–87.

17. Bataille recalls that at the time he was 'far from alone in thinking that Sartre's attitude was tiresome', and that by falsely accusing him of conspiring against communism, Sartre had inadvertently 'reinforced the Communist position in the realm of literature' which Bataille in fact did 'not believe Sartre himself agrees'. See Bataille, "The Age of Revolt," in WS, 176. The article was originally published as a review of Albert Camus' *The Rebel* in *Critique* 55 (1951). More discussion of the Bataille-Sartre dispute can be found in Edward Greenwood, "Literature: Freedom or Evil? The Debate between Sartre and Bataille," *Sartre Studies International* 4.1 (1998): 17–29; and Françoise Meltzer, "On the Question of Aufhebung: Baudelaire, Bataille

and Sartre," *RCCS Annual Review: A Selection from the Portuguese Journal Revista Crítica de Ciências Sociais* 0 (2009): 110–24.

18. See Bataille, "On the Subject of Slumbers," in WS, 49; "Notes on the Publishing of 'Un Cadavre,'" in WS, 32; and "Surrealism from Day to Day," in WS, 41.

19. Bataille, "Method of Meditation," in US, 77.

20. Stuart Kendall, *Georges Bataille*, 124. Bataille et al., *L'Apprenti Sorcier: texts, letteres, documents, 1932-1939*, ed. M. Galletti (Paris: Editions de la Différence, 1999), 124.

21. Bataille, "Appendix: The Author's Foreword [1957]," in BN, 127.

22. Bataille, "The Sacred Conspiracy (1936)," in VE, 179.

Chapter 1

Bataille, Nietzsche, Lacan, and the *Real* of Erotics

> Language does not exist independently of the play of taboo and transgression. That is why if philosophy is to tackle all problems as a single whole it must start from an historical analysis of taboo and transgression.
>
> —Bataille, *Erotism/Death and Sensuality/A Study of Eroticism and the Taboo* (1957), 276

Bataille felt eroticism could count as the standpoint through which to grasp humanity as a whole, based on his understanding of how making a taboo of our sexual and aggressive aspects also gives them an erotic hue, generating then the desire to transgress even at the price of death. This is much in keeping with Lacan's notion of a 'tight bond between desire and the Law', where 'transgression in the direction of *jouissance* [enjoyment]' is actually 'supported by the oppositional principle' of the 'forms of the Law' (SVII, 177) – the transgression of which gives the most direct, immediate satisfaction of the drives by broaching what is usually elided from symbolic articulation, which he calls *the real*. As such, an ethics of psychoanalysis can be formed on the basis of recognizing such occluded realities, *in* the real, to delimit the harmful consequences that excessive unconsciousness of them can cause.

This chapter considers how the *erotics* of the real implicit in the taboo–transgression correlation definitively formulated in Bataille's 1957 *Eroticism* can augment the *ethics* of the real emerging from Lacan's clinic.[1] Assisting this is Lacan's proclamation in his 1959–60 *Seminar VII, The Ethics* of *Psychoanalysis*, that ethics must go 'more deeply into the notion of the real', rather than into 'the ideal' as per the 'superficial opinion' of Western moralism – whose 'notion of nature is different from ours', Lacan must add, in over-assuming the 'exclusion of all bestial desires' from its ideal of 'human fulfilment' (SVII, 11, 13). Then there is Nietzsche's 1886 *Beyond Good and Evil* declaration that with 'intrepid Oedipus eyes' we ought to examine *human* nature as we have 'the rest of nature', 'to translate man back into nature', such that we are 'deaf to the siren songs' of any hyper-ideal world imagined wholly beyond the earthly, animal body and its senses, as a metaphysical source accessible through a pure immortal soul (BGE, 230).

Invoked, then, between Lacan and Nietzsche is a *real* ethics, *of* the real – as opposed to an imaginary ethics, *caught* in the imaginary.[2] But what Bataille will enable is a focus on how the taboo structures of morality can be transgressed in a *complimentary* erotic process that returns for us the rest of nature – the *real* of nature as *jouissance*[3] – and how non-Platonic cultures had developed sacred myths and rituals for its structured affirmation. I argue that an erotics of the real – of sublimated *drives* beyond usual pleasures – can restore living *openness* to something more of the originary erotics observable in pre-Platonic Greece. By tracing then the *loss* of this eroticism through the subsequent Platonic, Christian, and Modern Science epochs that Nietzsche's revaluations of the Good also tend to centre on, what emerges is an extended genealogical understanding of how the brothels of Paris, for instance – *figuratively* speaking – could become for Bataille true churches again.[4]

1.1 PALAEOLITHIC TRANSITION FROM ANIMAL TO HUMAN

This section will illuminate Bataille's taboo–transgression relation in terms of Lacan's tri-partite episteme of the real, symbolic, and imaginary – clarifying the latter with the nature-to-culture, or *animal-to-human*, and back-again dynamic that in Bataille entails transgression. Then Nietzsche will be brought in to consider how the tragic age of the Greeks might master this *correlative* process of taboo-*and*-transgression: through a religious-erotic later lost with Socrates and Plato, and exacerbated by Christianity.

It is in his *Eroticism*, and the earlier unpublished version of it that makes up Vol. II of *The Accursed Share* (1952), that Bataille depicts our Palaeolithic 'transition from animal to human' (E, 30) as having occurred through *taboos* being placed on aspects of nature pertaining to 'death and sexuality' (E, 61) – equating these with 'violence' (E, 40). He notes how it is through such taboos that we first built up 'the rational world', but there remains 'an undercurrent of violence'; for 'Nature herself is violent', he adds, especially for a 'rational being who tries to obey but who succumbs to stirrings within' that are insufficiently brought 'to heel' (E, 40).

For Bataille, then, it is as such via our 'negation of nature' (AS II, 61), our '"No" to nature' (E, 61) – as 'the animal that does not just accept the facts of nature' but 'contradicts them' (E, 214) – that we first transitioned from animal to human, creating thus a culture *out* of nature. He registers such negations not only more generally on licentiousness and murder but also specifically on things such as 'excreta' (E, 57), 'nudity' (E, 170, 214), 'incest' (E, 51, 197), 'the corpse' (E, 44-7, 57, 71), 'child birth', 'menstruation', and the 'blood' which 'in itself is a symbol of violence' (E, 54) – the *distancing* from which humanizes a world of work founded on respect for taboos, a bourgeoning consciousness of mortality, and the concomitant developments of tools for controlling and understanding nature via an ever-lengthening 'chain of cause and effect' (E, 44).[5]

This new world, said by Bataille to 'cut' us 'off from violence which tended in the opposite direction' (E, 45), invokes the *symbolic* register of Lacan. This is the register of *language*, used to communicate the law, morality, knowledge, and reason made possible by the space created by taboo, to found an *order of things* that every newborn in a sense repeats our species entry into. As Lacan put it in his 1953 article 'The Function and Field of Speech and Language in Psychoanalysis', 'Man thus speaks, but it is because the symbol has made him man' – noting how it is the incest taboos and corresponding injunctions to exogamy that have helped 'superimpose the reign of culture over the reign of nature', for instance, by imposing the names that 'institute the order of preferences and taboos that knot and braid the thread of lineage through the generations' (Éc, 229–30). In moments such as these, Marcos Zafiropoulos also marks Lacan's debt to Mauss's ethnology on the 'birth of the symbolic', and in particular to 'Lévi-Strauss's introduction to the posthumous edition of Mauss's *Sociologie et Anthropologie*' – along with their shared debt to the father of French Sociology, Émile Durkheim (1858–1917), of whom Mauss was both pupil and nephew.[6]

'Besides', Bataille remarks, referring back to the present, 'what are children if not animals becoming human' (AS II, 65) – following here the Freud who suggests for children that 'something quite similar occurred' at the start of 'the prehistoric epoch of the species as a whole', at 'the beginnings of morality, religion and social order', while noting also the 'horror of incest', and 'enormous sense of guilt', that linger on from this to feed the resistances of those adults who 'refuse to allow themselves to be reminded of it'.[7] In eschewing such resistances himself, however, all this will recall for Bataille how 'interminable millennia correspond with man's slow shaking-off of his original animal nature' – and how 'he emerged from it by working, by understanding his own mortality, and by moving imperceptibly from unashamed sexuality to sexuality with shame, which gave birth to eroticism' (E, 31).

With this erotic we come to the brute fact of instinctual existence, that 'what comes under the effect of repression returns', as Lacan puts it Freudianly, 'in symptoms and a host of other phenomena' (SIII, 12) – where Bataille's stress is on how the latter include the erotic which is taboo's 'expected complement', 'just as explosion follows upon compression', and where the 'compression is not subservient to the explosion, far from it; it gives it increased force' (E, 65). Here with this explosive force we discover the notion of *transgression*, which, as complementary counterpoint of taboo – *and as gift* – Bataille attributes to the 'oral teaching' of the anthropology of Mauss, whose printed work bore it out 'only in a small number of significant sentences' (E, 65).[8] It is also entailed in one of Bataille's first important articles, 'The Notion of Expenditure (1933)', where it is articulated in terms of a 'principle of loss', 'unproductive expenditure' or 'consumption', and where the examples listed are: 'luxury, mourning, war, cults, the construction of sumptuary monuments, games, spectacles, arts', and finally 'perverse sexual activity', that which is 'deflected from genital finality' (VE, 118).

Bataille's own distinctive focus is on how the impetus for such transgression comes from the object of taboo gaining its distinctive *erotic* hue as desire dams up, and is even in part *damned*, or *accursed:* making it the paradoxical object of anguish and awe that lifts primitive mind high onto the religious plane. This plane is the *imaginary* register, linked to the *post-symbolic* sense of the real in Lacan, which is often simply contracted as 'the real' given its strikingness, as indicated by his remark on 'shame' in his later seminar on *The Other Side of Psychoanalysis*, where he states: 'You know from me that this means the real' (SXVII, 180). This *shame* of 'the other side [*l'envers*]' (SXVII, 182), along with what Lacan also denotes as 'anxiety, signal of the real' (SX, 160-1), suggests the *prior* operation of taboo *on* the real, and thus also the prior operation of the symbolic. And with Bataille we can clarify that the real, here, as this object of anxious, erotic shame, is not just nature but us *returning* to it – or it returning *to us* – after having been uprooted from it while remaining 'still uprooted' as 'the first uprooting is not obliterated' (AS II, 90), but rather leaves an affective trace. This is what Bataille observes to render the nature returning *transfigured* in the imaginary, into something sublime: 'poetic and divine though animal' (E, 153).[9]

Bataille's warning on this sublime, however, is to 'not be misled by the appearance of a return by man to nature' (AS II, 90). In a way much in keeping with Lacan's notion of a constitutive 'dehiscence' in our 'relationship to nature', that can never seamlessly be refilled[10] – Bataille describes what we return to as 'the natural world mingled with the divine', through 'the human world, shaped by a denial of animality or nature, denying itself, though not returning to what it had rejected in the first place' (E, 85). Later in *Eroticism* he adds that 'the sacred world is nothing but the natural world persisting insofar as it cannot be entirely reduced to the order laid down by work' – wherein 'it transcends' (E, 114–5). And it is here that we get another illumination of the *post*-symbolic sense of the real in Lacan, included in what Bataille himself calls 'the concrete totality of the real' in his own search for 'terminological exactness' (AS II, 117), so as to include the real's returning in the metaphorizing affects of the mind's sacred, sublime *imaginary* – which is how for Bataille, as opposed to the 'standpoint of work', and thus taboo, 'our animal nature preserves the values of subjective experience' (E, 158).

Bataille also articulates this experience in the context of the festival in volume II of his *Accursed Share*. In a section evocatively headed, 'The Festival Is Not Just a Return to One's Vomit', returning nature is now characterized in terms of the 'meaning' it invokes, when the impulses we ordinarily 'refuse' finally become sanctioned (AS II, 90). 'In any case', he remarks, 'these impulses cannot be mistaken for those of animals' (AS II, 90) – not any more, or not directly, given the potential complexity of the narratives unfolding. And this is why, making use of his striking heading, he affirms that what we return to has the 'opposite meaning' to 'a return by man to his vomit' (AS II, 90) – that is, to something expelled through nausea, taboo, fear, or disgust that remains as such thereafter.

Lacan and Nietzsche are relevant here – both of whom have much praise for the Greek tragic festival because of the *depths* of its meaning-making wisdom: enabling *not* just release but a growing mindfulness of the drives, too. This praise is in stark opposition to the Plato of *Gorgias* 502b–d, whom Lacan cites in his seminar on *Transference* for where 'tragedy is touched on' only to be abruptly 'executed in three lines among the arts of flattery as one rhetoric among the others' – as if there is 'nothing more to be said' (SVIII, 82). Here Plato has Socrates suggest that tragedy aims merely 'to gratify the citizens', to 'neglect the common good for their personal interest' and thus 'treat them like children', with no regard for whether this 'makes them better or worse'[11] – but Lacan disagrees: For 'the hero trembles before nothing', Lacan's *Ethics* affirms, 'crossing not only all fear but all pity' to show us just 'where the pole of desire is', such that 'the subject learns a little more about the deepest level' (SVII, 323). This is also how for Nietzsche tragic art communicates an ecstatic victory, a 'display of fearlessness in the face of the fearsome and questionable' (TI IX, 24).

Bataille would concur with Lacan and Nietzsche in noting that 'classical tragedy' is 'most engaging when the character of the hero leads' *directly* towards 'destruction', by daring to look it 'straight in the face'; but what Bataille's distinct focus is able to further contend is that 'here eroticism is analogous to a tragedy', insofar as our normal or usual taboos are transgressed in a ruinous expenditure, literally here 'at the price of a sacrifice' (AS

II, 107, 109, 119). This recalls the 'joy in destruction', in the 'sacrifice of its highest types' (TI X, 5), that was for Nietzsche the *Dionysian* tragic-effect or catharsis. But it also invokes Freud's remarks in *Beyond the Pleasure Principle* on how we 'do not spare the spectators' the 'most painful experiences' when it comes to artistic play 'in tragedy', that 'can yet be felt by them as highly enjoyable' – where here for Freud it is through 'an instinct of mastery', where remembering, *repeating,* the tragic or traumatic real is very much to empower and become 'master of the situation' (SE18, 16–7). This is what *drives* us beyond usual pleasures, delimited by taboo, such that we ourselves are deepened, extended – and it is thus that Nietzsche concludes, when thinking of our *pre*-Platonic Classical Greeks, that 'Pleasure in tragedy characterizes *strong* ages and natures' (WP, 852).

Such a strength pertains to the initial paradox of eroticism where, Bataille observes, we *negate* our dependence on animality yet at some point fail, 'for this negation is fictitious' (AS II, 92). The fiction, however, cuts both ways: For while in transgression we seem now to be 'renouncing independence' from animality, we are rather in the momentary *sovereignty* of the drives part of a cycle of repetition hurtling around towards completion, the 'culmination of a movement towards autonomy which is', for Bataille, whether on the way up or down, or in or out, 'forevermore, the same thing as man himself' (AS II, 91). But this double movement of autonomy in taboo-*and*-transgression was lost in the later deference to Socrates of Plato, which set itself *against* the erotic-real of our repressed animality and sought no further truck with it – fixing the gaze instead on a Good made Sovereign across all times, such that we, beneath its awnings, could only ever be reduced to slaves.

1.2 DEATH OF TRAGEDY FROM SOCRATES' INCOMPETENCE

Lacan's commentaries on Nietzsche's texts are few, so it is imperative to at least register his *Transference* seminar position that 'it is nevertheless indisputable, and Nietzsche put his finger on it', concerning 'Socrates' profound incompetence every time he broaches the topic of tragedy' – that when Nietzsche discovered this 'it went to his head' and his first work '*The Birth of Tragedy* grew out of it, as did all his subsequent work' (SVIII, 81–2). This section will explore Nietzsche's critique of Euripides in his 1872 *Birth of Tragedy* for allowing Socrates' influence to destroy classical tragedy's Dionysian basis. This will capture the taboo–transgression co-relation of Bataille shifting from its original classical-archaic form to its subsequently distorted form – where the imaginary of the Good extolled by the Platonic

Socrates seeks to buttress the symbolic *over-against* the real: as if to repress the real of bodily animality even across all spaces.

In Bataillean terms, Nietzsche finds Euripides using tragedy *not* so much to transgress taboos but rather to reinforce them – shifting thus from the coequal taboo-*and*-transgression to a taboo *on* transgression, by making tragedy more self-conscious, moral and rational, which requires *not* the brief suspension but the continuing of taboos. This is such for Nietzsche that although Euripides' final play *The Bacchae:* written 'in the evening of his life' (BT, 12) to premier posthumously in 405 BC – has Dionysos, whom Bataille calls 'the god of transgression' (TE, 70), retuning to destroy those who denied him: It is more a return of the repressed *as* repressed, as symptom savage and cruel, than it is a sublimated outlet of the drives ennobled by Apollo, the 'shining one' (BT, 1), to whom Nietzsche has Dionysos paired.

By referencing the shining one, '*Der Scheinende*' (BT, 1), Nietzsche is invoking Apollo's Homeric appellation of *Phoibus*, although in Delphi Apollo was also known as *Pythios* from the serpent which rotted there after he slew it.[12] Tracing the signifier to the Greek, here, Πύθων (*Pythōn*) takes a verbal form, πύθω, which means literally 'to rot', while the neighbouring πυθμήν (*pythmēn*) suggests the 'bottom' of seas and caves where serpents dwell, or the 'base' of a vessel like the '*legs*' of a tripod'.[13] And it was Erwin Rohde, Nietzsche's fellow professor in philology, who suggested that this *Pythios*, or python, slayed by Apollo and left to rot, was at some point equated with Dionysos himself but only by an 'untrustworthy witness' – with the weight of evidence suggesting, rather, that Dionysos was not buried as *Python* 'under the *Omphalos*' but 'in the ἄδυτον [*adyton*]', the innermost shrine, right 'by the tripod'.[14] This is whence Roberto Calasso can later poeticize of how Dionysos takes over the site each winter while Apollo enacts his 'nordic quest among the Hyperboreans', citing 'Plutarch, priest of Delphic Apollo', who observed that 'Dionysos was just as important in Delphi as Apollo', as 'neither can do without the other', as 'neither can be there all the time' – with Calasso also sanctioning the slippage of 'Python, a snake', with 'Dionysos, the god generated by Zeus when in the form of a snake and escorted by virgins who tied snakes around their foreheads like ribbons'.[15]

To further explain this key condensation of Apollo-Dionysos, Nietzsche notes that when it comes to the risk of having our 'savage natural instincts unleashed' – where that 'horrible witches brew of sensuality and cruelty' mixes itself up with 'extravagant sexual licentiousness' – what creates the 'immense gap which separates the Dionysian Greek from the Dionysian barbarian' (BT, 2) is precisely the moderation of Apollo: to beautify, subject to measure, lucidity and 'self-knowledge', so that there was 'nothing in excess' (BT, 4). Rohde himself had even affirmed – in that 'admirable work' *Psyche*

Lacan expresses deference to in his *Ethics* for analysing 'antiquity's different conceptions of the immortality of the soul', and recommends that 'psychoanalysts ought to have read at least once' (SVII, 250, 284) – that when Dionysos is finally introduced to Athens by the Delphic oracle it is as already reconciled with Apollo, making him thus 'gentler and more civilized', 'pruned and moderated', whereupon he would go on to find a 'wide-reaching influence' on all Greece.[16]

Alas for Euripides, Nietzsche bemoans, 'the deity that spoke through him was neither Dionysos nor Apollo, but an altogether newborn demon, called Socrates' (BT, 12). And Socrates, for Nietzsche, was that 'other spectator who did not comprehend tragedy and therefore did not esteem it' (BT, 11), whose 'moralism' (TI II,10) was thus *other* to any affirmation of the drives in their inscrutable realness. 'And because you had abandoned Dionysos, Apollo had abandoned you' (BT, 10), Nietzsche calls to Euripides directly – for by *The Bacchae*, 'when the poet recanted, his tendency had already triumphed. Dionysos had already been scared from the tragic stage' (BT, 12).

Nietzsche senses the symptom in Euripides' depiction of the holocaust wrought by Dionysos on the people of Thebes – because it is, he tells us, 'what we are told by a poet who opposed Dionysos with heroic valour throughout a long life' but ends with 'a glorification of his adversary and with suicide, like a giddy man who, to escape the horrible vertigo he can no longer endure, casts himself from a tower' (BT, 12). Viewed from the Bataillean optic, what is occurring here is the *denial* of periodic rituals for adequate transgression: those where 'under the charm of the Dionysian', as Nietzsche first saw, the 'nature which has become alienated' celebrates 'her reconciliation with her lost son' (BT, 1) – such that when normally refused animal needs now *do* return, it is of their own volition, with an excess of violence, savagery, and cruelty, beyond the pale of Apollonian control.

Something is thence lost from within the structure of taboo-and-transgression, with, Nietzsche notes, 'cool, paradoxical thoughts, replacing Apollonian contemplation – and fiery *affects*, replacing Dionysian ecstasies' (BT, 12). With regards to a more finely balanced structure, Lacan had also observed that previously societies had once 'lived very well by reference to laws that are far from promoting their universal application', but rather 'prosper as a result of the transgression of these maxims' (SVII, 78). This was part of the 'potlatch' economy or form of exchange, of which Lacan assumes his seminar is 'well enough informed' and can see 'is not simply the privilege of primitive societies' (SVII, 235). It is what Bataille's 'Notion of Expenditure' article notes was the rival gift giving, sacrifices, or 'spectacular destruction' that was first 'identified by Mauss under the name *potlatch*, which he borrowed from the Northwestern American Indians who provided such a remarkable example of it' (VE, 121) – where, Lacan observes, thinking of how 'vestiges' of this can still *return* in some way, the 'open destruction' of goods could enable a 'maintenance and discipline of desire' in defiance of our usual workaday taboos in the ethical register of utilitarianism, but structured and delimited to be 'carried out consciously and in a controlled way' (SVII, 235).

While Mauss had remarked upon the often 'marked agonistic character', 'essentially usurious and sumptuary', of potlatch among tribes of the American Northwest, he had also documented the numerous 'intermediate forms' in the exchange of gifts 'where emulation is more moderate', such as in the 'ancient Indo-European world, and especially among the Thracians', along with parts of today such as 'our presents of thanks, banquets and weddings', and 'simple invitations'.[17] When it comes to other vestiges of this practice returning, however, Lacan compares the festivals of the feudal Lords of the Narbonne region of twelfth-century France – who rivalled each other to 'destroy the most' goods consumed as part of the festivities but also 'animals and harnesses' – with the more savage and recent 'massive destruction' of the two world wars which were done uncontrolled and unconscious of this potlach tendency, operating and exploding out of them nonetheless (SVII, 235).

It is, moreover, with Socrates' fifth-century BC intervention into tragedy, thanks to Plato's subsequent fourth-century writings of his teacher in philosophy, that our abilities for conscious control and open experience of this practice begins to wane, as we enter what Lacan calls 'the longest transference, giving this expression its fullest import, that history has ever known' (SVIII, 7). Transference for Lacan is a belief-state projected onto an analyst as the one 'supposed to know' (SXI, 232). And as such with Plato's Socratic transference, the *profound incompetence* within, on what Bataille calls literature and theatre's 'symbolic representations of tragic loss' (VE, 120), was later adopted by Christendom – so that when it came to tragedy, it 'didn't know' (SVII, 236), which is how Lacan characterizes the modern subject: as neither do we *know*, as this transference eventually becomes our own.

Bataille decries the ensuing forfeiture of the sacred-erotic transgression as the 'dualist evolution' (TR, 72) in his 1948 *Theory of Religion*, published posthumously in 1973 – but he also takes this up in his 1949 *Accursed Share* (AS II, 133) and 1957 *Eroticism* (E, 122), in the context of critiquing Christianity.[18] Now with Nietzsche we can locate this binary dualist turn, where Dionysos is bad and Apollo good, such that transgression cannot allow any proper return from the latter to the former, to the death of tragedy through the philosopher Socrates: acting as both 'agent' and 'symptom', Nietzsche notes, of 'the dissolution of Greece' (TI II, 2) which was subsequently universalized in Plato – with the Christianity to follow itself called by Nietzsche, because of this exacerbating binary structure in the tellingly titled 1886 *Beyond Good and Evil*, a 'Platonism for "the masses"' (BGE, P).

This was not the same as the dualism of the Gnostics Bataille earlier discussed in his 1929 *Documents* article 'Base Materialism and Gnosticism' – which 'in an almost bestial way', Bataille suggests, 'no matter what were its metaphysical developments, introduced a most impure fermentation into Greco-Roman ideology' (VE, 46), especially once the latter was under the sway of the Platonic idealist turn. For this Gnosticism, Bataille notes, which had its origins mainly in 'Persian' or 'Zoroastrian dualism' (VE, 46-7), was motivated by 'a sinister love of darkness' and a 'monstrous taste for obscene and lawless *archontes* [rulers]' (VE, 48) – with matter and evil itself seen as 'an *active* principle having its own eternal autonomous existence' (VE, 47) – which is different to the idealism Bataille characterized as comparatively 'monistic', in that it rather 'saw matter and evil as degradations of superior principles' (VE, 47). Bataille's aim, here, was to develop a *base* materialism to counter the idealist notion of matter presupposed even in other materialisms, to include again the *real* elements commonly left out. It is what Hollier thus calls Bataille's *'dualist materialism'* that is based *not* on any spirit–matter binary but on the restored taboo–transgression dynamic: with taboos governing the *profane* time of work, and transgression governing the *sacred* time of religion, whereupon the excluded parts consciously return – which tragic art, within its *original* Hellenic religious traditions, allowed a superlative space for.[19]

In *Birth of Tragedy* Nietzsche senses what would irk a Socrates, Euripides, and Plato in the original Greek religion, wherever it bore 'accents of an exuberant, triumphant life in which all things, whether good or evil [*böse*], are deified' – such that 'whoever approaches these Olympians with another religion in his heart', Nietzsche observes, searching not for aesthetic beauty but only 'moral elevation', 'disincarnate spirituality', or 'charity and benevolence', will soon be 'discouraged and disappointed, for there is nothing here that suggests asceticism' (BT, 3).[20] But the subsequent substitution of the *ascetic* for the aesthetic by Platonism is precisely the 'dual attitude' (E, 138) later criticized by Bataille, whose *Theory of Religion* itself noted that 'originally, in the divine world, the beneficent and pure elements opposed the malefic and impure elements, and both types appeared equally distinct from the profane' (TR, 69). And it was only later, he adds, in 'a dominant movement of reflective thought, the divine appears linked to purity, the profane to impurity' (TR, 69), as eventually 'the divine becomes rational and moral and relegates the malefic sacred to the sphere of the profane' (TR, 72).

Bataille calls this 'dualism' of a puritan-sacred and an impure-profane 'a shifting of boundaries and an overturning of values' – as before, an 'immanent sacred is predicated on the animal intimacy of man', *accessible in transgression*, 'whereas the profane world is predicated on the transcendence of the object, which has no intimacy', relying as it does *on taboo* to hoist the mind free of immanence for the 'manipulation of objects', 'relations with objects, or with subjects regarded as objects' via 'reason and morality' (TR, 71).[21] Then with Plato, although neither he nor Socrates are named here by Bataille, 'the intellect or concept' is 'situated outside time, is defined as a sovereign order, to which the world of things is subordinated, just as it subordinated the gods of mythology' – and this is such that now only 'the intelligible world has the appearance of the divine', but it is as *'forever* separated from the world of the senses', as 'outside', over-against, and 'opposite the sensuous world' (TR, 73).[22]

This inflationary dualism criticized here by Bataille is what can be further grasped genealogically through Nietzsche's critique of Socrates' effect on Euripides in art. For they 'brought the masses onto the stage' (BT, 80), Nietzsche observes, with their 'civic mediocrity, on which Euripides built all his political hopes', which again requires the incessant functioning of moral-rational taboos – such that gone were the 'demigod', the 'drunken satyr', the 'formerly only grand and bold traits', replaced with the everyday, workaday herd that 'philosophized, managed land and goods, and conducted lawsuits with unheard of circumspection' (BT, 11).

Life increasingly imitates this new art, as its new ideals buttress, from a Sovereign Good beyond the sky, the symbolic *over-against* the real to *repress* at all times. For Bataille this is even what 'reintroduces evil as a major force', when repressions fail and the repressed returns in ever more monstrous forms, as 'the sleep of dualism is also a reduction to the order of things that leaves no opening except towards a return to violence' (TR, 79). Lacan's *Transference* seminar critique of Plato's *Symposium* is also quite pertinent here, where Socrates' preaching of an Eros cleansed of flesh, that *inflates* Diotima's ladder of love up towards the Good, is met with the return of a drunken Alcibiades, Socrates' pupil and handsome beloved, to raze this inflated dualism to the ground. This is for Lacan the 'eruption' or 'upheaval' of the real (SVIII, 66) which, despite 'the fine stories, as fascinating as they may seem', about an 'ultra-world' or 'mirage' in the *beyond*, 'suffices to bring us back to reality [*réel*]' – *as it really is* (SVIII, 132).

How *It* really is was wonderfully metaphorized by the Olympian deities, whom even Lacan calls 'the real gods' (SVIII, 161) and where 'the gods belong to the field of the real' (SXI, 45), as ever *staged* in the Apollo-Dionysos dynamic – prior, that is, to the Platonic whitewash that meant the real could only return of the banal dialectic between neurosis-*and*-perversion, like the Socrates-*and*-Alcibiades show of *Symposium*, and akin to what Nietzsche, at Athens' decline, called 'two decadence movements running side by side' (WP, 427).[23]

Alcibiades here becomes the barbarian Dionysos of Euripides, repressed by Socrates instead of moderated by Apollo so always-already wild, bent on destruction. And this is why for Lacan 'Socrates' daemon is Alcibiades' (SVIII, 160), embodying the artificially elided elements of 'the real gods' that could also appear 'in the guise of something that would cause a ruckus', such as 'theft, fraud, and adultery', not to mention 'impiety' (SVIII, 161–2). But without a sufficient aesthetic outlet for the drives, all this ruckus worsens in the Christendom to come, which the later Bataille will come to decry as the 'sovereignty of taboos' at their most 'clear cut' (E, 136) – as 'absolute' (E, 126) – which only 'deepened the degree of sensual disturbance by forbidding organized transgression' (E, 127).

1.3 TABOO ON TRANSGRESSION FROM YAHWEH'S IGNORANCE

To understand Christianity, Nietzsche's genealogy traces it to its Hebraic roots. Here I will combine it with Lacan's analysis of the Judaeo-Christian theme to explore Bataille's own apropos of his articulation of 'the basic interrelation of taboo and transgression, opposite and complementary concepts' (E, 196). The key for this is Lacan's *Seminar XVII* invoking of 'Yahweh's ferocious ignorance', towards 'religious practices' founded on 'sexual knowledge' that 'blends supernatural agencies in with nature itself' (SXVII, 136). For although Yahweh, unlike his later Christian version, can still exhibit violence – as per Freud's casting of him in *Moses and Monotheism* (1939) as originally an 'uncanny, bloodthirsty demon' (SE23, 34) – this impurity is already *cleansed* of libido. Lacan's acumen in tracking what for Nietzsche is this cleansing's '*denaturalizing* of natural values' (AC, 25) – whence 'morality as anti-nature' becomes '*hostile to life*' and a 'castration' of our ability to properly 'spiritualize, beautify, deify a desire' (TI V, 1–2) – is to see in Freud's thesis of a primal-father's murder and *repetition* on totems, then Moses, and finally Jesus a 'hysteric's desire' (SXVII, 129) to castrate now our aggressive *and* sexed aspects via Oedipal imaginaries. For Lacan, however, it is also this 'castration' that *produces* the primal father, which 'determines the father as this impossible real', to begin with (SXVII, 128–9).

Referring to Freud's 1913 *Totem and Taboo*, whence *Moses and Monotheism*'s primal-father thesis drew, Bataille couches this in his own anthropological terms as the 'psychoanalytical hypothesis which attributes the transition from animal to human to a postulated murder of the father by the brothers' – where afterwards 'the brothers, jealous of each other, maintain the taboos on relations with their mother or sisters that their father imposed in order to keep them for his own use' (E, 200). Freud's idea was that the brothers maintain the incest taboos as none were strong enough 'to take on the father's part with success' (SE13, 144) – this 'violent and jealous father who keeps all the females for himself and drives away his sons as they grow up' (SE13, 141), obstructing thus 'their craving for power and their sexual desires' (SE13, 143).

Lacan, however, will come to disagree in his later *Seminar XVII* on *The Other Side of Psychoanalysis*. For he finds Freud's idea of 'putting the omnipotent father at the origin of desire' (SXVII, 129) – somehow linked to Moses, Jesus, and Oedipus through an 'acted-out instead of remembering' (SE23, 89) repetition of murders with the tightening of taboos the result each time – 'adequately refuted by the fact that he was extracting its master signifiers from the hysteric's desire' (SXVII, 129). This is where the master is paradoxically invented in the locus of the Father as something to cut down, 'govern', and 'reign over' (SXVII, 129), as if his own reign prior to this 'were real', 'necessarily happened' and 'where everything began' – whereas for Lacan a father usually has 'only the most distant of relationships' with the master: for 'it is he who works for everybody' (SXVII, 100), and 'not the slightest trace has ever been seen of the father of the human horde' (SXVII, 113). Lacan in fact wonders if this hysteric's discourse 'isn't where the invention of the master began' (SXVII, 129).[24]

Bataille's position is similar to Lacan's, observing: 'Really Freud's myth brings in the most fantastic guess work yet it has the advantage over the sociologists of being an expression of living compulsions' (E, 200) – noting even how in '*Totem and Taboo* Freud, because of his superficial knowledge of ethnographical data, nowadays much less vague', erred in his view of the taboo on corpses in thinking it countered 'the desire to touch', which was 'doubtless no greater in former times than it is today' (E, 47). In terms of the primal father myth, Bataille will add that 'Lévi-Strauss expresses it neatly' in suggesting Freud 'gives a fair account not of the beginnings of civilization, but of its present state', uncovering thence 'in symbolical form an inveterate fantasy' (E, 200).[25] That is, going back to Lacan, Freud's myth is a fantasy symptomatic of 'castration', of the 'real operation' of repressive taboos introduced by the *incidence* of the signifier 'into the sexual relationship [*rapport du sex*]' (SXVII, 128-9) – a fantasy, then, which retro-projects both the violent incestuous desire of and for the inflated master-father (transgression), *and* its required violent rejection (taboo-law), that together constitutes the unconscious structure of Judaeo-Christian nuclear families: a compromise formation where both positive and negative compulsions are frozen together as an Oedipal complex in time.[26]

Bataille's complaint about Lévi-Strauss is only the tendency to Freudianly found the whole transition from nature to culture on the incest taboo, which is 'just one aspect of the general taboo' (E, 51), to the neglect of others coequal in value on death, nudity, dejecta, and blood. By speaking of nature-to-culture, moreover – rather than *animal-to-human* – Bataille's sense is that Lévi-Strauss is merely 'setting one abstraction beside another' (E, 214), and omitting thus the 'drama in which they oppose one another', as 'a laceration that exposes the whole of divided being' (AS II, 52), occurring wherever 'man and animal nature confront each other as the totality of being is rent asunder' (E, 213).[27]

Lacan's aim in *Seminar XVII* to go *beyond* 'everything in the same basket as Oedipus' and the 'cock-and-bull story' of primal murder – to see it as Freud's 'strange Christocentrism' and 'dream' that needs to be 'interpreted' (SXVII, 114, 117, 137, 176) – signals a similar intent to *not* reduce us to the incest taboo. Later Lacan can be found claiming to 'metaphorize' as incest the relation 'truth maintains with the real'.[28] But one should also factor in Nietzsche's genealogy, which suggests that what is really murdered, sacrificed, or 'castrated' with the Judaeo-Christian unfolding is not some hyper-hetero ape and his Hebraic substitutes but 'the erudite culture' of Greek and Roman nobles, and the gods *and* goddesses of *Hellenismos*, by the slavish *ressentiment*, 'bad conscience', and 'petty envy' that continues to unduly press normativity today (AC, 59; GM II, 23–4). Bataille's own acumen is to stress how lost in the Christian universalization of Yahweh's *ferocious ignorance,* which went Eastwards also with a later Islamic version, and combining with Socrates' *profound incompetence*, is the erotic rituals of transgression that were once the very domain of religion: pursuant to the *originary* sacred that mixed the pure with the sexed impure of repressed animality, returning them then as 'deified nature' (AS II, 131).

Bataille is keenest to mark in his 1957 *Eroticism* that Christianity alters this by leaving 'transgression condemned', 'condemned out of hand' as 'sin', as 'evil' (E, 127, 262), and in doing so conceals 'that the sacred and the forbidden are one, that the sacred can be reached through the violence of a broken taboo' (E, 126). Previously in the 1952 volume II of *Accursed Share* he noted that in forbidding transgression Christianity now 'took up in a renewed form the movement that set the first men against nature', and 'revived within themselves the original drama that was the transition from animal to man' – *but with no route back* – rendering thus 'repudiated the pagan world in which transgression counterbalances the prohibition to form the totality' (AS II, 135-6). This is why later in his *Eroticism* Bataille will be compelled to most emphatically decry that 'in the Christian world the taboo was absolute', which nevertheless could never cease to paradoxically eroticize what it repressed as the desire dammed to bursting point, meaning 'Christianity in its turn deepened the degree of sensual disturbance by forbidding organized transgression' (E, 126–7).

For Bataille, then, 'misunderstanding the sanctity of transgression is one of the foundations of Christianity' (E, 90). But Lacan's 1959–60 *Ethics* seminar also marks the disturbance this creates in citing Paul's as precisely 'the Law which causes sin' (SVII, 170), which 'causes our desire to flare up' even as a 'desire for death', as it 'takes on an excessive, hyperbolic character' (SVII, 83-4). And so as *not* to 'leave us clinging to that dialectic', and to produce something that merits the title of an 'ethics of psychoanalysis', Lacan declares that 'we will have to explore that which, over the centuries, human beings have succeeded in elaborating that transgresses the Law, puts them in a relationship to desire that transgresses interdiction, and introduces an erotics that is above morality' (SVII, 84).[29]

This declaration must be stressed, and through Bataille's eroticizing my aim here has been just that, because with Christianity we *forget* that an ethics must preserve a space for an erotics, which for Lacan is akin to how in 'having lived for a long time under Christian law', 'we no longer have any idea what the gods are' – something which he requires we remedy by practising 'a little ethnography' (SVII, 259).[30] For the gods once *sanctioned* transgression, rendering its erotics guided, but now they have taken-flight – which is what makes Christianity for Bataille 'the least religious religion of them all', insofar as it 'sets its face against eroticism and thereby condemns most religions' (E, 32), able itself to sanction transgression only in the alleged *'felix culpa* [happy fault]' (E, 262) of 'the ignominious death on the cross' (AS II, 136). This is also the 'central image' that Lacan will describe as leaving desire 'literally poisoned', 'pursued throughout the world by Christian missionaries', 'crucifying man in holiness for centuries', as it 'absorbs all other images of desire in man with significant consequences' (SVII, 262).

Lacan, then, later in his *Ethics*, refers to the 'inner catastrophes' of 'neurosis' that are forever stemming from the demand be always 'doing things in the name of the good, and even more in the name of the good of the other' – as repressed 'desire keeps coming back, keeps returning, and situates us once again in a given track' (SVII, 319). But Bataille will also stress the concurrent 'contempt for animals' involved, forging a 'perceptible link' with such 'victory of morality and the sovereignty of taboos', which is 'this morality pushed to its logical conclusion', as accordingly 'the attributes of deity vanish from the animal kingdom' (E, 136–7). Even a saviour's birth, now, cannot directly involve what we share with other mammals: 'private parts, the hairy ones to be precise, the animal ones' (E, 143), as Bataille most bluntly puts it – draped over for evermore by the most ambiguous of virginities.

We are a long way here from Zeus's divine rapes, where he would *expressly* take the animal form: whether a swan for Leda, a serpent for Semele, or a shimmering white bull for Europa.[31] And as perhaps echoing in Lacan's later dictum of there being 'no sexual relation' (SXVII, 116), Bataille will also chide the Christian attempts to now *deny* their fear of sex in a 1952 congress of Carmelites, who interestingly invited other orders along with 'religious historians and psycho-analysts' (E, 221).[32] For Bataille notes that in their concern to show that 'fear of sexuality was not the mainspring of the Christian practice of continence', things were progressing so that 'Schopenhauer's simplifications were readily accepted' of the sexual impulses being merely 'Nature's purpose working through them' – but 'no one bothered to reflect that "Nature" behaved in a ridiculous way' (E, 222, 232). Such idealized notions of nature are precisely what Bataille debunks with his striking articulations of how 'the sexual channels are also the body's sewers' – and how our vanity is very much offended when we 'connect the anal orifice with them' and, like Augustine, recollect how 'we are born between faeces and urine' (E, 57–8).

If the Carmelites, then, insist on a 'harmony between sexuality and life' it is, for Bataille, only by *narrowing* it to 'certain limits', where 'outside these it is forbidden' (E, 230) – reduced to the procreative form, and 'limited to marriage' (E, 238), heterosexuality and monogamy, to give it transcendental significance. 'Transcendental?' Bataille riposte, 'That means denying its horror, the horror connected with earthly reality' (E, 224) – where again for Bataille nature even *invites* an element of 'horror' as it 'brings together and even in part mingles the organs' of 'sexuality and dejecta' (AS II, 62).[33] Lacan would in fact concur in his 1969–70 *Seminar XVII* in suggesting that 'signifiers are not made for sexual relations', that once our consciousness of and through taboo has formed 'once the human being is speaking, it's stuffed, it's the end of this perfection, this harmony, in copulation – which in any case', Lacan adds, 'is impossible to find anywhere in nature' (SXVII, 33). Perhaps it is no accident, then, that where Bataille in *Eroticism* chides this narrowing transcendentalism of priests and monks is a photo of a statuette, of an Alexandrian 'temple prostitute', attributed to the 'Jacques Lacan collection' (E, 224) – whom he earlier thanks as among 'a great many friends' for their 'active support' in finding 'relevant documents' (E, 9).

Lacan's own 1959-60 *Seminar VII* riposte to the idea of a transcendental Good in nature – which 'from the origin of moral philosophy' we find 'since Plato, certainly since Aristotle, and down through the Stoics, the Epicureans' and 'Christian thought itself in Saint Thomas Aquinas' (SVII, 221) – is again to 'consider how far that notion of nature is different to ours', as it entails 'the exclusion of all bestial desires from what is properly speaking human fulfilment' (SVII, 13). In his 'Discourse to Catholics (1960)' lecture of the same period, moreover, he similarly rebukes the narrowing altruistic notion of genital-relations promoted even by some of his fellow psychoanalysts, for *repressing* the 'fundamental perverseness of human desire' – while later in his 'Triumph of Religion (1974)' conference he again calls the speaking-being a 'sick animal', 'ravaged by the Word', which Christianity only seeks to 'cure' by 'drowning the symptom in meaning' so as 'to repress it', so as to 'not perceive what is not going well'.[34] Nevertheless, as his Alexandrian *temple* prostitute can only acknowledge, *pre*-Christian-Platonic cultures had a way of narrowing much less, while affirming much more, of what of our libidinal animality Christendom felt the need to so repress and drown with transcendental compensations in an inflated imaginary. In noting, moreover, '*nobler* uses for the invention of gods' than the 'degeneration of the imagination' involved in the 'self-crucifixion' of the last two-millennia, Nietzsche himself stresses that this is 'fortunately revealed even by a mere glance at the *Greek gods*', roughly half of which were also feminine, and all 'in whom *the animal* in man felt deified and did not lacerate itself, did not rage against itself!' (GM II, 23).

Regarding, then, our own distinct hue of animal beauty and the irrepressible desire for it within – given *divine* affirmation in Greco-Roman contexts not only in prostitution but also in homoerotics and the orgy – Bataille notes that for the Christian 'there is a halo of death about it that makes its beauty hateful' (E, 237).[35] It is the 'snare of the devil', which is 'at once hateful and desirable' as the 'lure of forbidden fruit', which Bataille observes now 'stands out more sharply', with 'harsher flavour', because of the strictest taboos which left so much of sex 'guilty and sin-laden' (E, 234, 237-8, 270). Hence 'flesh is the born enemy of people haunted by Christian taboos', while they live as if dead, waiting for death to give them life by 'calculations' on an after-world which for Bataille will always 'confer a miserliness, a poverty, a dismal discipline on the ascetic life of no matter what religion or sect' (E, 92, 251).

'Man must die to live eternally', as Bataille quotes a Father Tesson as 'speaking for the whole Church', with an 'ambiguousness of vocabulary' (E, 235) that also resonates with Lacan's notion of a 'second death' in the afterlife, if the soul were to be seduced by 'the phenomenon of the beautiful' (SVII, 260). Henceforth will Bataille conclude that Christians bank with their ultimately selfish calculations on each soul's salvation as 'forever divided, arbitrarily distinct from each other', and 'arbitrarily detached from the totality of being with which they must nevertheless remain connected' – violating thus forever in this 'atomization of totality' the sacred *return* 'from isolation to fusion, from the discontinuous to the continuous', and to the 'totality of the real' and 'continuity of being' implicit of the sacred-erotic Dionysian path forever 'marked out by transgression' (AS II, 117; E, 13, 120).

1.4 CAPITALISM'S CURIOUS SERVICE OF GOODS

The atomistic soul of Christianity, like much in our subsequent modern era, now takes a secular form. The detached soul becomes the individual, and this an empirical matter. This section argues that the transgressions of modern capitalism, fuelled by the advances in science, have more in common with the *disturbed* transgressions of the Christian age than they do with those sacred of the Hellenic. It suggests capitalist transgression is a secularized descendent of 'sin' because of its still degraded nature. But first I begin with Bataille's critique of sex-positivism in his *Eroticism* chapter 'Kinsey, the Underworld and Work' (E, 149). From here I will then broach and connect Lacan's split-subject, Nietzsche's ascetic ideal, and a modern capitalist world *pre-destined* in such a way that everything already is symbolic.

As Kendall records, when Bataille first read the Kinsey reports in 1948 'he leapt' for the translation rights but without success, producing instead the review for his journal *Critique,* later reprinted as a chapter of *Eroticism*.[36] It is within it, moreover, that Bataille suggests the 'originality' of the Kinsey Reports, published on the *Human Male* in 1948 and *Human Female* in 1953, is 'to discuss sexual conduct as one discusses things' (E, 152). Here 'sexual activity is treated statistically like external data', but Bataille's sense is that 'the doubts' cast by some on the scientificity of 'the results' are over 'technical and superficial', *commending* the authors instead for their 'precautions' (E, 151). This praise is because following the obscene strictness of Christian taboo, the reductionism of the Kinsey team was key for recovering knowledge of the sexual and repairing the damages done to reason, what Freud referred to as the 'intimidation of the intelligence' that fixes us in states of 'psychical infantilism' (SE21, 84–5), wrought by the Church on all such matters. Bataille thus concludes, 'The sexual behaviour of our fellows has ceased to be so completely hidden from us because of this gigantic enquiry' (E, 151).

Bataille's only complaint with this enquiry, with its admittedly 'often senselessly clumsy business of bringing man's sexual life down to the level of objective data' (E, 152), is with the assumption that now taboos can be dismissed as irrational altogether. He writes, 'We are faced with a voluminous collection of facts remarkably well assembled', by 'methods' that are 'brought to a high pitch of efficiency, though it is harder to admire the theories they spring from' (E, 156). And this is because 'for the authors sexuality is a normal and acceptable biological function in whatever form it appears', only 'religious principles restrict this natural activity' (E, 156). But such an assumption will not do for Bataille because there is a sense where sexuality is not just transgressive relative to Christian taboo, but relative to the order of things in general.[37]

What the authors miss, then, when it comes to libidinal restrictions is 'the factor of work', and Bataille repeats his formulation that it is first and foremost 'by work man orders the world of things and brings himself down to the level of a thing among things', as a 'means to an end', in 'opposition to animal nature' (E, 157). But without taboo, Bataille must add, 'animal darkness would still hold sway' (E, 161), but also without work, which is the very reason for taboo, as even shown for Bataille in Kinsey's class results. This is where only 'in the underworld alone, where no work is done and where behaviour in general adds up to a denial of humanity do we find 49.4%' of the people surveyed reaching the seven orgasms a week said to be 'the normal frequency in nature – the animal nature of the anthropoids' (E, 158–9). Other classes had only '16.1% to 8.9%' (E, 159).[38] Regardless, Bataille remarks, 'we are animals anyway', and 'cannot help the animal in us persisting and often overwhelming us', with our 'sexual exuberance demonstrating how animal life persists' (E, 150).

That the 'facts of sex' are not just 'things', moreover, or *wholly* reducible to an external aspect, is, for Bataille, also revealed in Kinsey's finding that 'beyond the desired result lie consequences' they 'did not anticipate' – namely the 'private feelings as opposed to things that the Reports suggest must exist beyond the graphs and curves', pointing to 'the memory of deep wounds, frustrating pain, unsatisfied desire, disappointments, tragic situations and utter catastrophe' (E, 152, 154). What Bataille is suggesting here is that while Christian taboo indeed makes the problems more acute, it is not alone responsible for the traumas of the real inherent *within* nature itself – and soon enough 'the authors themselves knew what abyss yawned beneath the facts they report' (E, 155).[39]

Lacan's remarks on Krafft-Ebing and Havelock Ellis are akin to Bataille's on Kinsey here, in noting 'not the failure of a method, but the choice of a failed method', and dismissing it in the context of understanding desire as merely a 'so-called scientific objectivity' (SVII, 194). Bataille's own aim, moreover, is to broach such curtailing limits of science apropos of his greater understanding of the interrelation of taboo-and-transgression. And in this he reproaches scientism, positivism – and indeed sex-positivism – for neglecting the original functions of religious eroticism, which, he complains, 'are closed books to us if we do not locate them firmly in the realm of inner experience', where in fact 'we put them on the same level as things known from the outside if we yield albeit unwittingly to the taboo' (E, 37).

This 'unwittingness' implies that rejecting taboo is secretly the consequence of the sustained functioning of taboo – shutting us off from *inner-*experience, making *it* unconscious. But 'the worst of it' for Bataille 'is that science whose procedures demand an objective approach to taboos owes its existence to them but at the same time disclaims them because taboos are not rational' (E, 37). This again is from taboo continuing to function unconsciously in a secularized form, which, Bataille notes, 'acted on behalf of science in the first place' in removing 'the object of taboo from our consciousness by forbidding it', the 'disturbing object' – the Lacanian object a[40] – so as to attain for us 'that calm ordering of ideas without which human awareness is inconceivable' (E, 38). And it is in this sense that, despite his due respect, Bataille must still lament how 'in science the scientist himself becomes an object exterior to the subject, able to think objectively', because generally 'he could not do this if he had not denied himself as a subject to begin with' (E, 37).

Lacan in his 1953 *Écrits* article, 'The Function and Field of Speech and Language in Psychoanalysis', must also lament 'the subject who loses his meaning in the objectifications of discourse', calling it 'the most profound alienation of the subject in our scientific civilization', which 'we encounter first when the subject begins to talk to us about himself' (Éc, 233).[41] Bataille even senses 'professorial philosophy' (E, 260) to share this alienating objectifying tendency, for 'emotions put it out of joint', and we find 'superiority in one field bought at the expense of relative ignorance in other fields', as 'everyday philosophy becomes a little more of a specialized discipline like the others' (E, 253).

Bataille suggests that a 'reaction against this cold and rigid aspect of philosophy is characteristic of modern philosophy as a whole', say, from 'Nietzsche to Heidegger' – insofar as it finds itself caught 'in an impasse' where the very 'discipline' it requires leaves it also unable to 'embrace the extremes of its subject', eliding thence 'the outer most reaches of human life' such that 'it is doomed to failure' (E, 259). 'Yet what significance can the reflections of mankind upon himself and on being in general have', Bataille asks, 'if they take no account of the intense emotional states?' – discerning here 'the specialist's peculiar narrow-mindedness' even as it tries to be 'the sum of knowledge', for 'it does not even aim at being the sum of experiences' (E, 254). And so, Bataille concludes, with a 'clear conscience, even with a feeling of getting rid of a foreign body', 'some muck', or 'source of error, it leaves out the intense emotion bound up with birth, with the creation of life as with death' (E, 258-9) – and in doing so for Bataille, from the optic here of his *heterology*, is both forgetting and ensuring that 'the truth of taboos is the key to our human attitude' (E, 38).[42]

Here we encounter a more general critique where for Lacan, too, it must be admitted that the discourse of science *and* the university produces 'the *Spaltung* [splitting] of the subject', a 'divided subject' (SXVII, 104, 148) – one that is *split off* from its subjective truth in desire's signifying montage of the drives, which is always 'remembering, historicizing', and irreducible to 'need and reason' (SVII, 208–9). For while 'the discourse of science' has a place for everything, Lacan bemoans, it also 'leaves no place for man' (SXVII, 147) – which even invokes Nietzsche's earlier critique of science's tendency to 'unselfing and depersonalization' in its pursuit of 'disinterested knowledge' (BGE, 207), where actually it is 'despiritualizing' (TI VIII, 3), hiding from, and denying itself under the same 'ascetic ideal' or nihilism of hitherto Christian-Platonism, as merely *'the latest and noblest form of it'* (GM III, 23).

Lacan can thus depict the shift to modernity as going from the Sovereign Good of Plato and Aristotle and God of the Good of Christendom to the 'service of goods' of today: to the service of consumer and technological goods for the use, abuse, and alleged 'satisfaction of all' (SVII, 292) – which, however, can never integrate or properly acknowledge the Freudian Thing, or fill the gap of its momentous loss. 'We don't seem to have produced integral man yet' (SVII, 208), Lacan's 1959-60 *Ethics* Seminar nigh mockingly concludes: For when it comes to the 'human sciences', as they *condescend* to 'form a branch of the service of goods', Lacan will forewarn that 'implied here is a no less systematic misunderstanding of all the violent phenomena that reveal that the path of the triumph of goods in our world is not likely to be a smooth one' (SVII, 324).

Lacan's *Seminar VII* comments above are best understood with his later *Seminar XVII* reference to 'the capitalist's discourse, with its curious copulation with science' (SXVII, 110) – insofar as 'science got its money', its funding and grants, by promising to *apply* its findings 'to put all kinds of machines, gadgets, contraptions, at your service' (SVII, 325).[43] This is where it can be of added value to bring in Bataille's own critique of modernity for its inexorable capitalism, to cast light further into this *curious copulation* disclosed by Lacan, which Bataille in fact discusses at length prior to *Eroticism* in his 1948 *Theory of Religion* and 1949 volume I of *The Accursed Share*.

Making use of Max Weber's 'famous studies' (AS I, 195), Bataille traces capitalism back to Luther's Protestantism – who initially 'formulated a naïve, half-peasant revolt' – and then to Calvin, whose subsequent 'reactions were those of a jurist familiar with business matters', who thus 'expressed the aspirations of the middle class of the commercial cities' (AS I, 115).[44] Here is where the lack of a properly sacred erotic transgression on the Christian inner ethical plane is *externalized* further into the political sphere, such that earthly deeds among the order of things are reduced to accumulation, governed by work and more respect for taboos. This opposes any sacrificial festive function given 'to the use of excess resources, or rather to their destruction', Bataille notes, 'at least insofar as they are useful' (AS I, 120) – referring to the non-productive potlatch type expenditure, transgression, or *gift* that retains a divine about it. Bataille will mark how part of the latter had at least survived with 'the Roman Church', in their 'contemplative idleness', 'ostentatious luxury', 'splendour of ceremonies and churches', and 'forms of charity' to make good the losses for the poor (AS I, 122-3). 'Shining through the world of pure utility that succeeded it', Bataille concludes, 'where wealth lost its immediate value, it still radiates in our eyes' (AS I, 122).

But Luther denied 'the idea of merits gained by these means', as Bataille explains, for basing himself on 'the Gospel's principle of hostility to wealth and luxury', Luther was incensed by 'the possibility of gaining heaven by making extravagant use of individual wealth' (AS I, 121). This is because Luther saw the transgressive squandering of surplus involved as a profane self-aggrandizement, *deflating* what to him, Bataille notes, was the 'decisive separation between God and everything that was not the deep inner life of faith', thus rendering 'everything that we can *do* and *really* carry into effect' on this earth 'futile' or 'culpable' (AS I, 121). Calvin, then, extends what for Bataille is this 'utter negation' by seeing the pursuit of profit, made possible by work, taboos, and thus some self-denial, as governed *not* by any greed but by 'diligence and industry', and thereby asserts the 'morality of commerce' – for even in Luther, Bataille recalls, however futile or culpable, earthly activity 'must still be subject to moral law' (AS I, 122). Consequently, in the capitalism emerging, fuelled by the advances in science and 'the rise of industry' (TR, 87), the aim of accumulation became *only more* accumulation – shifting us thus from what Bataille discerned as the 'former, static economy', which 'made a non-productive consumption of excess wealth', to one which only ever 'accumulates and determines a dynamic growth of the productive apparatus' (AS I, 116).[45]

Bataille even marks how 'Calvin rejects merit and works no less firmly than Luther', but with principles 'articulated a little differently', and 'more consequences' (AS I, 123). And this was such for Bataille that now 'the reformed Christian had to be humble, saving, hardworking', and 'bring the greatest zeal to his profession, be it in commerce, industry or whatever' – as values herein were 'overturning', 'withdrawn', and only 'given to the virtues that have their basis in utility' (AS I, 123). How better to show this than the size of one's wallet? – *not* now as 'a way of attaining salvation' but 'as a proof salvation has been attained' (AS I, 123), as Bataille notes in citing Tawney, as the obscure *God rewards the rich* doctrine of predestination emerges.[46] This doctrine, moreover, is much to the contrary of what Lacan in *Seminar VIII* suggests is the traditional 'Christian curse that what is most worthwhile is forever refused to the rich' (SVIII, 60), also phrased as the 'Christian truth that the kingdom of heaven is off-limits to the rich' (SVIII, 49) – as epitomised in Jesus being purported to have said that 'it is easier for a camel to pass through the eye of a needle than for a rich man to enter the kingdom of God'.[47]

Instead we arrive now at what Lacan calls the 'rich Calvinist' doctrine, referring to how 'Calvinist theology' deems as 'one of the elements of moral guidance that it is on Earth that God rewards the people he loves with plentiful goods', that 'observation of the divine commandments brings success here on earth', and, moreover, will always 'bear fruit in all of sorts of enterprises' (SVIII, 57). As long as the wealth did not attract a 'halo of splendour', Bataille would add, and was paradoxically limited to 'useful works' – one could here become as obscenely rich as one pleased by professing only to be taking pride in their 'attachment to a profession', 'the desacralization of human life', and 'the glorifying of God' through negation of one's 'own-glory', through the 'relegation of mankind to gloryless activity' (AS I, 124).[48]

With immediate spending now considered waste, one invested *only* in more production, causing ever more uncontrolled destructions as our newly disavowed drives again re-emerge without our prior knowledge, affirmation, or consent. Here violence continues the *ferocious ignorance* of Yahweh, the *superego* as Sovereign Good, savaging within, projecting without, but now in the name of profit! Bataille concludes, 'the revolution effected by the Reformation has, as Weber saw, a profound significance: It marked the passage to a new form of economy'; for 'by accepting the extreme consequences of a demand for religious purity it destroyed the sacred world, the world of non-productive consumption, and handed the earth over to the men of production', which 'inaugurated the world of the bourgeoisie, whose accomplishment is economic mankind' (AS I, 127).

Bataille's *Theory of Religion* will thus lament how here we are '*reduced to the order of things*', and 'more estranged' now 'than ever before' – in a world 'that no longer knows what to do with its products', surrendered to a movement 'no longer controlled' (TR, 93–4). How could one in fact know, or control? – when, Bataille must add, 'capitalist society reduces what is human to the condition of a *thing* (of a commodity)' (AS I, 129). For this is such to appear that *everything already is symbolic*, and the sheer imaginary of this reduction veils the irruptions of the returning real in the guise of Law growing ever more violent by the day.[49]

The physical destruction of the environment is the direst effect of this forced reduction – given, Lacan notes, that it 'threatens' not just culture or civilization but 'the planet itself as a habitat for mankind' (SVII, 104). For as Richardson puts it, while capitalism cannot itself escape wasteful-useless expenditure, its refusal to properly acknowledge this is what 'turns it into an accursed form', externalized in 'imperialistic wars and destructive violence', assuming 'uncontrollable and potentially catastrophic forms' – for missing still is 'sacred being devoted to life enhancement', through a 'joyous surpassing of limits', serving the 'real needs of mankind', rather than 'the market', with its ever begrudging 'eye upon an ultimate accumulation'.⁵⁰ Bataille would only add to this that while this monstrous capitalism, which in its 'pure form' expressed the austerity of 'time is money', was 'implicit in the first formulation' (AS I, 125–6), of 'self-denial, which in Calvinism is the affirmation of God' (AS I, 136) – at the time 'what was needed was less to give complete freedom to the natural impulses of the merchants than to tie them to some dominant moral position' (AS I, 125). For 'it was only in England, in the second half of the seventeenth century', 'that Puritans linked the principle of the free pursuit of profit to the Calvinist tradition' – as thereupon the 'independence of economic laws was posited', Bataille concludes, and the 'abdication of the moral sovereignty of the religious world on the plane of production came to pass' (AS I, 125).⁵¹

The violence of this is no doubt real but always 'rationalized', and rarely understood: The consequence of our prior systemic *flight* from the real through two-thousand years of an inflated dualism. Hence, the moralists who hustle only for ever *more* flight, castration or lack, continue to feed the problem without realizing it. And here 'a crook is certainly worth a fool', as Lacan quips of the political, noting how the 'gathering of crooks into a herd' yields the 'collective foolery' that 'makes the politics of right-wing ideology so depressing'; whereas by a 'curious *chiasma*', he hastens to add, 'the "foolery" which constitutes the individual style of the left-wing intellectual gives rise to a collective "knavery"' (SVII, 183) – which is arguably more depressing still.⁵²

This is where Zupančič in *The Shortest Shadow*, in the first book-length work to attempt the 'short circuit' of bringing Nietzsche's thought back into relation with Lacan's to challenge the orthodoxies surrounding them, writes of *sublimation* as the counter to ideology here mis-presenting itself as 'reality principle', 'empirical fact', or 'biological, economic necessity'. For sublimation gets us *closer* to the real which is left out of 'reality', does *not* turn away in the name of some pre-existing Father ideal or Good, but creates a stage so that prohibited drives and passions can be re-seen as something valuable, so as to challenge the criteria of morality and reformulate anew.⁵³ I have shown how in Bataillean terms it is precisely eroticism that is the lure towards this sublimated 'ethics of the real', earlier framed in Zupančič by a reading of Lacan with Kant, which now sheds any Christian residue or masochist sense of duty by recovering prohibited animality as sacred, naturally desired, and affirmed – rather than as 'pathological' – as the lost but ever latent origin that restores the joy to *jouissance*, and allows us to rethink the relation of taboo and transgression in a more analytically attuned and optimal way.⁵⁴

The next chapter will consider how Bataille's 1928 erotic novella *Story of the Eye* might metaphorize a break from such repressive taboo hitherto that profits from externalizing destruction. While abreast, now, of a genealogy restoring the erotic to its proper place – like the dawning days of *Hellenismos* – I conclude by throwing to the Bataille whose contribution apropos of the equiprimordiality of taboo-*and*-transgression, and its more optimal functioning in days and nights and gods and plays gone by, must continue to *resonate* across the myriad discourses, and unconscious formations, until something better with *it* can be done.

> The various forms of human life have superseded each other and we finally see how the last step must be taken. A gentle light, not the full glare of science, shows us a reality difficult to come to terms with compared to the reality of things; it makes possible a silent awakening.
> —Bataille, *Eroticism* (1957), 163

NOTES

1. In her reading of Lacan with Kant, Alenka Zupančič calls 'ethics of the Real' not an orienting towards the real but an attempt at acknowledging the real as already operative in ethics making it by nature 'disturbing' and 'excessive'. My approach is closer to her next book which reads Lacan more with Nietzsche, so as to locate the infinite regress of this super-egoic closure not as something of a 'revolution' by Kant but a consequence of the ascetic ideal she notes occurring 'in the whole history of Christianity'. By incorporating Bataille's erotics my aim is to even further overcome the monstrous, moralizing return of the repressed this neurotic asceticism causes, rather than universalize, rationalize, and essentialize its symptoms as Nietzsche diagnosed to still occur throughout German idealism, including in Schopenhauer. I discuss the inherent nihilism of Schopenhauer's pessimism vis-à-vis the differences between Nietzsche and Freud here in section 4.1. For Nietzsche's debunking of the mythical 'real' of idealism from Plato to Kant and beyond, couched in terms of Lacan's treatment of the problem of sublimation inherited from Freud, see also section 2.3 of Themi, *Lacan's Ethics and Nietzsche's Critique of Platonism*, 36–40. Zupančič, *Ethics of the Real: Kant, Lacan* (London: Verso, 2000), 4–5; and *The Shortest Shadow: Nietzsche's Philosophy of the Two* (Cambridge, MA: The MIT Press, 2003), 50.

2. For Marc de Kesel's critique of the notion of an ethics of the real in Zupančič and Žižek, along with Mari Ruti's response that an ethics of sublimation or desire and an ethics of the real need not be posed as mutually exclusive – particularly insofar as we can elevate the object of desire to the level of the Thing (*das Ding*) to overcome oppressive social forces – see chapters 5 and 6 of *Unconscious Incarnations: Psychoanalytic and Philosophical Perspectives on the Body*, eds. B. Becker, J. Manoussakis, D. Goodman (Milton Park: Routledge, 2018), 76–112.

3. As Lacan's term for *maximal* enjoyment *beyond* usual pleasures, *jouissance* requires transgression; as he stresses in his *Ethics* Seminar: 'without a transgression there is no access to *jouissance*' (SVII, 177).

4. Bataille writes: 'My true church is a whorehouse – the only one that gives me true satisfaction' (G, 12). Michael Surya suggests that for Bataille 'the girls are god's

saints, whom he loves'. Surya, *Georges Bataille: An Intellectual Biography*, trans. K. Fijalkowski, M. Richardson (London: Verso, 2002), 84.

5. David Allison also notes how taboos function 'within this horizon' of labour to order nature. Allison, "Transgression and the Community of the Sacred," in *The Obsessions of Georges Bataille*, eds. A. Mitchell, J. Winfree (Albany: SUNY Press, 2009), 85–7.

6. Zafiropoulos, *Lacan and Lévi-Strauss or The Return to Freud (1951-1957)*, trans. J. Holland (London: Karnac, 2010), 5–6, 44, 106, 138–9, 158.

7. Freud also remarks on this recapitulation of the species in every infant, where 'impressive analogies from biology' can show us that an 'individual's mental development repeats the course of human development in an abbreviated form', in his 1910 essay on Leonardo da Vinci. See Freud, "The Resistances to Psychoanalysis (1925)," in SE19, 220–1; and *Leonardo da Vinci and a Memory of his Childhood*, in SE11, 96–7.

8. Richardson notes that by 1931 Bataille is 'considerably widened by attending the lectures of Marcel Mauss on anthropology'. Richardson, *Georges Bataille*, 20–1.

9. Charles Shepherdson discusses how this post-symbolic sense of the real 'only exists as a result of symbolization', as 'an effect of the symbolic order' that is 'not reducible to it' and 'not at all equivalent to reality'. For discussion of this in terms of a *return of the repressed* due to a neuroticized attempt at symbolization, see Themi, *Lacan's Ethics and Nietzsche's Critique of Platonism*, 12, 14. Shepherdson, *Lacan and the Limits of Language* (New York: Fordham, 2008), 38.

10. See Lacan, "The Mirror Stage as Formative of the *I* Function as Revealed in Psychoanalytic Experience (1949)," in Éc, 78; "Aggressiveness in Psychoanalysis (1948)," in Éc, 94; and Dylan Evans, *Introductory Dictionary of Lacanian Psychoanalysis* (London: Routledge, 2005), 71–2. I must also thank an anonymous reviewer for pointing out this term in Lacan's early work.

11. Plato, *Gorgias*, trans. W. D. Woodhead, in *The Collected Dialogues of Plato: Including the Letters*, eds. E. Hamilton, H. Cairns (Princeton: Princeton Press, 1989), 285.

12. See Paul Raimond Daniels, *Nietzsche and the Birth of Tragedy* (Durham: Acumen, 2013), 45.

13. See entries πυθμήν, πύθω, and Πύθων in Henry G. Liddell and Robert Scott, *A Greek-English Lexicon* (Oxford: Clarendon Press, 1996), 1551–52.

14. Rohde and Nietzsche had both become classics professors under Friedrich Ritschl at Bonn and Leipzig, remaining for a time close thereafter. For more on the history of their friendship and the relationship of their work, see Alan Cardew, "*The Dioscuri*: Nietzsche and Rohde," in *Nietzsche and Antiquity: His Reaction and Response to the Classical Tradition*, ed. P. Bishop (Rochester: Camden House, 2004), 458–73. Rohde, *Psyche: The Cult of Souls and Belief in Immortality among the Greeks*, trans. W. Hillis (Eugene: Wipf-Stock, 2006), I, 97, 110; II, 287–8. See also the entry ἄδυτος in Liddell and Scott, *A Greek-English Lexicon*, 25.

15. Calasso, *The Marriage of Cadmus and Harmony*, trans. T. Parks (New York: Vintage, 1994), 148–9.

16. Rohde, *Psyche*, II, 288.

17. Mauss, *The Gift: The Form and Reason for Exchange in Archaic Societies*, trans. W. D. Halls (New York: Norton, 2000), 6–7.

18. Richardson suggests one is 'well-advised' to take *Eroticism* as the entry point into Bataille, as a 'clearly written' summation of his 'overall themes'. Richardson, *Georges Bataille*, 133.

19. Hollier notes that the profane-sacred distinction is central to Bataille's confrontation with the numerous 'forms historically taken by dualism' such as 'Good and Evil', 'the intelligible and the sensible', 'the transcendent and the immanent', and 'the high and the low'. Michèle Richman documents how this profane-sacred distinction was established in Durkheim's 1912 *The Elementary Forms of Religious Life*, and notes the role he and his nephew-student Mauss had in 'promoting an ethnographic awareness among the dissident surrealists who first collaborated on the eclectic art review *Documents* (1929–31), to which Mauss contributed', who would later come together with the *Collège de Sociologie* (1937–39) Bataille founded with Roger Caillois and Michel Leiris, who also 'had been students of Mauss'. Hollier, "The Dualist Materialism of Georges Bataille," trans. H. Allred, *Yale French Studies* 78 (1990): 130–1, 127. Richman, *Sacred Revolutions: Durkheim and the Collège de Sociologie* (Minneapolis: University of Minnesota Press, 2002), 3.

20. Daniels notes that such gods exhibit *real* human desires: strengths *and* flaws. E. R. Dodds suggests they are *projections* of real inner-states, personified by the poets as intervening from without. Daniels, *Nietzsche and the Birth of Tragedy*, 51. Dodds, *The Greeks and the Irrational* (Berkeley: California University Press, 1951), 14–5.

21. This is also Lacan's *split* or 'divided subject' (SXVII, 148).

22. Richardson notes that Bataille's *Theory of Religion*, whence these citations come, is 'important' but initially the 'most difficult' to understand. Richardson, *Georges Bataille*, 133.

23. Nietzsche also expresses admiration for Alcibiades' seductive qualities (BGE, 200) – while Lacan notes his 'highly remarkable absence of fear of castration' (SVIII, 157). For analysis of the continued relevance of the Hades-Persephone myth for female sexuation in contemporary media forms, see Alison Horbury, *The Persephone Complex: Post-feminist Impasses in Popular Heroine Television* (Basingstoke: Palgrave-Macmillan, 2015).

24. A full discussion of Lacan's *Seminar XVII* linking of the hysteric's fantasy to the Judaeo/Christian primal-father myth of Freud's *Moses and Monotheism* can be found in Themi, *Lacan's Ethics and Nietzsche's Critique of Platonism*, 87–97. For how certain feminist discourses can suffer from this hystericization in their complaints about patriarchy and the gaze, 'where male becomes a synonym for a sadistic father/master figure', invented paradoxically as something to reign over, see Horbury, "What does Feminism Want?" *Continental Thought & Theory: Journal of Intellectual Freedom* 1.3 (2017): 578, 582.

25. Bataille cites from Lévi-Strauss, *Structures Elémentaires de la Parenté* [Elementary Structures of Relationship] (Paris: Presses Universitaires de France, 1949), 30.

26. This is why Lacan paradoxically concludes that 'fantasy dominates the entire reality of desire, that is, the law' (SXVII, 129). Perhaps the key tell of the Judaeo/

Christocentric retro-projection at stake is the absence of bisexuality in the protagonists of the primal myth, which fails to tally with Freud's own 1905 *Three Essays on the Theory of Sexuality* (SE7, 141–8, 166, 220). See also the cross-referenced 1908 article 'Hysterical Phantasies and their Relation to Bisexuality', in SE9, 166.

27. Paul Smith observes that it is Bataille's insight into the erotic drama here that disrupts the structuralist 'nature/culture opposition' from *in*-between – preserving thus the actuality of our 'inner experience'. Smith, "Bataille's Erotic Writings and the Return of the Subject," in *On Bataille: Critical Essays*, ed. L. Boldt-Irons (Albany: SUNY Press, 1995), 233–4.

28. Lacan, "L'étourdit," trans. C. Gallagher, *The Letter* 41 (2009): 44.

29. Zupančič also notes vis-à-vis Nietzsche and Lacan where Christianity's bearing of the ascetic ideal allows no play for transgression in taking the side of law, wherein it rages against sensuality and corporeality to constitute a deepening of cruelty as a puritanical mode of enjoyment. 'Something has changed in the juncture of Law and enjoyment', she remarks – where, first and foremost, 'Nietzsche recognizes this mode of enjoyment in the whole history of Christianity'. My approach takes this further by incorporating Bataille's focus on the mutating structures of eroticism into Lacan's ethics and Nietzsche's genealogy – to begin, thus, not with Christian or even Platonic structure but with those preceding from the initial Palaeolithic transition to the classical-archaic Greek. Zupančič, *Shortest Shadow*, 49–51.

30. Famously it was Bataille, Caillois, and Leiris, who first took what Richman calls this 'ethnographic detour' in their founding of the College of Sociology in the late 1930s – the early gatherings of which Roudinesco records were also held in Lacan's apartment. Richman, *Sacred Revolutions*, viii. Roudinesco, *Jacques Lacan*, 136.

31. For exploration of the amorousness of Hellenic deities involving 'rapes, preceded by animal metamorphoses', see Calasso, *Marriage of Cadmus and Harmony*, 3, 5, 47, 52–3, 126–7, 136, 152, 205.

32. Bataille also resists some of the 'over-hasty' sexual reductions of contemporary psychology on mystics, as the foreclosed sexual drive here returns on another level for the subject, at least in their heads, rendering the accompanying physical sensations 'extrinsic to their experience' (E, 225–6). Amy Hollywood, with aid of Lacan's concept of 'not-all [*pas-tout*]', also defends against the charge of Sartre and Beauvoir that Bataille's own mysticism is a search for imaginary wholeness. Hollywood, *Sensible Ecstasy: Mysticism, Sexual Difference, and the Demands of History* (Chicago: The University of Chicago Press, 2012), 15–6, 35, 65, 113–4, 120, 149.

33. Freud also cites '*inter urinas et faeces*' in 1912 when locating some of the causes of impotence in how 'the excremental is all too intimately and inseparably bound up with the sexual' due to the unchangeable 'position of the genitals'. Freud, "On the Universal Tendency to Debasement in the Sphere of Love," in SE11, 189.

34. Lacan, *Triumph of Religion, preceded by Discourse to Catholics* trans. Fink (Cambridge: Polity Press, 2013), 44, 67, 71–2, 74, 77.

35. Bataille adds that the Christian-modern view of the orgy 'must at all costs be rejected', for it assumes a lack of 'modesty' instead of the sacrifice that 'demands equality among the participants', despite the 'differences between individuals and the

sexual attraction connected with those differences' (E, 117, 129). In his earlier 1944 work *Guilty* he discloses both orgy and brothel as religious sites of erotic fusion, despite the modern context maintaining a sordid aura around them – within which, he writes: 'I escape the illusion of any solid connection between me and the world' (G, 12–13).

36. Kendall, *Georges Bataille*, 181.

37. James Shields suggests that in reacting against Christianity, Kinsey commits the naturalistic fallacy: that 'whatever is, is right', and that 'all sex is good'. Shields, "Eros and Transgression in an Age of Immanence: Georges Bataille's (Religious) Critique of Kinsey," *Journal of Religion and Culture* 13 (1999): 178, 180.

38. Contrary to Kinsey's 'insistence', Shields agrees that work, not religion, hinders the most sexual release, as evidenced in Kinsey's own data. Shields, "Eros and Transgression in an Age of Immanence," 180.

39. Freud concludes something similar in his 1912 analysis of psychical impotence, suggesting 'something in the nature of the sexual instinct itself' prevents us from 'complete satisfaction', due to the impulses to incest, sadism, coprophilia, and the contrast of moral vanity with the implacable animality of 'the genitals themselves'. Freud, "The Tendency to Debasement in Love," in SE11, 188–9.

40. Evans notes that object *a* as 'the object of desire' for Lacan is both 'cause' and origin of desire, what the partial drives anxiously circle around, and what is left over after symbolic prohibition, returning as a 'surplus enjoyment [*plus-de-jouir*]' beyond a specific 'use-value'. Evans, *Introductory Dictionary of Lacanian Psychoanalysis*, 124–5.

41. In analysing Lacan's 'Freudian Thing' article from two years later, Adrian Johnston also marks Lacan's tendency to want to formalize psychoanalysis by use of mathematics (Éc, 362): as per the structuralist programme to formalize the foundations of the human sciences and the 'French neo-rationalist "epistemology"' which equates scientificity with mathematization – where such formalization is seen to counter alienation within ideology and the 'discourse of opinion' (Éc, 348). While this tendency does not occupy the entire terrain of Lacan's thought, and in its excesses risks regression to a kind of Pythagorean-Platonist metaphysical fantasy in its eschewing of the empirical, it does mark out a point of difference between Lacan and Bataille. A comparison of Lacan's more mathematics-centred positive comments on science with Nietzsche's more empiricist-centred view, including the signs of nuance found on both sides, can be found in sections 6.2 and 6.3 of Themi, *Lacan's Ethics and Nietzsche's Critique of Platonism*, 117–27. Johnston, "The Freudian Thing, or the Meaning of the Return to Freud in Psychoanalysis," in *Reading Lacan's Écrits: From 'The Freudian Thing' to 'Remarks on Daniel Lagache,'* eds. D. Hook, C. Neil, S. Vanheule (New York: Routledge, 2020), 62, 30.

42. As Jean-Louis Baudry puts it, 'Science, resulting from the realm of work, can only be developed within the delineated realm of taboo where desire is diverted and the subject...laid bare by transgression – is buried'. Baudry, "Bataille and Science: Introduction to Inner Experience," in *On Bataille*, ed. Boldt-Irons, 277.

43. Zupančič links the difference between master and slave morality in Nietzsche to the modern shift Lacan sketches here between the dominance of the master's

discourse to that of the university. However, master morality for Nietzsche was already destroyed as soon as Christianity was adopted, and previously already waning in Antiquity as Platonism became more popular. Thus, the decline of the Nietzschean master cannot be equated with the shift from feudalism to the industrial revolution and Enlightenment. I will discuss in sections 3.3, 6.2, and 6.4 how Bataille conceives the notion of sovereignty of feudalism to itself be a fake 'moralizing (enslaving) sovereignty mired in Christianity' (AS III, 368). A full discussion of Lacan's *Seminar XVII* shift from the master's to the university's discourse, including their relation to the analyst's and hysteric's discourse, can be found in section 6.1 of Themi, *Lacan's Ethics and Nietzsche's Critique of Platonism*, 108–17. Zupančič, *The Shortest Shadow*, 44.

44. Weber, *The Protestant Ethic and the Spirit of Capitalism*, trans. T. Parsons (New York: Scribner, 1958).

45. Jean Piel suggests that Bataille's own 'Copernican change' here beyond *restricted* notions of scarcity, growth, and utility is from his focus on the *general* economy of 'the living masses in its entirety – where energy is always in excess and which must unceasingly destroy a surplus', because 'the sun's rays, which are the source of growth, are given without measure'. An epoch is thereby structured by how it uptakes this surplus, excess, or 'accursed share'. In comparable terms, Zupančič dismisses those who reject Nietzsche's critique of the ascetic ideal as no longer relevant to our postmodern late-capitalist hedonist world, because Christian asceticism still involved a specific mode of enjoyment 'beyond the pleasure principle', a *surplus* enjoyment consequent to an initial renunciation, whose mode has merely changed on the surface in our today without any overcoming of its sadomasochistic structure. Piel, "Bataille and the World from 'The Notion of Expenditure' to the Accursed Share," in *On Bataille*, ed. Boldt-Irons, 102–3. Zupančič, *The Shortest Shadow*, 47–8, 50–1.

46. Bataille quotes from R. H. Tawney, *Religion and the Rise of Capitalism*, 2nd ed. (New York: Penguin Books, 1947), 109.

47. See *Matthew* 19: 25, *Mark* 10: 25, *Luke* 18: 25.

48. For Zupančič's discussion of the Calvinist turn to predestination, the 'hyperactivity' it causes, and the decline of the old masters of wealth via Weber, Nietzsche and Lacan (but not Bataille), see *The Shortest Shadow*, 41–3.

49. Žižek suggests that Bataille's Law-transgression dialectic overlooks a 'Kantian philosophical revolution' that makes *Law itself* transgressive. However, Nietzsche points to Kantianism as a retrograde Christianity (AC, 10–12), Lacan even notes its fixation on 'pain' (SVII, 80), and Bataille's greater articulation of the taboo–transgression relation, used to frame the genealogical analysis here, shows Christianity's disturbed violence preserved in capitalism as a symptom of a still *degraded* transgression and a 'Law' unworthy of the name – far from its more optimal form in Greece's tragic age. Later Žižek seems to remove the Dionysian *base* of the real by seeing it only as 'the monstrous aspect of the Apoliniac itself', 'gone awry, exploding in its autonomy', again suggesting *loss* of the more optimal taboo–transgression or Apollo-Dionysos dynamic, when the *profound incompetence* of Socrates on tragedy was idealized by Plato and *exacerbated* by Christianity, after combining with *Yahweh's*

ferocious ignorance. I have argued here that it is with aid of Bataille's focus on eroticism, and its original role in religion, that we can more successfully overcome the latter foreclosures. Žižek, *The Puppet and the Dwarf: The Perverse Core of Christianity* (Cambridge, MA: The MIT Press, 2003), 56; *The Parallax View* (Cambridge, MA: The MIT Press, 2006), 95; "Ideology III: To Read Too Many Books is Harmful," in *Lacan.com* (2007), 4, http://www.lacan.com/zizchemicalbeats.html (accessed July 3, 2020).

50. Richardson, *Georges Bataille*, 94–5.

51. Jean-Joseph Goux suggests today's consumerism is so wasteful it undermines Bataille's critique of it as hyper-productive. Noys responds that the 'unproductive expenditure' of Bataille 'cannot be reduced to the losses of capitalism' because it is not 'how wasteful or destructive' a society is but '*how* it goes about dealing with the accursed share' – which Goux even acknowledges in saying 'it is not the quantity of waste' but the 'mode of waste' that is 'the difference'. Noys suggests Goux was trying to extract a 'purified' accursed share, failing which was its reduction back into the restricted economy of capitalism. Goux, "General Economics and Postmodern Capitalism," trans. K. Ascheim, R. Garelick, *Yale French Studies* 78 (1990): 210, 223. Noys, *Georges Bataille*, 118–9.

52. Zupančič is again correct here in rejecting the dismissal of Nietzsche's critique of the ascetic ideal as irrelevant to our postmodern hedonistic era, where complaints about permissiveness and sexualization seem to take on the complexion of the kinds of moral panics that marked the Dark Ages of Christendom. The aim is to encourage the overcoming of the ascetic ideal by learning more about the real it *still* denies, falsifies, forecloses, and acts-out blindly as a means to 'enjoy' – to make its primary repressed material re-available for sublimation – not simply restore an earlier more recalcitrant (Christian) version of it. Although Žižek suggests Bataille's 'passion for the real' is 'obsessed with communism and fascism' and mistakenly opposes communism, I will show here in chapter 6 how a closer, more sustained reading of Bataille reveals him as much more nuanced than this implies, aiming from the 1930s to *expand* Marxism by incorporating other valuable traditions in French sociology, German philosophy, and psychoanalysis. As a Hegelian Lacanian of the left, Žižek is in his own way doing something similarly expansive with Marxism himself. Richardson, however, suggests that for Bataille the left must develop a sacred to 'counter' that of fascism, rather than compete with capitalism on its strength of 'economic utility', by equating us in the process 'with state domination and needs' and 'onerous duties' that neglect 'the importance of mankind's drives'. For Richardson, moreover, Bataille is only misread in this as an 'advocate for unlimited excess' and transgression 'in isolation from a sense of order', as if taboo were not coequal to his thought. Familiar with this misreading in 1946, Bataille himself states: 'People wrongly think that I am a nihilist interested only in Dionysian excess' – acknowledging in this that while at times he may have 'left a false trail', it was only in seeking 'the implications and significance of Nietzsche's experience', which opens most fully for him 'from a collapse' he is compelled to speak to, *from the inside*, as a 'repetition'. Zupančič, *The Shortest Shadow*, 47. Žižek, *The Puppet and the Dwarf*, 55; *The Parallax View*, 95. Richardson, *Georges Bataille*, 92–3, 23. Bataille, "The Problems of Surrealism," in WS, 101.

53. Zupančič's 2003 work was followed by my 2014 *Lacan's Ethics and Nietzsche's Critique of Platonism* which establishes the connection between Lacan and Nietzsche in a more thoroughly detailed and systematic way. I also explore this connection in terms of the initial proximity between Nietzsche and Freud here in chapter 4, tracing the divergences amidst the confluences from the Germanophone to the Francophone context where we find respectively the more Nietzschean Bataille and more Freudian Lacan. Zupančič, *The Shortest Shadow*, 77.

54. In her earlier 2000 work *Ethics of the Real*, Zupančič uses Lacan's *Seminar XI* to stipulate desire not so much as a configuration of the polymorphous perversity of the component drives and partial objects: as per Freud's *Three Essays on Sexuality* which utilizes the Latin 'libido' for 'desire' (SE7, 135, 170, 218, 231–2, 237) – but rather as something closer to a defensive fantasy against 'the Real of enjoyment', using this to pose a shift from an ethics of desire to one of the drive and the real between Lacan's *Seminar VII* and *XI*. Towards the end of the work, however, Zupančič notes that nevertheless 'at the heart of desire a possible passage opens up towards the drive', and 'one might therefore come to the drive if one follows the "logic" of desire to its limit'. The difficulty in preserving a hard distinction between desire on the one hand, and the drives-in-the real on the other, is that different desires have different aims, objects and thus initial proximities to the truth or real of the drives and enjoyment – as is evident in comparing, say, the puritan ascetic myths of Judaeo/Christian-Platonism with those of the earthly Homeric divinities, where for Nietzsche the latter serve as an 'instinctive deifier' of the bodily drives and senses *here* in nature, rather than dream of the kind of anti-world 'beyond' by which Plato is dubbed 'the great slanderer of life' (GM III, 154). I expound the distinction implicated here between the mythopoetic products, 'desires', and fantasies of weak sublimations (which elide and hide from the real) and those of strong sublimations (which are able to face and affirm the real) extensively in Lacano-Nietzschean terms in section 2.3 of *Lacan's Ethics and Nietzsche's Critique of Platonism*, 36–40. Zupančič, *Ethics of the Real*, 235, 243.

Chapter 2

Metaphorizing the Split Gaze of Bataille's Story of *Eye*

In the context of seeking a cure with 'Dr Borel, one of the first French psychoanalysts' (TE, 205) – while also challenging the idealist uses of Freud and Sade by surrealist contemporaries such as Breton – Bataille published a novella of his own in 1928 entitled *Story of the Eye* under the pseudonym 'Lord Auch', meaning literally 'Lord to the shithouse [*aux chiottes*]' (SE, 76). As Hollier was to put it, with 'Bataille's first writings a break was produced whose locus was this psychoanalysis', which implied confrontation, because where 'Breton proposes a use for psychoanalysis, Bataille proposes an inscription of perversion'.[1] Tried, then, in precisely this kind of fire, Bataille goes on to weave together in literary form what could be read as an earliest formulation of what would later become some of his most significant pronouncements about his milieu and its proposed amelioration. But this should come as no surprise, for as ffrench records, 'the fictional texts are imbricated in the theoretical writings, and vice versa', with the fictions thus coming from the same 'impetus that produces the more pedagogically oriented texts such as *The Accursed Share* or *Eroticism*'.[2]

We saw in chapter 1 how Bataille felt taboos had become unreflectively ossified over the course of time, meaning our erotic transgressions of such taboos today were condemned to degradation in a way that eschewed the sacred-erotic sites of our communal past. Such sites were once the stuff of religion, where myth and metaphorization took place. But it is also where, as Lacan would say, the '*jouissance* [enjoyment]' prohibited by taboo 'doesn't hush up' but finds its *Other* mode to speak: for the 'first effect of repression is that it speaks of something else', as a *return* of the repressed, which is 'what constitutes the mainspring of metaphor' (SXX, 61–2). And so, it is ever of interest to re-examine what our myths or fictions might be metaphorizing today, lest we neglect their meaning.

This chapter examines the meaning of the eye metaphor in Bataille's *Story of the Eye*. But it begins with Barthes' seminal 1963 essay on the topic, 'The Metaphor of the Eye', to offer then, with aid of Lacan's similarly formal linguistic approach to analysis, a more detailed fleshing out of the metaphor and metonymy disclosed within. The aim is also to explain here why Barthes counter-intuitively calls *Story* neither sexual nor phallic, nor a matter for depth-psychology, and to show how incorporating Lacan helps to demonstrate how the transgression of taboos is matched by transgression at the level of language to surface what is usually excluded *in the real*. Next, the chapter delves deeper into the content side of Bataille's *Story*, showing how the formal distance established can be an optimal vantage though which to disclose a clear picture of the desire at play, but only when aided by further engagement with Lacan's psychoanalysis and Bataille's own philosophical works on the erotic. The aim, here, in going beyond the formalism of Barthes, is also to consider how the violence of *Story* stages the battle lines against taboos that repress the drives to the point of explosion. Finally, the chapter turns to the treatment of Sade's 'Sovereign Man' in Bataille's definitive 1957 *Eroticism*, and argues that the violence inflicted upon a priest's *eye* in *Story*'s denouement metaphorizes a crossing of the bar of resistance towards the *gaze*. This is apropos of the specially ossified taboos of Christianity on the fluidity of the *real*, in what amounts to an immolation of the super-egoic *eye* of bad conscience, by the *re*-eroticizing Bataillean *gaze*.

2.1 SURFACE FORMALISM: METONYMIC CROSS-CUTS OF METAPHORIC CHAINS

Story of the Eye is not a deep work. Everything in it is on the surface.

—Barthes, 'The Metaphor of the Eye'[3]

This section examines Barthes' 'Metaphor of the Eye' article from the journal *Critique* Bataille founded after the war, in the special issue released upon his death, to consider how within it Barthes' linguistic approach sheds light on Bataille's *Story*. Ffrench in fact suggests that by emphasizing 'the structural quality' of the 'transgressive eroticism' of Bataille's *Story*, Barthes inaugurates the consideration of it 'as a *text*', rather than simply as 'a piece of surrealistic pornography' – meaning that one cannot read it 'except in relation to Barthes, today'.[4] The aim here, however, will also be to see how incorporating the similarly formalistic approach of Lacan to Freudian psychoanalysis might take such a reading as Barthes' much further still.

Barthes famously divides the *Story* into 'two chains of metaphor, that of the Eye...and that of tears' (ME, 123). The *Eye* is then given as 'primary metaphor of the poem' (ME, 121), as it is '*varied* through a certain number of substitute objects' along what, Barthes notes, 'the science of linguistics' teaches is the paradigmatic axis of 'selection' from a fund of 'similar' significants (ME, 120). It takes us from *round-white* eye to *round-white* egg, moon, testicle, buttock, or saucer. Only this, Barthes adds, means 'a second chain springs from it, made up of all the avatars of liquid', such as 'tears, milk in the cat's saucer-eye, the yolk of a soft-boiled egg, sperm or urine' (ME, 121). But the last two can be specifically invoked because seated in a cat's *saucer-eye* of milk, in the first erotic play between Bataille's narrator and the character Simone, is the latter's sex: as signalled by the evocative phrase, 'Milk is for the pussy' (SE, 10).[5]

This phrase relies on a colloquialism for vagina, but with milk there instead of the normally associated genital fluids, coming from a *round-white* saucer doubling as an eye, we come to what for Barthes is the key to Bataille's eroticism from the linguistic perspective: namely 'metonymical interchange' (ME, 126), in the 'transfer of meaning from one chain to the other *at different levels of metaphor*' (ME, 125). Here Barthes observes how the 'transgression of values that is the avowed principle of eroticism is matched by – if not based on – a technical transgression of the forms of language' (ME, 126), which is how Bataille can write 'drinking my left eye', an 'eye sucked like a breast' (ME, 125), as if milk would come, or eyes were nipples. This is what for Barthes creates a 'forced *syntagma*' (ME, 126), where a syntagma is usually 'the plane of concatenation and combination of signs at the level of actual discourse (e.g. the *line* of words)', as opposed to the *paradigm* or vertical axis 'for each sign of the syntagma', which is 'the fund of sister – but nevertheless dissimilar – signs from which it was selected' (ME, 127). And it is the forcing or interchanging of which that creates what Barthes calls 'the violation of a limit to the signifying space', which enables, 'at the level of speech, a counter-division of objects, usages, meanings, spaces' (ME, 126). This is such that eventually for Barthes what the 'play of metaphor and metonymy in *Story of the Eye* makes it possible to transgress is sex' – *sex itself* – which he suggests is *not* 'the same as sublimating it' through the usual channels, but 'rather the contrary' (ME, 126).

> She played gaily with words, speaking about broken eggs, and then broken eyes, and her arguments became more and more unreasonable.
> —Bataille, *Story of the Eye*, 34

A further example Barthes gives to support his schema is the above shift from 'break an egg, put out an eye', to 'break an eye, put out an egg' – where again, he explains, we 'tamper with the correspondence between the two chains', and 'instead of pairing objects and actions' within 'traditional affinity', we 'dislocate the association' such that 'the syntagma now becomes crossed' (ME, 124). This is what might explain the peculiar erotic charge of Simone, Barthes observes, later 'biting the bull's testicle like an egg or inserting it in the body', or 'cutting up or putting out an eye or using one in sex play' (ME, 125). For all of this forcing-crossing culminates in a dramatic final scene where Simone demands a priest have his eye cut out so she can put it in herself, such that Bataille's narrator would see there 'the wan blue eye of *Marcelle*' (SE, 67), a 'ravishing blonde girl' and the 'purest and most affecting' (SE, 12) of all the friends they had corrupted, 'gazing' at him 'through tears of urine' – as 'streaks of come' would frame the convulsing of Simone's final 'urinary spasm, and the burning urine streamed out from under the eye down to the thighs below' (SE, 67).

The utility of Barthes' formal schema is perhaps to create the right amount of intellectual distance in the face of what Bataille's narrator even calls the 'horror' and 'disastrous sadness' of these 'dreamy visions' (SE, 67). And in doing so, such formalism can also be preserving thus what Lacan calls the 'sovereign signifierness' of the speech that proffers in his 'Instance of the Letter in the Unconscious' article, apropos of his translating of Heidegger (Éc, 438)[6] – the deflationary *logos* of which in Bataille's case, Barthes notes, is occupied with 'demolishing the usual contiguities of objects' so that 'the world becomes blurred', its 'properties no longer separate', but 'spilling, sobbing, urinating, ejaculating', and forming its '*wavy* meaning' (ME, 125).

For Barthes this meaning is very much to *facilitate* what in Bataille is the erotic transgression of values with a language that itself signifies transgression, of the usual 'relationships of contiguity' between the two metaphoric chains of 'controlled difference' – such as eye, egg, saucer, urethra, with tears, yolk, milk, urine – which the 'metonymy that interchanges them immediately sets about abolishing' (ME, 125). Ffrench suggests that metonymy here in Barthes is thus 'an operation "within" metaphor', not its binary opposite, which actually 'undoes it as a vertical paradigm' – with metaphor 'collapsing into metonymy', and 'the vertical always falling to the horizontal'.[7] This is what allows Barthes to claim that '*Story of the Eye* is not a deep work', that 'everything in it is on the surface' (ME, 123). But it is also what allows him to eschew what he calls 'depth psychology', which might more properly be understood here as *wild-analysis*: the kind that only allows one to see 'as its "secret"' some 'sexual fantasy' (ME, 122) that could tell us more about the idiosyncrasies of a particular reader than about the great thinker-creator we find in Bataille.[8]

Lacan can also be of value here, insofar as he occupies a place between Freudian analysis and structuralist linguistics, by famously applying the latter to the former – but also *vice versa* – in his seminal works of the 1950s.

Russell Grigg notes how this is done via Lacan's inscription of Saussure's and Jakobson's linguistics into the 'primary process' in Freud, where 'condensation' now becomes metaphor, and 'displacement' is metonymy.[9] And with such interventions Lacan will also warn of the dangers of too hastily leaping from the signifier straight to the signified, as if the bar of resistance that separates the two realms were no longer in place, or completely transparent to all. In his 1955–56 seminar on *The Psychoses*, for instance, he complains of those for whom 'it is always the signified' that will 'draw attention' in their 'analyses', which are thereby 'misrecognizing that it's the signifier that in reality is the guiding thread', the 'instrument by which the missing signified expresses itself' (SIII, 220–1).

This shift in emphasis from signified to signifier is also taken up in Lacan's 1957 'Instance of the Letter in the Unconscious', where again it is the 'incessant sliding of the signified under the signifier' that 'comes to the fore' (Éc, 419), 'which is always happening (unconsciously, let us note), in discourse' (Éc, 425), and for Lacan much to the contrary of the 'illusion that the signifier serves the function of representing the signified', or 'that the signifier has to justify its existence in terms of any signification whatsoever' (Éc, 416). Later Lacan remarks that the signifier and signified of the 'Saussurian algorithm are not in the same place', that one would be 'deluding' oneself to believe one were 'situated in their common axis, which is nowhere' (Éc, 430–1) – which again can speak to Barthes' desire *not* to plunge so wildly into depth-psychology apropos of Bataille's text but to register, rather, a 'kind of open literature out of the reach of all interpretation', that 'only formal criticism can – at a great distance – accompany' (ME, 122).[10]

With this formal but perceptive distance in place, then, with aid of both Lacan and Barthes, we can observe the latter noting that there is a sense where Bataille himself has 'doomed every attempt at deciphering his poem to partial failure by giving (at the end of the book) the sources (they are biographical) of his metaphor' (ME, 122). This claim might at first appear odd, insofar as the revelations Bataille gives, the very results of his own psychoanalysis with Borel, might be said to be the very aim of depth psychology; but again, it should only be the *wild* type analysis that Barthes here has thought to see doomed. For as Foucault was to put it, Barthes' 'application of structuralism to literature' was to avoid its hasty reduction to the personal problems and history of the writer, but also its inflation to a 'very general' cultural analysis – by focussing instead on the 'particular specificity', at the 'level of writing', to recognize 'literature *as* literature' in a way that 'goes beyond the individuals who reside within its space', or its sublating into 'all the other cultural productions'.[11]

Barthes' other counter-intuitively anti-psychoanalytic assertion that 'the erotic theme is never directly phallic', that 'what we have here is a "round phallicism"' that 'in no way nominates the sexual in the first term in the chain' – that 'there are no grounds for saying that the metaphor sets out from the genital to end up at apparently asexual objects as egg, eye, or sun' (ME, 122) – can also speak, moreover, to what Lacan notes is the 'pre-genital' base of the libido, referring to its 'eternal polymorphism, with its world of images', of the partial drives-*and*-objects that are 'associated with the different stages from the oral to the anal', in their ever-flowing active and passive oscillations, confluences, and divergences around 'the genital' (SVII, 92). For Lacan also adds the 'scopic' and 'invocatory' to the more traditional oral and anal partial drives, with these four now perennially *constituting without completion* the genital organization emerging in the later Oedipal-phallic phase, as something never completely stabilized, or wholly dissolved, in a pure and perfect sexual relation by way of a 'natural metamorphosis' (SXI, 180–1, 200).[12]

Lacan in fact himself states in his 1965–66 *Seminar XIII* on *The Object of Psychoanalysis* that Bataille's '*L'histoire de l'oeil* [*Story of the Eye*] is rich in a whole texture that is well designed to remind us' of precisely the 'fitting together, the equivalence, the interconnection of all the o-objects and their central relationship with the sexual organ' (SXIII, 20: 247). But with this central relationship Lacan is not at all *reducing* the o-objects or part-objects, also known as objects *a*, to the genital relation, as little as Barthes himself should be denying them any relation at all, as indicated when he later states that still 'by virtue of their metaphorical dependence eye, sun, and egg are closely bound up with the genital' (ME, 125). Thus, being invoked here is how the *later* genital relation never fully subsumes its *pre*-existing and constituent partial drives, but only provides a temporal synthesis at best, memorialized by an implacable instability that is key to Lacan's later dictum that 'there is no sexual relation' (SXVII, 116) – that is, that there is no absolute, pre-ordained harmony between the sexes, or even between the subject and their own sex, at the genital stage that supersedes the polymorphous-perversity of the earlier constituent parts.[13]

This reordering or resituating of the genital phase back into its pre-existing constituent parts can now shed light on Barthes' ostensibly overstated claim that there is nothing sexual-genital, per se, *grounding* the 'perfectly spherical metaphor' as a 'simple thing signified', or 'as the first term in the chain', where each of its terms is rather just 'the significant of another term' (ME, 122). For Barthes notes how Bataille reveals to us in his postface that it is 'the very equivalence of the ocular and the genital that is original, not one of its terms', insofar as 'the Eye' is revealed by Bataille 'to have been the Father himself, blind, his whitish globes turned up in their sockets as he pissed in front of the child' (ME, 122). This, Bataille tells us, is because in his Father's blind, syphilitic state, he could neither make it to the toilet nor notice when his fascinated child was watching him make use of 'a small container at his armchair' (SE, 72).

Thus, it is the *equivalence* of ocular and genital as whole *primal scene*, and not as a singularly determinate or easily reducible sexual fantasy, signified, meaning or thing, that leads Barthes to affirm if not overstate apropos of Bataille's metaphor that 'the paradigm begins nowhere', despite how 'the Eye, whose story it is, appears to predominate' (ME, 122).[14] And indeed we find Bataille further revealing in his postface that 'the image of those white eyes from that time' was linked for him 'to the image of eggs', which 'explains the almost regular appearance of urine every time eyes or eggs occurs in the story' (SE, 72).

The place of balls in the series also originates here, insofar as they may have been visible with a roundness to match the eyes and eggs – an association culminating in the bullfight where Simone is offered the raw balls of the first bull sacrificed, described as a 'white dish containing two peeled balls, glands the size and shape of eggs', and 'faintly bloodshot, like the globe of an eye' (SE, 51). Bataille in fact confesses in his postface, entitled 'Coincidences' – and noting how he read *Story*'s depiction of a bullfight to a friend 'who is a doctor' (SE, 71), referring to his sessions with Borel – to not initially having connected the balls to the cycle of '*eggs and eyes*' (SE, 71). And this is what had left Bataille himself forced, then, before his analysis, to explain such 'extraordinary relations by assuming a profound region' where 'certain images coincide', 'the completely obscene ones', on which 'the conscious floats indefinitely' – and confessing thus to being 'unable to endure them without an explosion or aberration' (SE, 71).

But the urine that forms the explosive second or liquid chain of the primal scene, also linked to the eye by the roundness of the urethral opening and rim, takes an added sense in Bataille's pubertal phase – where he invokes an Oedipal development, and, through rivalry now *for* the Mother, comes to express disgust for the father who 'sometimes left shit on his trousers' (SE, 73). This is where urine becomes expressly linked to the feminine figures of the *Story*, particularly Marcelle, although Bataille suggests it is an exaggeration 'to say positively that Marcelle is basically identical' with his 'Mother' (SE, 73). Such links pertain to how after his father finally went mad, his mother, after being subjected to a particularly vile scene, 'suddenly lost her mind too', resulting in 'several months in a crisis of manic-depressive insanity', accompanied by 'absurd ideas of damnation and catastrophe', that led her to hang herself (SE, 73–4). But unlike Marcelle, who also hung herself after going mad subsequent to an ostensibly vile scene, 'they managed to revive her', his mother, that is, after which she then tried to drown herself in a creek – which is where Bataille found her, 'drenched up to her belt', as if her 'skirt was *pissing* the creek water' (SE, 74).

As ffrench puts it, 'the mother's madness and subsequent attempts at suicide follows point for point the narrative of Marcelle's insanity and subsequent death'. But here he must also mark 'a conflict between a structuralist reading' of liquidity, linked to the tears of the eye as a 'purely permutational and combinatorial', and that of Bataille's own expressly more psychoanalytic linking of it to the *phallic* urine of his paternal *and* maternal childhood memories, which return to mind as a kind of literary, phenomenological *meta-seeing*.[15]

Marcelle herself had only asked to be locked in a wardrobe naked during an orgy, stirred by the sight of Simone's entreating of a boy, 'Piss on me . . . Piss on my cunt' (SE, 16). And suddenly, Bataille's narrator would tell, 'Marcelle was pissing in her wardrobe while masturbating' (SE, 17), such that Simone and he would later fantasize about having her 'with her dress tucked up', in a 'bath tub half filled with fresh eggs', so she could 'pee while crushing them' (SE, 33). But this is only once they had broken her out of the sanatorium she was sent to when they forgot to let her out of the wardrobe right away: whence she was found, drenched and sobbing, 'in the make-shift pissoir that was now her prison' (SE, 17), when the orgy was discovered by the parents and 'police had to be called, with all the neighbours witnessing the outrageous scandal' (SE, 18).

2.2 DEPTH CONTENTS: THE VIOLENCE OF THE EYE'S TRANSGRESSION

Just prior to recollecting the mother's suicide attempts, Bataille's postface offers a further disclosure of explanatory significance: namely, that when his father first went mad and was 'literally howling in his room', Bataille 'went for the doctor, who came immediately', while his father kept 'endlessly and eloquently imagining the most outrageous and generally the happiest events' (SE, 73). This culminates in a moment where the doctor had 'withdrawn to the next room', with the mother, presumably to give his diagnosis, while the father 'shrieked in a stentorian voice': 'Doctor, let me know when you are done fucking my wife!' (SE, 73).[16] For Bataille records this as in a 'split second' having 'annihilated the demoralizing effects of a strict upbringing' – leaving him with 'something like a steady obligation, unconscious and unwilled', to find an 'equivalent to that sentence in any situation', which to him also 'largely explains *Story of the Eye*' (SE, 73).

This opens out more into the *content* side of the transgression in the *Story*, what Barthes had even called the 'transgression of values that is the avowed principle of eroticism' (ME, 125), which thus far we have tracked apropos of the formal linguistic transgression that matched it, via Barthes, but also

Lacan. Now, without at all eschewing the stabilizing structure of *distance* this formal approach has garnered, I delve deeper into the content side of things, to see what further light might be cast apropos of the *Eye*'s meaning.[17]

Lacan himself claims, in the limited comments we have of his regarding the *Story*, that it is 'a book published anonymously by one of the most representative personages of a certain essential uneasiness', in what is 'supposed to be an erotic novel' (SXIII, 20: 246). But this unease which, for Lacan, is specially 'anxiety, signal of the real' (SX, 160–1), is critical to understanding the violence depicted in *Story* – a transgressive yet anxiously erotic violence that is ultimately inflicted upon the eye itself: first, when the matador 'Manuel Granero (a real person)' has his eye put out by the horns of a bull, an event Bataille tells us he 'actually witnessed' (SE, 71), while Simone inserts a bull's ball in herself; and second, when at the *Story*'s denouement Simone inserts the enucleated eye of the priest in herself, whence the narrator sees it 'gazing' at him as the 'eye of *Marcelle*', crying 'tears of urine' (SE, 67).

Arguably in the *Story* throughout we have seen nothing but the metaphorization of violence on the eye, whether in the form of eggs being crushed while peed on by Marcelle in the bath, or flushed and peed on by Simone in the bidet or toilet (SE, 33). There was also Simone's cracking of an egg with 'her buttocks' after the narrator placed it 'on the hole in her ass', smearing his face 'abundantly in her ass' while his 'come shot out and trickled down her eyes' (SE, 14); or Simone's biting of the bull's raw ball as if it were an egg, staining her face 'blood-red' (SE, 53). But the key to what this violence metaphorizes is perhaps in Bataille's 1943 preface from *Le Petit*, where he expressly invokes 'the eye of the conscience' (SE, 76). For this can form a link between the enucleated eye of the 'blond priest' (SE, 57), whose eye it is in the final scene, and the eye of the 'blonde girl' (SE, 12), Marcelle, whose eye the narrator sees there – as both of them occupy a place of rigidity concerning prevailing taboo on sexual possibilities.

The eye of the matador can also be seen in this context – insofar as he is there to slay the bull, symbol of the raw animal power of the drive, which he incites by waving his red-rag towards. Perhaps, then, the sight of frigid girl and pious priest was also a kind of red-rag to the driving force of Simone and narrator?[18] This is where Bataille's work on the history of eroticism is of great value, sketching out as it does a genealogy of the *loss* of a more optimal correlation of taboo-*and*-transgression, during the concomitant loss of the *manifestly* erotic function of religion as the metaphysics of Monotheism took hold.[19] For as Bataille was to put it in his 1957 *Eroticism*, in the form of a condensed formula: 'Primitive religious feeling drew from taboos the spirit of transgression. Christian religious feeling has by and large opposed' (E, 118). Previously, however, the usual taboos placed on sex and death for the purposes of self-preservation would be temporally suspended by the gods, in the sacred-erotic moment of the festival – allowing both for propitious release of pent-up drives and knowledge of them, in a moment of communal sublimation and celebration. The optimal functioning of this taboo–transgression correlation was what was disclosed by Nietzsche in his 1872 *The Birth of Tragedy* as the Apollo-Dionysos dynamic of pre-Platonic Greece – a disclosure that influenced Bataille greatly.[20]

'We must not forget', Bataille must restress, 'that outside of Christianity the religious and sacred nature of eroticism is shown in the full light of day', with 'sacredness dominating shame' – where temples from Greece to 'India still abound in erotic pictures carved in stone in which eroticism is seen for what it is, fundamentally divine' (E, 134). But Christianity turned against these sacred-erotic sites of transgression, especially the orgy, seeking to impose the violent operation of taboo nigh across all times. For it was 'the religious side of eroticism that mattered most to the Church', Bataille records, 'the one that called forth her full wrath' (E, 137). This meant an equally violent force from the drive itself would then emerge to re-oppose, to root such taboo out, held in as it was by sadistic emotions of shame, fear, ignorance, and guilt: for, Bataille laments, 'reason alone could not define those shifting limits authoritatively enough' (E, 63). This double movement of rigidly forced taboo and explosive returning transgression is basically the violence of Bataille's *Story*, with the anxiety signalling the *real* soon to re-emerge – where the protagonists we find in Simone and narrator would rather attack such fixated taboo at its foreign source, than allow it to regerminate within as such.[21]

Regarding the violence that is not always literal, the act of urination is indeed most striking, which Simone would direct when 'she pissed on her mother', who had 'gazed' at them 'with such dismal eyes' (SE, 15); on Marcelle's corpse, when she 'drenched the face' because the 'open eyes' were 'irritating', and 'those eyes, extraordinarily, did not close' (43); on the priest's clothes, when she 'crouched down and pissed on them like a bitch' and 'wanked and sucked him' while the narrator 'urinated in his nostrils' (61); or on her playmates or self (11, 21, 33), when 'she soaked her dress in a long convulsion that fully denuded her' (42). There was also the 'tiny trickle' when she 'pissed down her leg' on the 'tomb of Don Juan', who caused them great mirth by founding there a church after 'repenting', by burying himself 'under the doorstep so that the faithful would trudge over his corpse' (SE, 56). What we have here is a metaphorization of the overthrowing of taboos holding the fullness of desire in abeyance, as indicated when Simone – whom their playmate Sir Edmund calls 'the simplest and most angelic creature ever to walk the earth' (SE, 55) – responds to the narrator's questions during her convalescence after a fall that not only did egg mean *eye*, because the 'white of the egg was the white of the eye, and the yolk the eyeball', but *urine* also meant to 'terminate, the eyes, with a razor, something red, the sun' (SE, 34).[22]

This *Sun* can call to mind 'the idea of the Good', famously metaphorized as such in Plato's 'Story of the Cave' of *Republic*[23] – the same Sovereign Good that Lacan notes in his 1959–60 seminar on *The Ethics of Psychoanalysis* has been 'the philosopher's stone of all the moralists' (SVII, 96), 'since Plato, certainly since Aristotle', and right 'through Christian thought itself' (SVII, 221). This is the Good that artificially *narrows* the limits of what may count as pleasure, guarding them zealously with threats of punishment or pain, such that Bataille's narrator will describe 'decent people' as having 'gelded eyes', who can 'savour the "pleasures of the flesh" only on condition that they be insipid' (SE, 42).

Lacan's 1964 *Seminar XI* dynamic of 'the eye and the gaze' is also of value here, articulating as it does 'the split' between the eye of perception and the sexed gaze of the real, wherein 'the drive is manifested at the level of the scopic field' (SXI, 73). For here is a '*Spaltung* [splitting]' to match the 'divided-subject' later discussed by Lacan in his 1969–70 *Seminar XVII* apropos of science, everyday morality and work, governed by the respect for taboos that can always *repress* so much of ourselves *to* the unconscious, and lead to the demand for *its* analysis (SXVII, 104, 148). Noys for one even poses the proximity between Bataille's transgressive, 'subversive image' and Lacan's eye-gaze split of *Seminar XI*, complaining how often this is overlooked when, in analysing the 'distortion of vision as an act of desire', the focus is only on Lacan's early 1949 article on 'The Mirror Stage' which sees the gaze as a 'mirroring effect of the mother's look'. Todd McGowan, in comparable terms, also complains of the influence of film theorists who metonymically seized on Lacan's early article to thereby reduce the gaze to a sadistic desire for mastery. For this omits the way the gaze itself can appear in the real for Lacan *as* an '*objet* a', (SXI, 105), wherein '*it shows*' (SXI, 75), to look back and joyfully shatter any ill-conceived narcissism at the level of the ego syntonic, by returning *that* which has been split, 'where the subject falls' (SXI, 76).[24]

This *split*, Lacan observes, still in *Seminar XI*, is the gap or 'lack that constitutes castration anxiety' (SXI, 73) – insofar as we may fear the real of the drive approaching, but also being *separated* from it too much.[25] Thus, what we have metaphorized with a quasi-repetitive insistence in Bataille's *Story* is the returning of the eye in some form to the separated sexed real of the partial drives and objects of the gaze – whether by flushing an egg down the toilet after Simone was upon them peeing or 'plopping' (SE, 35); the enucleation of a matador by a bull where the eye becomes the bull's ball in Simone's vagina (as discussed in Foucault's 'Preface to Transgression'), or the most directly violent snuffing of the priest whose eye ends up, in the very same *hole-in-the-real* of Simone, as the eye of Marcelle.[26] This 'eye of the conscience' (SE, 76), of everyday morality fixated on the repressing action of taboo, in such scenes becomes complete in its topsy-turvy movement, set in motion *by* taboo, when transgressively returning to the gaze *in* the real[27] – wherein we can find it staring back at us, as object, through the *tears of urine* framed by Simone's 'flesh, in the midst of fur' and 'streaks of come', that 'helped give that dreamy vision a disastrous sadness' (SE, 67).

In psychoanalytic terms, as well as in terms of *the gaze as object*, this dreamy vision also points to Lacan's sense that 'the symptom is a metaphor' (Éc, 439) – where the 'symptom here is the signifier of a signified that has been repressed from the subject's consciousness' – whence it is re-avowable only via 'deciphering' (Éc, 232). For the unease or anxiety, metaphorized as violence here, is a symptom that not only speaks to the distorted taboo–transgression correlation disclosed by Bataille's philosophy of the erotic, but also to what Lacan notes is the 'ambiguity and double causality of the symptom as a compromise formation' (SVII, 110).

We see this ambiguity in Simone's final erotic scene being described as containing images of 'disastrous sadness' (SE, 67), despite its erotic pornographic contents[28] – but also when the narrator earlier is walking the beach, having fled the scandal of the orgy, and marks within how the 'violent agitation' of his 'phantasms of Simone and Marcelle took shape with gruesome expressions' (SE, 20). Then there is the moment when shortly after reuniting with Simone, he notes how their 'sexual dream kept changing into a nightmare', their 'desire to fuck' linked to their 'most violent desires' through Marcelle's 'piercing cries' – that is, through 'her smile, her freshness, her sense of shame that made her redden and, painfully red, tear off her own clothes and surrender lovely blond buttocks to impure hands' (SE, 21–2).

What this ambiguity expresses, then, is the 'compromise' formation that Freud saw in articles such as his 1908 'Hysterical Phantasies and their Relation to Bisexuality', where he discerns how a 'libidinal and a repressive impulse' can in fact oppose each other *simultaneously* in the symptom. This is what Freud illustrates with a patient who 'pressed her dress up against her body with one hand (as the woman), while she tried to tear it off with the other (as the man)' – as a case of where the 'simultaneity of contradictory actions serves to a large extent to obscure the situation, which is otherwise so plastically portrayed in the attack' (SE9, 165–6).

Now we can see what is *otherwise so plastically portrayed* by Bataille's metaphorizing is both the repressive impulse of taboo and the libidinal impulse for its transgression: the double movement of which we can even see *as* Marcelle, in what the narrator notes was her 'unusual lack of will power' when coaxed into a 'tea with some other friends', in what became their fateful orgy – despite her being otherwise so 'timid and naively pious', and having 'blushed so deeply' at seeing them (SE, 15).

Her shame was all the more acute for having previously been lured into a ménage à trois, when she chanced upon Simone and narrator in the sexual act, atop a cliff by the sea – where, stunned by the sight, she 'suddenly collapsed and huddled in the grass amid sobs', but was soon persuaded to join with great vigour as 'two young mouths fought over' the 'ass', 'balls', and 'cock', and 'a brutal frenzy drove' the 'three bodies' (SE, 12). What we find here is Simone and narrator refusing to internalize the *eye* of bad conscience – identifying instead with the libido to attack the sources of where repression would come: whether a stern parent, a frigid subject, or ultimately a Christian priest, his institutional paraphernalia, and surrounds.

2.3 SADE'S SOVEREIGN MAN: THE RAPE OF PRIEST'S EYE BY THE GAZE

This section looks at the issue of violence where it takes its most direct form in the *Story*. It focuses on the actual acts of death and assault suffered not only by Marcelle and Priest, or the matador and bull, but also by an 'apparently very young and very pretty' cyclist Simone and narrator hit with a car, her head 'almost totally ripped off by the wheels' (SE, 11), and a 'petite and luscious streetwalker from Madrid', who, locked in a 'cramped, windowless pigsty' for their amusement, 'collapsed in a pool of manure under the bellies of the grunting swine' (SE, 46). Given the sadism, it is imperative to look at the chapters in Bataille's *Eroticism* on Sade himself entitled 'De Sade's Sovereign Man' and 'De Sade and the Normal Man' (E, 164–97). For it is here that we may find the final piece of the puzzle that is the wandering metaphor of the *Eye* – apropos of the violence it both sees and suffers.

Bataille in fact raises the question of whether we do or not 'wear our sadism like an excrescence which may once have had meaning' but has now 'lost it' – which today can 'easily be eradicated at will, in ourselves by asceticism, in others by punishment' – for it may be that we are 'concerned on the contrary with a sovereign and indestructible element of mankind, yet one that evades conscious appraisal' (E, 184). Bataille will thus stress the imperative of the '*normal* man of today to become aware of himself and to know clearly what his *sovereign* aspirations are in order to limit their possibly disastrous consequences' (E, 185). And on this basis, as an ethics of self-knowledge, of a Delphic *know thyself*, not only does Bataille provide a commentary on Sade and conclude that 'by describing these instincts in a masterly fashion' he has 'contributed to man's slow-growing awareness of himself' (E, 183) – he also gives expression to his own violence in *Story of the Eye*, but in a way that I suggest signifies a deeper *crossing* towards the *gaze*, in response to the ossified taboos of Christianity, lingering as a thick residue on the fluidity of the *real*.[29]

Let us first examine the cyclist death near the start of *Story*, which is not only surprising because of her innocence and beauty, but also because Simone and narrator 'nevertheless...waited a long time before copulating', right where they had 'parked a few yards beyond, without getting out, fully absorbed in the sight of the corpse' (SE, 11). Here the 'horror and despair at so much bloody flesh' is described as 'nauseating' but also 'very beautiful', and 'fairly equivalent' to the impression Simone and narrator have upon 'seeing one another' (SE, 11) – leading to the evocative description of Simone's 'natural' sensuality, 'tall and lovely', as 'suggestive of all things linked to deep sexuality, such as blood, suffocation, sudden terror, crime', insofar as she 'so bluntly craved any upheaval' (SE, 11). But all this will come to signify for Bataille the still *compromised* relation of transgression and taboo at what can be called a Sadean transitional stage. For in *Eroticism*, Bataille notes, 'De Sade knew nothing about the basic interrelation of taboo and transgression', as 'opposite and complementary concepts', but nevertheless he 'took the first step' in intuitively linking 'erection and ejaculation with the transgression of the law' (E, 196).

This is what Lacan in his own *Ethics* calls the '*jouissance* of transgression' (SVII, 195), that which is always linked to the law or taboo it crosses, after also announcing he 'would talk about Sade' (SVII, 191). But it is in pursuing this relation between 'desire and the law' that Danny Nobus suggests 'Lacan entered a tacit dialogue with Georges Bataille' and his notion of eroticism, via Sade's literary invocation of the violence of desire as 'the problematic part of ourselves' (E, 273) – with Bataille's work thus forming an 'essential yet unacknowledged backdrop' for Lacan's 1963 *Écrits* article 'Kant with Sade', which was even first published in the journal *Critique* shortly after Bataille's death.[30]

In this Sadean sense, Simone and narrator would be like Sade's literary characters such as: 'Clairwill, the heroine Juliette's companion in debauch', whom Bataille finds is scolded for committing crime 'in the flush of enthusiasm', instead of the preferred 'cold blood' (E, 172–4); or Amélie and the Borchamps who, 'hoping for a monster execution', betrays 'all the members of a conspiracy which he himself has plotted', which actually 'delights the young woman' (E, 175). But even though Bataille's *Story* is from the earliest part of his oeuvre, Sade's couples preferring to plan the greatest of crimes with the coldest of blood, for extra *jouissance* – without such an established *complementary* role for taboo – seems to surpass by far the general countenance of Simone and narrator, who seem to metaphorize something more that is happening.

Nobus further suggests that the lack of complementarity is also what unites 'Kant with Sade' as failures for the Lacan who again here, Nobus will stress, is 'following in the intellectual footsteps of Bataille, yet without ever mentioning him by name', when arguing that 'desire and the law are not antagonistic forces, but rather interdependent components of a single bipolar psychic system'. Nobus adds to this that Lacan here is 'extending a principle he had also found in Freud'.[31] But as was Bataille himself in a sense, considering the 1921 *Group Psychology* essay he so admired, where Freud marks how 'a periodical infringement of the prohibition is the rule', as is shown by 'the institutions of festivals' which are 'excesses provided by law' that are much desired because of 'the release they bring' – ending in 'the transgression of what are at other times the most sacred commandments' (SE18, 131).

Freud's earlier 1913 *Totem and Taboo*, also known to Bataille and noted in this context by Nobus, too indicates awareness of this complementary structure, but from shared anthropological sources such as Durkheim, Frazer, Hubert, and Mauss – wherein Freud notes that for primitive mind the power prohibiting wishes and 'the apparently more important one of inducing him to transgress the prohibition' are two functions that 'can be reduced to one', as the recollection of a forbidden act seems to *coincide* with its temptation (SE13, 30–1, 34). In a clinical sense, this tight bond between law (taboo) and desire-enjoyment (transgression) again speaks to repression and return of the repressed as two sides of the same coin, expressed in Lacan's 'Kant with Sade' article as 'Law and repressed desire are one and the same thing' (Éc, 660) – which in response to the ascetic ideal of Christian ideology is where the superego as Law secretly takes on the perverse injunction to enjoy (transgress), as was already formulated in essay II of Nietzsche's *Genealogy of Morals*.[32]

This perverse fusion is illustrated for Nobus where Kant's moralism 'does not eradicate desire, but merely represses it', and thus simultaneously sustains and inflames it, which risks declining from the highest good to the most radical evil; whereas for Sade, Nobus concludes, there is equally no such thing as a raw, unmediated or 'pure' natural desire, free of any interdependence on 'the symbolic Other of language and the law'.[33]

Lacan himself will even confess in his *Ethics* seminar, just three years prior to his 'Kant with Sade', to be 'thinking of Georges Bataille' with the idea that Sade's value here remains the 'power to open up the possibility of the assumption of being on the level of immorality' – for Lacan contends that the many 'treatises and rationalizations' offered by Sade's characters, often 'dubbed digressions' from a 'loss of suggestive tension', suggest an 'approach to a centre of incandescence or an absolute zero that is physically unbearable' for both the 'reader and writer' (SVII, 201). It is in this sense for

Lacan that while Sade is the latent truth of Kant (Éc, 646), with Lacan later saying 'I make Kant into a flower of Sadism [*fleur sadique*]', the opposite can also be true, that Kant is the latent truth of Sade, making Sade into an inadvertent flower of moral masochism in his literary *crusading* for the real as impossible – all because of an as yet insufficiently clarified inter-relation between law (taboo) and desire (transgression).[34]

With respect to Bataille's *Story*, however, the cyclist's death, 'apparently very young and very pretty' (SE, 11), can also invoke for Bataille the primitive logic of sacrifice, which in *Eroticism* is where the 'victim dies and the spectators share in what the death reveals' – that 'for us as discontinuous beings death implies the continuity of being', that is, of the continuity 'of all existence with which the victim is now one' (E, 82). In the chapter of *Eroticism* entitled 'Beauty', moreover, Bataille marks also how the victim is 'chosen so that its perfection shall give point to the full brutality of death' (E, 144), which is akin to the sexual act in invoking the 'contrast between the pure aspect of mankind and the hideous animal quality of the sexual organs' (E, 144). This is because both sex and death mean dissolution back into the continuity of the *real* of nature, that from which we have *distanced* ourselves via taboo: the transgression of which, through highest possible points of contrast acting as lure, as points of vertigo, brings the *cycle* most starkly to mind – which for Bataille again takes the erotic and 'connects it with the nostalgia of lost continuity' (E, 146), and how 'to despoil is the essence of eroticism', meaning 'beauty has a cardinal importance, for ugliness cannot be spoiled' (E, 145). In the chapter entitled 'The Object of Desire: Prostitution', then, with precisely this contrast of high and low in mind, Bataille concludes, 'we are faced with the paradox of an object which implies the abolition of the limits of all objects, of an *erotic object*' (E, 130).

Here we might consider the assault of the 'streetwalker from Madrid' (SE, 46), initially surprising not just because she is 'petite and luscious' (SE, 46), but also because her profession does not appear to represent the fixation of taboo at all. But this surprise connects to the misreading of Bataille as aiming to fully obliterate taboo, rather than restrain it to its more optimal relation *with* transgression.[35] For Bataille marks the degradation sex work falls into to actually be the *consequence* of Christianity's fixation of taboo, forcing the drive to nigh shun taboo altogether in response, with no other choice, as in 'low prostitution' (E, 134) which the Church, while burning the others for referencing the sacred, allowed to continue so that 'the degradation of prostitution was stressed and used to illustrate the nature of sin' (E, 137). Previously prostitutes were in contact with 'sacred things', and in 'surroundings themselves sacred', Bataille recalls, had a 'sacredness comparable with that of priests' (E, 133) – again showing how taboo had coexisted *with* transgression in a sacred-erotic coupling. Only this called forth the Church's 'full wrath' (E, 137), for rivalling its own paltry purpose. Hence, 'Witches were burnt, low class prostitutes allowed to live' (E, 137) – and this is how in Bataille the streetwalker is connected to the later assault of the priest: It is from connecting by default to the Church's fixation of taboo which destroyed any sacred-erotic transgression, and pointed to the perverse effects this censorship caused as what it was built to combat.[36]

In turning now to the final assault of the priest, Don Aminado, in the climactic moment of violence of *Story*, we reach thereby the heart of the matter: The source of the all-seeing 'eye of the conscience', which Bataille bemoans as the most 'desperate image for remorse' (SE, 76), radiating as it does from the eternal panopticon of the Judaeo-Christian God himself, fixating taboo while promoted by his emissary Priest in the guise of unconditional love. This is an *agapic* love cleansed of flesh and *eros*, for as Bataille put it in *Eroticism*, 'flesh is the born enemy of people haunted by Christian taboos', as it 'signifies a return' for them to an always 'threatening freedom' (E, 92). It is also why in their final improvised ceremony, as a kind of Black Mass, Simone, narrator, and their other companion Sir Edmund, restore the Church's rituals back to the erotic truth of some bodily substance – undoing the reaction-formations against the latter by injecting things such as semen and urine.

They make the priest erect while hearing confession, when Simone confesses to masturbating while giving it to him, 'so that the long cock stuck out, pink and hard' (SE, 60). They make him 'come on the hosts in the ciborium', because they 'smell like come' and thus really are 'Christ's sperm in the form of small white biscuits' (SE, 61–2). They make him urinate in the chalice and drink it, because if the wine used were really the '*blood* of Christ' it would be '*red*' instead of 'only *white*', so really they are 'quite aware that this is urine' (SE, 62). Then they snuff him at the moment of climax, when Simone manages to 'squeeze his throat' so that 'the cock stood on end', and the narrator had 'no trouble fitting it into Simone's vulva' (SE, 64) – linking here definitively death with sex. But not before again invoking the *eye*, this time through the legs of a fly, that irritated Simone by having 'perched on the corpse's eye', whence it was 'agitating its long nightmarish legs on the strange orb' – whereupon Simone 'took her head into her hands and shook it, trembling', while seeming to 'plunge into an abyss of reflection' (SE, 65).

'Do you see the eye?' – she asked in coming to: 'It's an egg'; 'I want to play with this eye'; 'tear it out at once, I want it!' – and Sir Edmund obliged with a 'pair of fine scissors from his wallet' (SE, 66). And soon Simone was fondling it, feeling the 'caress of the eye over the skin', slipping it into the 'profound crevice of her ass' from which it spat like a 'stone from a cherry' (SE, 66). This is where the narrator finally 'fucked her hard', while Edmund rolled the eye 'between the contortions' of their 'bodies', 'bellies', 'breasts', and 'buttocks', whence Simone took and 'slid it' into her vagina such that Bataille found himself facing what he imagined he was 'waiting for in the same way that a guillotine waits for a neck to slice' – '*gazing* at' him 'through tears of urine' (SE, 67). No tears of blood, here, like an Oedipus lamenting a crime, or a Mary lamenting a world of sin through the eyes of a Lord, but tears of urine – as all the contiguities of previous events are interchanged in one final metonymy, at the different levels of the metaphor of the *Eye*, that keeps the relations with the real here resolutely *to* the surface.

This is the final image which for ffrench intersects vision and liquidity, as 'the *eye pisses* and *looks* at the same time' – signalling then the 'liquefaction of reality' and its transgressive 'transformation into a flux', where 'light is liquid' and 'the real, as what is *seen*, flows'.[37] But Freud had earlier connected 'urethral erotism' to 'ambition' (SE21, 90), in a footnote of his 1930 *Civilization and Its Discontents*, and the task here has also been to discern what the *ambition* of Bataille through his main characters has been. Later Bataille himself will mark the solid-fluid dynamic as a version of Apollo and Dionysos (AS II, 144) – as, I suggest, is Lacan's eye and gaze – signalling, then, the desire of Bataille for a return of Dionysos, of the properly erotic gaze which was artificially reduced by Christianity to the sadistic role of evil-eye. This is of course the opposite effect on the gaze than that which was wrought by Apollo, which Lacan in *Seminar XI* even notes is part of 'the pacifying, Apollonian effect of painting', where, through beautification, something 'given not so much to the gaze as to the eye' involves 'the abandonment, the *laying down*, of the gaze' (SXI, 101) – rather than, say, its repressive inflammation.

By way of conclusion, then, concerning what Bataille's eye metaphor means, here we might again reference Lacan's theorization of metaphor and metonymy from his 1957 *Écrits* article on 'The Instance of the Letter in the Unconscious'. For here metonymy is disclosed as 'caught in the rails', of 'eternally extending towards the desire for something else' (Éc, 431) – that is, as always passing from object to object which are *parts* substituted for an *elided* (w)hole that is 'the Freudian Thing' itself (SVII, 132) – an elision, Lacan notes, 'by which the signifier instates lack of being in the object relation', and the 'maintenance of the bar' or 'resistance of signification', in 'relations between signifier and signified' (Éc, 428). Even Barthes had to concede that while *Story of the Eye* 'is a metaphorical composition' (ME, 120), within it 'Bataille's eroticism is essentially metonymic' (ME, 125). But Lacan observes that metonymy is where 'perverse fixation' occurs, as a 'suspension of the signifying chain' (Éc, 431) – which here would hearken to Bataille's primal *scene* of his father's blind syphilitic upturned eye while urinating, while his fascinated child is secretly and jubilantly *watching* – precisely there where Lacan would say a 'screen memory is immobilized and the fascinating image of the fetish becomes frozen' (Éc, 431).

This is the paternal memory later overlaid by that of Bataille's mother *looking* like she was *pissing* the creek water, subsequent to his father's re-sexualization of her right before his son's *eyes* when implying the doctor was fucking his wife – ensuring thus the recurrence of the erotic copulations of *difference* between the eye and liquid substitutions in the text.[38] But because Bataille has his characters not merely passing between what Lacan calls the 'service of goods' (SVII, 324) – that is, the consumer goods and moral goods that govern their accumulation; or, incidentally, between merely 'natural' objects of various kinds – I suggest the way the *eye* passes metonymically between objects such as egg, saucer, sun, or ball, *does* conjure the whole Freudian Thing. For as shown with Barthes, this metonymy is itself substituting at cross-cut levels of different objects ('break an eye', 'put out an egg', 'light (the sun) pours down', 'drinking my left eye', 'like a breast' (ME, 124–5)), that are themselves already metaphorical in their substitutions by being *condensations*: where, for Lacan, 'condensation is the superimposed structure of signifiers in which metaphor finds its field', and its 'connaturality with poetry' (Éc, 425).

As Hollier had observed, Bataille's entries on 'Mouth', 'Eye', and 'Big Toe' in the *Documents* journal of the same period as *Story of the Eye* (1928–31), precipitated by his analysis with Borel and critique of surrealism over its idealist uses of Freud and Sade, show the same impulse of 'lexicographical organ removal' – making such organs the 'locus of a semantic concentration through which the part takes on the values that are tied to the whole', as a 'condensation (concentration) of all of humanity'.[39] But the Freudian notion of condensation is precisely where Lacan intervenes linguistically with his notion of *metaphor*: observing here how through the 'substitution of signifier for signifier' we get not so much the misplaced displacement but the 'crossing of the bar' of resistance and the 'emergence of signification' – where, Lacan suggests, 'between the enigmatic signifier of sexual trauma and the term it comes to replace in a current signifying chain, a spark flies that fixes a symptom', in which 'flesh or function is taken as a signifying element' (Éc, 429). This is why I conclude that the meaning of the round-white *Eye*, as enigmatic signifier: linked to flesh or function of *seeing*, or 'peeing', with beams of *liquid*, as metaphoric symptom – is the Gaze. The metaphor of eye is there as symptom to eventually be signifier of the gaze: the *erotic* gaze that is ultimately this eye-metaphor's signified when situated back in the fluidity of the *real*, *in* the unconscious, and its genealogical play of the emergence and elision of the memorialized drives through time.[40]

In terms of the violence depicted, I argued it metaphorizes *progress* over the erotic fictions of Sade that the priest is the only figure of a most direct torture violence: for many of the other acts depicted can be pleasurable *simulations* of transgression between consenting adults, offering much needed release – once, that is, the dictatorship of the priest's eye, the super-ego 'I' of fixated taboo, bad-conscience, ascetic identification and internalization is annulled.[41] For as Bataille noted in his final 1961 work, *The Tears of Eros*, on the history of erotic expression: 'The Middle Ages assigned a place to eroticism in painting: it relegated it to hell!' – for painters had to work 'for the Church', for whom 'eroticism was sin', meaning it could only figure as 'representations of hell', as 'something condemned', as 'repulsive images of sin'; that is, 'it did not enter a world ready to welcome it', the passions depicted were 'distorted', 'piously cursed' – and from that time often, Bataille laments, but including in his earliest work here discussed, 'we have found ourselves facing the terrible alliance between eroticism and sadism'.[42] I showed, thereby, why a priest's fictional enucleation, rape and murder metaphorizes a satisfying denouement of *Story of the Eye*.[43] It is Bataille in his characters transitionally working to improve the conditions of *jouissance* by exposing negation at its source – something that is paramount for an ethics that seeks to understand and prosper the human condition, through a restoring of its sacred-erotic dimension, *in* the field of aesthetics.

The next chapter will consider what kinds of aesthetic criteria may be further extracted from such of Bataille's erotic interventions into the artistic world, beginning with his striking confrontation with Breton's more idealist surrealism. In the meantime we bid our leave to the Priest's all-seeing eye, of a 'God' of what Lacan calls ultimately a 'ferocious ignorance' towards 'sexual relations' and 'sexual knowledge' (SXVII, 116, 136), portending to love, finally returned to the *real* of the gaze, via Simone – metaphorized also against the alleged purity of Marcelle – such that through the poetics of Bataille we can *see far more truth* about the libido and its polymorphous base, and its intensification of that signifying place, and far more optimally genuine ways of employing *it*.

> Poetry leads to the same place as all forms of eroticism – to the blending and fusion of separate objects. It leads us to eternity, it leads us to death, and through death to continuity. Poetry is eternity; the sun matched with the sea.
>
> —Bataille, *Eroticism* (1957), 25

NOTES

1. Hollier, *Against Architecture*, 84, 107–9. Bataille explains the perverse transgressive meaning of his pseudonym 'Auch' in his later 1943 preface to *Story* from

Le Petit. Bataille, "W.C. Preface to *Story of the Eye from Le Petit: 1943*," in SE, 76. See also Bataille, "*The Little One* [Le Petit] by Louis Trente," in *Louis XXX: The Little One* and *The Tomb of Louis XXX*, trans. Kendall (London: Equus Press, 2013), 35–40.

2. Ffrench, "Bataille's Literary Writings," in *Georges Bataille: Key Concepts*, eds. Hewson, Coelen, 190.

3. Barthes, "The Metaphor of the Eye," trans. J. A. Underwood, in Bataille, SE, 123. Repeat citations ME.

4. Other contributors to the special 1963 issue of *Critique* besides Barthes included Foucault, Sollers, Blanchot, Klossowski, Mason, Leiris, and Métraux. Ffrench, *The Cut: Reading Bataille's Histoire de L'Oeil* (Oxford: Oxford University Press, 1999), 6–7. See also Revue *Critique* 195–6 (1963): *Hommage à Georges Bataille*.

5. Deborah Cullen notes that *Les assiettes, c'est fait pour s'asseoir* means literally 'the plate' or 'seat is for sitting', as *assiettes* means both plate and seat but the pun is lost in English where 'words for "plate" and "seat" are very different', leaving translators thus to the imagination. The cross-lingual connotation of 'ass' in English might have helped with this. Noah Chasin, "Interview: Deborah Cullen," in *Bataille's Eye/ICI Filed Notes 4*, ed. Cullen (Santa Monica, CA: Institute of Cultural Inquiry, 1997), 16–7.

6. William Richardson discusses Lacan's translation of Heidegger's 1956 essay on Heraclitus's *Logos* to examine any compatibilities of Heidegger's thesis, where Being is interpreted as 'language itself in its origins', with Lacan's notion of an unconscious 'structured like a language' – which, however, refers more to the human subject than it does to the Cosmos as such. I discuss Lacan's *Seminar VII* debunking of an inflationary connection between the microcosm of the subject and the macrocosm of the universe at large, in the context of Aristotle's notion of an alleged Sovereign Good embedded within nature, in section 1.2 of Themi, *Lacan's Ethics and Nietzsche's Critique of Platonism*. Richardson, "Heidegger and Psychoanalysis?" *Natureza Humana* 5.1 (2003): 17. Lacan, "Trans. of *Logos*, by Martin Heidegger," *La Psychanalyse* 1 (1956): 57–79. Heidegger, "Logos (Heraclitus, Fragment B 50)," in *Early Greek Thinking*, trans. D. Krell, F. Capuzzi (New York: Harper and Row, 1975), 59–78.

7. Ffrench, *The Cut*, 11.

8. Freud's 1910 '"Wild" Psychoanalysis' article warns of such dangers, emphasizing psychoanalysis's 'extended' notion of the sexual that 'goes lower and also higher than its popular sense' by stressing 'the mental factor' (SE11, 222–3).

9. Grigg, *Lacan, Language, and Philosophy* (Albany: SUNY Press, 2008), 151–2.

10. Susan Suleiman, for example, notes how Andrea Dworkin conversely 'flattens' Bataille's *Story* into 'pulp pornography' which 'prevents her from noticing differences', or a 'more significant questioning', and 'obliges her to see, in every book she reads, simply more of the same thing'. Noys also notes Dworkin's 'desire to categorize and condemn' as 'violently reductive' in reading *Story* simplistically as 'an assault against women'. 'Woman', as the universal purity or innocence of

passive victimhood, is the one Lacan in *Seminar XX, On Feminine Sexuality*, suggests 'doesn't exist', saying 'there's no such thing as Woman, Woman with a capital W indicating the universal', which pertains to his thesis of the 'not-whole [*pas-tout*]' relative to the phallic function and lack of a naturally essentializing clean or moral 'sexual relationship' – of which he remarks: 'what do you expect? – if the sexual relationship doesn't exist, there aren't any ladies' (SXX, 57, 72). Horbury discusses further in Lacanian terms the way certain feminist discourses hystericize a master to castrate as if to abstract sexual difference to an equality as sameness in a puritan fashion, as per Althusser's depiction of ideology as the imaginary relation kept with the *real* conditions of existence. Suleiman, "Transgression and the Avant-Garde," in *On Bataille*, ed. Boldt-Irons, 320–2, 324. Noys, *Georges Bataille*, 88. Horbury, "What Does Feminism Want?" 582.

11. Barthes speaks to this *ad hominem* type issue further in his 1967 essay, "The Death of the Author," in *Image, Music, Text*, trans. S. Heath (London: Fontana, 1977), 142–8. Foucault, "Return to History," trans. R. Hurley, in *Aesthetics, Method, and Epistemology*, 420–1.

12. Evans tables each of the four partial drives along with their corresponding erogenous zones, partial objects and verbs respectively, for example: *drive*-oral, *zone*-lips, *object*-breast, *verb*-'to suck'; or *drive*-scopic, *zone*-eyes, *object*-gaze, *verb*-'to see'. My discussion of how the eye relates to the gaze *as object* is still to come. Evans, *Introductory Dictionary of Lacanian Psychoanalysis*, 48.

13. For more on the 'no sexual relation', see Evans, *Introductory Dictionary of Lacanian Psychoanalysis*, 181.

14. Suleiman refers to Hollier and Freud's *Wolf Man* case to suggest Bataille's primal scene is an express fantasy for castration by the father and passive anal relation with him such that 'the mother becomes superfluous'. This, however, understates how the mother can be the powerful identification point of this passive desire, as Freud suggests Wolf Man's primal scene 'puts himself in his mother's place' precisely because he 'envied her this relation with his father' (SE17, 78). Jean Dragon also sees Bataille's oedipal figures as too paradoxical to be 'phallocentric', but Michael Halley implies that in defusing the charge of 'phallocentrism' Barthes risks inviting the opposite prejudice, which is what Lacan would call getting 'carried away by the idea of an antiphallic nature, of which there is no trace in the unconscious'. Halley notes, for instance, the implacable phallicness of the liquid series in Barthes schema: the sperm and urine propagating not in circles but straight lines, in the *real*. Suleiman, "Transgression and the Avant-Garde," in *On Bataille*, ed. Boldt-Irons, 328, 333. Freud, *From the History of an Infantile Neurosis* (1918[1914]), SE17, 78. Dragon, "The Work of Alterity: Bataille and Lacan," *Diacritics* 26.2 (1996): 32. Halley, "And a Truth for a Truth: Barthes on Bataille," in *On Bataille*, ed. Boldt-Irons, 290. Lacan, *Television: A Challenge to the Psychoanalytic Establishment*, trans. J. Mehlman (New York: Norton, 1990), 134.

15. Ffrench, *The Cut*, 169, 171.

16. Anne Ciecko notes how this makes the mother 'now and forever a sexual being in her son's eyes', and where, after losing her mind, 'the writer even feared she might kill him', the reader of any 'pornographic narrative of sex and death cannot read the

story as mere fiction', but rather as the 'unspeakable potential source of Bataille's obsessions and fears'. Ciecko, "Notes on Desire: Bataille and Oshima," in *Bataille's Eye*, ed. Cullen, 35.

17. Marc de Kesel identifies Lacan's psychoanalytic ethics as aiming to 'maintain the right (imaginary and symbolic) distance in relation to the (real) "thing"', a distance that is *also a nearness* to the Freudian Thing or 'polymorphous-perverse libidinal base' – for escapist transcendence can be most caught up in the death-drive of all, such that 'the conclusion of Lacan's critique' for de Kesel is that 'what for centuries we have called the supreme good must henceforth be identified as radical evil'. De Kesel, *Eros and Ethics: Reading Jacques Lacan's Seminar VII*, trans. S. Jöttkandt (Albany: SUNY Press, 2009), 83, 94, 104, 172–4.

18. The term 'old rag and ruin' that Madame Edwarda gives to her sex on exposing it to the narrator of another of Bataille's erotic novellas, using her fingers to 'draw the folds of skin apart', and demanding that he 'see, look' (M, 150), might also be read in this context of waving a red-rag to a bull.

19. For a sustained critical treatment with Nietzsche, Freud, and Lacan of how religion was *denaturalized* and its erotic function reduced to sin over the course of the Judaeo-Christian-Platonic trajectory, see also chapter 5 of Themi, *Lacan's Ethics and Nietzsche's Critique of Platonism*, 58–63, 103, 131.

20. Andrew Stein records that from 1930 Bataille identified with 'Nietzsche's Dionysos' by making him 'more Sadean', as evidenced in '*Madame Edwarda* (1938), whose protagonist, a very licentious prostitute, claims to be god since moderns can come face to face with ecstatic loss and death beyond their control only through the gateway of vulgar sexual pleasure'. Stein also notes how Caillois, one of Bataille's cofounders of the College of Sociology along with Leiris, 'often stressed the parallels between Nietzsche's ideas on tragedy and ecstasy' and their 'contemporary ethnographic research into the sacred', which Caillois felt 'added to the theories of Freud' with a 'new general theory of the instincts'. Noys suggests 'the most important early event' for Bataille was indeed 'his reading of Nietzsche in 1923, described as "decisive"' – while Giulia Agostini also marks the 'discovery of Sade in 1926', 'shortly after'. Stein, "The Use and Abuse of History: Habermas's Misreading of Bataille," *Symplokē* 1.1 (1993): 28, 31. Noys, *Georges Bataille*, 6. Agostini, "Nietzsche," in *Georges Bataille*, eds. Hewson, Coelen, 61.

21. Nadine Hartmann notes Bataille's aim to *remobilize* transgression to retrieve our enriched animal nature of the sacred that Christianity repudiated as pagan. But in attempting to criticize his articulation of the feminine aspect of desire, she seems to invoke the 'Woman with a capital *W* indicating the universal' of Lacan's *Seminar XX* that does *not* exist as *whole* (*pas-tout*) outside the Christian puritan fantasy of the sexual relation (SXX, 57, 72–3), wishing to conceive Madame Edwarda as a 'quintessentially untouchable' and 'categorical unattainability' in an 'apotheosis' – as if to *reelevate* her to the virgin Mary – rather than inscribe the real of perversion as Bataille does in *lowering* God to the 'whore' and the *eye* of her sex (M, 150). Horbury also marks the foreclosure of what analysis can teach about *being* 'the object of desire', and the particularities of the pleasures entailed, whenever the signifier 'feminism' is invoked – functioning as a Judaeo-Christian superego to *censor* 'a woman's

enjoyment in the gaze' and 'in being an erotic object'. Hewson notes that where the sacred is made to *oppose* 'the sensible world' and rendered pure as the Good, as 'in Plato', is the 'sleepy position' of the *dualist* turn to transcendence criticized in Bataille's *Theory of Religion*, where 'reason and morality are opposed to passion and self-interest with a view to the conservation of the order of things' – and where, Bataille laments, there is the dual equation of 'good and the mind and the other that of evil and matter', resulting only in 'a sovereignty of servitude' (TR, 77). Hartmann, "Eroticism," in *Georges Bataille*, eds. Hewson, Coelen, 138, 143. Horbury, "What Does Feminism Want?" 568–9, 580. Hewson, "Religion," in *George Bataille*, eds. Hewson, Coelen, 168.

22. Michèle Richman notes how the bodily dejecta in Bataille's *Story* always 'signal a moment of sovereign rupture with the boundaries of personal homogeneity'. Richman, "Spitting Images in Montaigne and Bataille for a Heterological Counterhistory of Sovereignty," *Diacritics* 35.3 (2005): 57–8.

23. In his 'Rotten Sun' article two years later for *Documents*, Bataille discusses the sun as having 'the poetic meaning of mathematical serenity and spiritual elevation', but with a marked *Icarus* aspect ever warning against getting too high, or 'too close'. I discuss this further here in section 3.1. Plato, *Republic*, trans. P. Shorey, in *The Collected Dialogues of Plato: Including the Letters*, eds. E. Hamilton, H. Cairns (Princeton: Princeton University Press, 1989), VI, 508; VII, 514–17. Bataille, "Rotten Sun," *Documents* 3 (1930): 173–4, in VE, 57–8.

24. Noys, *Georges Bataille*, 31–2. Lacan, "The Mirror Stage as Formative of the *I* Function as Revealed in Psychoanalytic Experience," in Éc, 75–81. McGowan, *The Real Gaze: Film Theory after Lacan* (Albany: SUNY Press, 2007), 1, 4–8.

25. Noys seems to reject the notion of castration here in Lacan for narrowly reducing to sexual difference, lack, or 'the body', to reject any assimilation of the Lacanian real as impossible with the heterogeneous of Bataille. But actually Lacan also widens the notion of castration to mean the subject's *entry* into language, along with their sudden *ejection* from its imaginarization, which requires both the installation *and* transgression of taboo and thus is much closer to Bataille's anthropological conception of a transitional 'laceration' from animal to human, or nature to culture, which need not retain such negative tones of closure, or assume the nature returned to seems exactly the same as that originally left behind. Possibly Noys has equated one of the metonymic misreadings of Lacan he has noted in 'Anglo-American academia' with Lacan himself, a move whose frequency McGowan has done much to remedy, with Laura Mulvey's reduction of the gaze to a sadistic male mastery over a passive feminine object coming in for particular criticism for its universalizing pretensions, failure to account for difference, and fixation to an ideologically infused consciousness at the price of the real. That said, McGowan's reading of Nietzsche's will to power as a desire for mastery vis-à-vis Foucault also perhaps greatly understates the sense of tragedy in Nietzsche, where the ultimate aim is ecstatic loss, to expend and discharge – *to gift* – rather than simply exploit and accumulate ever more power in a blind and unnuanced, unsublimated or compulsive fashion. This is even partly noted in McGowan's own paraphrase of Nietzsche's will to mastery as going beyond 'self-preservation', that is, beyond a mere mastery, narrowly conceived, with no

sacrificial or qualitative dimension. For Lacan's rereading of castration as a 'gateway through which the subject comes to language', linked historically to ritual sacrifice in our constituting from animal to human, see also Boothby, *Freud as Philosopher: Metapsychology after Lacan* (New York: Routledge, 2001), 176, 183. Noys, *Georges Bataille*, 31–2. McGowan, *The Real Gaze*, 2, 4, 8–9, 13, 15. See also McGowan, "Looking for the Gaze: Lacanian Film Theory and Its Vicissitudes," *Cinema Journal* 42.3 (2003): 27–47.

26. Foucault ends his Preface at the bullfight where 'the eye is returned back to its night', as Simone 'swallows a pale and skinless seed' ending with the 'urinary liquefaction of the sky' – where the Seville sun no longer *pours* light, having passed through the metonymic interchange disclosed by Barthes – connecting the narrator to the *immediacy* of the real as if 'to touch *her* [Marcelle] at eye level' (SE, 54). This Preface appeared in the 1963 *Critique* issue devoted to Bataille upon his death along with Barthes' essay. Foucault, "A Preface to Transgression," trans. D. Bouchard, S. Simon, in *Aesthetics, Method, and Epistemology*, 86–7.

27. Bataille attributes to Mauss on 'the history of religion' the discovery that taboo is 'not subservient' to explosive transgression but what 'gives it increased force', citing Caillois as definitively formulating this 'following Mauss's teaching and advice' (E, 65, 257). See Caillois, *Man and the Sacred*, trans. M. Barash (Chicago: Illinois University Press, 2001), 97–127.

28. Ffrench notes that Bataille's fictions are not strictly pornographic but rather 'narratives of the anxiety, shame, abjection and fear caused by the physical fact, the *real* of sex and desire'. Susan Sontag discusses *Story* from the optic of 'pornographies', as a case of those where 'inherent standards of artistic excellence pertain'. Suleiman suggests that because Bataille's eroticism meditates 'on its own Oedipal sources', the difference, ironically, is that 'between blindness and insight'. Ffrench, "Bataille's Literary Writings," in *Georges Bataille*, eds., Hewson, Coelen, 195. Sontag, "The Pornographic Imagination," in Bataille, SE, 83–4. Suleiman, "Transgression and the Avant-Garde," in *On Bataille*, ed. Boldt-Irons, 328.

29. Along with Halley, who rebukes Barthes for avoiding the final priest death scene, Suleiman suspects the focus only on the formalism of Bataille's *Story* artificially defends against its violent contents in the real, as a veritable 'averting of the gaze'. That said, the distorted content analyses such as Dworkin's that Suleiman broches also caution against eschewing formalism altogether, which Halley defines as 'commitment to textuality', 'emphasis on close reading', and 'scrutiny of forms as they appear on the page'. Richman notes how in *Critique* after the war Bataille develops an ethics of *dépense* (expenditure) that even conjoins Camus with Sade in a revolt against 'arbitrary and capricious' State violence. Halley, "And a Truth for a Truth," in *On Bataille*, ed. Boldt-Irons, 289, 291, 293. Suleiman, "Transgression and the Avant-Garde," in *On Bataille*, ed. Boldt-Irons, 319–22, 331, 333. Richman, "Bataille Moralist? *Critique* and the Postwar Writings," *Yale French Studies* 78 (1990): 146, 151.

30. Nobus, *The Law of Desire: On Lacan's "Kant with Sade"* (London: Palgrave-Macmillan, 2017), 85, 141. For a later distillation of this monograph, see also Nobus, "Kant with Sade," in *Reading Lacan's Écrits: From "Signification of the Phallus"*

to "Metaphor of the Subject," eds. S. Vanheule, D. Hook, C. Neil (New York: Routledge, 2019), 141, 145.

31. Nobus, *The Law of Desire*, 87; and "Kant with Sade," 145.

32. All this again stresses the importance of reading all of Nietzsche, Freud, Bataille, *and* Lacan together, to most fully grasp the *experience* they each were attempting to communicate for knowledge in their own variant ways. I discuss the relation of the quaternary Nietzsche, Freud, Bataille, and Lacan further here in chapter 4.

33. Nobus, *The Law of Desire*, 87–8; and "Kant with Sade," 141–2, 159.

34. Tiina Arppe suggests Bataille's focus in his 1957 *Literature and Evil* is 'on the impossibility of the experience which he sees Sade as pursuing' – in trying to maintain consciousness, as violence suppresses the differences between subject and object, and 'sexual frenzy (*jouissance*)' hits a 'summit'. Nobus also stresses for Lacan the difference between Sade's literary fantasy, expressed in his fictions as the absolute sadistic destruction of the Other, and that which governs Sade himself as a subject, the author 'not duped by his fantasy' (Éc, 656) who takes the pains of the Other upon himself – rejecting thus the reductive 'strict correspondence' between an author and their work in the question of 'the status and function of creative writing'. I discuss Bataille's *Literature and Evil* here in section 5.2. Lacan, *The Triumph of Religion* (1974), 83. Arppe, "Evil," in *Georges Bataille*, eds., Hewson, Coelen, 183. Nobus, *The Law of Desire*, 71, 145–6; and "Kant with Sade," 136–8, 159.

35. To counter this 'misunderstanding', Richardson cites Bataille stating that 'to shrink' from stability is as cowardly as 'to hesitate about shattering it', and that 'perpetual instability is more boring than adhering strictly to a rule'. Richardson, *Georges Bataille*, 23, 136. Bataille, G, 28–9.

36. Victoria Wohl depicts this via Foucault and Butler as when 'power does not prohibit but in fact incites and proliferates perversions', paradoxically calling for 'ever more penetrating and wide-reaching control'. In reading Freud's Schreber case, Lacan invokes Bataille's 'inner-experience' that 'God is a whore', restoring thus the foreclosed *sexual* aspect of religion, *in the real*. Wohl, "The Eros of Alcibiades," *Classical Antiquity* 18.2 (1999): 353–4. Lacan, "On a Question Prior to Any Possible Treatment of Psychosis," in Éc, 485, 488.

37. Ffrench, *The Cut*, 96–7.

38. Alan Bass discusses the emergence of the notion of 'castration' in such contexts as a fantasy of opposites foisted onto *difference* – creating fetishes (presence) as a compromise reaction-formation against phobias (absence). With his guillotine simile in the final image of *Story*, which Bataille writes he was 'waiting for in the same way that a guillotine waits for a neck to slice' (SE, 67), Bataille is perhaps invoking this process without reducing us to it, such that he leaves a way out. Bass, *Interpretation and Difference: The Strangeness of Care* (Stanford: Stanford University Press, 2006), x, 31.

39. Hollier, *Against Architecture*, 77–8, 84, 108.

40. Grigg notes how Lacan's theory of metaphor works best for substitution metaphors, but not appositive or extension metaphors, agreeing with Donald Davidson that the latter have no special determinate metaphoric meaning per se. Halley suggests that

by ultimately pointing to the presence of death in sex, the *eye* is paradoxically 'an empty metaphor' that 'symbolized no thing, a pure existent absence, the experience of irreality'. The eye as substitution for the gaze, however, which ultimately means the usually absent or excluded real, is here like the substitution of Booze's 'sheaf' for his phallus in the Victor Hugo metaphor discussed repeatedly by Lacan ('His sheaf was neither miserly nor spiteful'), in that the phallus connotes the function of castration and difference, and thus also the real. Perhaps a *Story of the Sheaf* remains to be written. Grigg, *Lacan, Language, and Philosophy*, 161–2, 164, 169. Davidson, "What Metaphors Mean," in *Inquiries into Truth and Interpretation* (New York: Clarendon Press, 1984), 261. Halley, "And a Truth for a Truth," in *On Bataille*, ed. Boldt-Irons, 292. Lacan, "The Metaphor of the Subject," in Éc, 758; "Instance of the Letter," in Éc, 422–3; and *Seminar III*, 218–9, 222–5.

41. Bass also marks via Nietzsche the origin of this 'slave morality' in the Platonic-Christian positing of ideal forms in a non-material world from which to denigrate the sensuous. Bass, *Interpretation and Difference*, 3.

42. Hewson and Coelen note the mature scholarship of Bataille's postwar work compared to the activist earlier texts. Horbury also links the medieval Death-and-the-Maiden theme in *Tears of Eros* (TE, 82–3) to the Hades-Kore myth of antiquity, noting the gradual loss of eroticism across time, the substitution of sadism, and its latent significance for sexuation still in popular media forms today. Hewson and Coelen, "Introduction," in *Georges Bataille*, eds., Hewson, Coelen, 19–20. Horbury, *The Persephone Complex*, 129–30.

43. I have shown also why Halley rebukes Barthes for eliding this scene from his analysis: for 'refusing to finish Bataille's story', by covering over the 'presence of absence', that he 'would just as soon skip'. Halley, "And a Truth for a Truth," in *On Bataille*, ed. Boldt-Irons, 292–3.

Chapter 3

Bataille, Nietzsche, Lacan, and the *Real* of Aesthetics

The previous chapter saw how Bataille's earliest published novella, the *Story of the Eye* of 1928, metaphorized an overcoming of the distorted taboo–transgression relation expressly characterizing Judaeo-Christian structure. Now I consider further the kind of aesthetic criteria that may be extracted from such of Bataille's interventions in the artistic world – from his early confrontation with Breton's surrealism to his later praise of prehistoric art – as a way of eventually leaping forwards, and *upwards*, to what he later took to be the sovereign level of Nietzsche's creative thought. Bataille describes this level as a 'moral summit' in his 1945 *On Nietzsche*, even though it is 'closer to evil than to good' in terms of traditional values, and corresponds 'to excess, to an exuberance of forces' with a 'maximum of tragic intensity', 'measureless expenditures of energy', and a 'violation of the integrity of individual beings' (ON, 17). Accordingly, the aim here will become to arrive at the maximum strength implied to furnish the aesthetic sphere with the restructuring it requires to be such a sublimated space for an eroticizing transgression.

First I examine Bataille's *Documents* era (1929–1931) critique of the ideals of beauty, taste, and of the boundary between high and low art. Waged in the context of accusing Breton of idealism, who in turn accused Bataille of perversion, this critique gives an important early indication of the kinds of aesthetics Bataille would oppose and, by implication, endorse.[1] Nietzsche's critique of Western idealism, and his major distinction between aesthetic states of *abundance* and *lack* that underpins it, will also prove of value to assess the dichotomies of high and low that can stifle our aesthetic debates – where one side of the binary is privileged over the other, and then reversed, in an equally reductive or misleading manner. Next, I examine Bataille's postwar turn to pre-history as central to his philosophical concerns, where he considers the Palaeolithic birth of cave painting to coincide with the passage from animal to human through our placing of taboos on animality, and then ritually transgressing them, in the sublime realm of aesthetics. Here for Bataille aesthetics becomes central for creating a secondary link between us and the animal world we *distanced* ourselves from, and it is also where kindred psychoanalytic concepts of sublimation and the real will be of use – for at the level of the unconscious drives there is still the demand for a direct enjoyment [*jouissance*], *in the real*, which, if not properly structured, can, as Lacan puts it, 'begin with a tickle and end in a blaze of petrol' (SXVII, 72). Finally, I turn to Bataille's positioning of Nietzsche's thought as the ultimate gift of subjectivity of the sovereign man of art, so as to suggest a criterion for aesthetic creation based on a sovereignty of the real. I will argue that this is something to be performed periodically *beyond* any reductively pre-given utilitarian purpose, governed by taboo, in the realm of labour and things.

3.1 DISSIDENT SURREALISM: BATAILLE'S *DOCUMENTS* CRITIQUE OF AESTHETICS

Before the war, in the *Documents* art journal he edited between 1929 and 1931 while embroiled in brutal dialectics with surrealist leader Breton, Bataille was reputed to have enacted a *transformation* of aesthetics – while earlier still, his most acknowledged precursor in Nietzsche had launched a striking intervention into aesthetics of his own, beginning with the seminal 1872 *Birth of Tragedy* and extending well into his final writings of 1888. This section brings together such of Bataille and Nietzsche's respective interventions into aesthetics, spanning almost a century between them (1872–1961) – within which the discoveries of psychoanalysis also took hold – to consider Bataille's *Documents* critique of aesthetics as only of *idealist* notions of beauty and aesthetics, and develops this by incorporating Nietzsche's critique of *both* sides of aesthetic dichotomies such as beauty and ugly, high and low. This will allow Nietzsche's celebrated 'backwards inference' of aesthetics to the physiological context of creating *in* the creator, 'from the work to the maker': amounting to the difference between an *abundance* of drive or a *lack* thereof (GS, 370)[2] – to ground Bataille's critique such that any combination of high and low qualities can in principle be part of a *positive* criterion for a real aesthetics, for an erotic aesthetics of the real.

Bataille's early critique of idealist aesthetics is best viewed in *Documents* articles such as 'The Big Toe', 'Rotten Sun', 'Formless', and 'The Language of Flowers' (VE). In the latter, for instance, he notes that while the visible parts of flowers signify 'ideal beauty', 'love', the 'beauty of girls' and 'human *ideal*' – as a reaching for the 'nobly elevated' – at the same time their 'ignoble roots wallow in the ground, loving rottenness just as leaves love light' (VE, 13). Similarly, in 'The Big Toe', Bataille notes the role of this toe in erecting the body 'straight up in the air like a tree', with a 'head raised to the heavens and heavenly things' – such as 'light and celestial space', as *principles* of good' – all of which requires, nevertheless, the 'firm foundation to the erection' given by the toe of 'this foot in the mud' (VE, 20). Then there is 'the sun' poeticized as 'the most elevated conception', meaning 'mathematical serenity and spiritual elevation', discussed in the article 'Rotten Sun' – called as such to note the *Icarian* tendency of reaching *too* high to get 'too close', 'causing failure and a screaming fall' as broke-wings of melted wax come crashing back to earth (VE, 57–8).

Bataille's point here is not to completely deny the heights and reverse privileges to fixate now on the lows, but to commend those aesthetic creations cognizant of the entire cycle between the two, what he calls 'a back and forth movement from refuse to ideal, and from ideal to refuse' (VE, 20–1). For this is an *eternal return* largely absent in 'academic painting', Bataille laments, which 'more or less corresponded to an elevation', but is still 'noticeable in the paintings of Picasso' – where what 'most ruptures the highest elevation' shares in the 'blinding brilliance' of the ascent, in the 'elaboration or decomposition of forms' (VE, 58).

Lacan also notes this of 'expressionist painting' in his *Seminar XI*, which, rather than the 'pacifying, Apollonian effect', takes us straight to the real, by way of a certain satisfaction in relation to the drive, of what is 'demanded by the gaze' (SXI, 101). But again, as Falasca-Zamponi puts it, what Bataille wanted here was not to completely shun Apollo but to facilitate 'an original discussion about the coexistence in nature of beauty and ugliness, formal and formless, normal and monstrous, high and low, ideal and material' – rather than simply 'reverse' our inherited and ready-made, pre-existing 'hierarchical principles'.[3]

We find further evidence of Bataille wanting to affirm the whole cycle between high and low in the apocryphal story concluding 'Language of Flowers', of the Marquis de Sade having the 'most beautiful flowers brought to him only to pluck off their petals and toss them into a ditch filled with liquid manure' (VE, 14). Even though, as Stoekl recalls, Breton used precisely this piece as grounds to attack Bataille for being a self-defeating 'excremental philosopher'[4] – Bataille seems well aware, as he puts it just prior to his portrait of Sade, that the 'substitution of natural forms for the abstractions currently used by philosophers will not only seem strange and absurd', but, 'moreover, threatens to carry one too far', and is 'absolutely unbearable for the most part' (VE, 14). Bataille's point is only that it is 'thanks to the miserable evasions' of those fixated on the high at the price of the low that there comes a 'troubling contempt' for all that is '*elevated*, noble, sacred' (VE,

14) – which, read with Freud, actually points to the self-defeating nature of *repressive* idealism: causing the distorted return of what was initially denied and thus 'withdrawn by repression from conscious influence', such that 'it proliferates in the dark', and thereby 'takes on extreme forms of expression'.[5]

In similar terms, Freud also rejects that in his analysis of the great *Leonardo da Vinci* he is only seeking to 'blacken the radiant and drag the sublime into the dust', affirming rather that there is nothing so great as to be immune from 'the laws which govern both normal and pathological activity with equal cogency' (SE11, 63). This is where Nietzsche's major aesthetic distinction between *abundance* and *lack* is of enduring value, for with it both wishing to fixate on the high at the price of the low, *and* vice versa, can be seen to express aesthetic states lacking in strength – whereas an abundance of strength would correspond to being able to affirm the whole cycle of high-and-low in some way like Bataille suggests, without recourse to either fixated idealism or morbid ugliness.

In the 'The Will to Power as Art' section of *Will to Power*, moreover – a key selection of his unpublished notes (WP, 794–853)[6] – we find Nietzsche further working his distinction to meet all the seeming paradoxes in aesthetics between 'high' beauty and 'low' ugliness, noting where it can be the former that signifies strength and abundance, and, depending on the context, where in fact it can be the latter. Greek tragedy becomes Nietzsche's exemplar of where pleasure in horrid themes, from incest and parricide to enucleation and loss, can nevertheless characterize 'strong ages and natures', 'strong enough to experience suffering as pleasure' – whereas those who turn away by citing their preferred 'taste for the pretty and dainty', could instead be suffering from the state of lack that 'belongs to the weak and delicate' (WP, 852).

In a later 1938 article focussed around Nietzsche, Bataille himself describes the tragic rites of Greece as 'a festival given in honour of horror-spreading time', which even 'depicted for gathered men the signs of delirium and death whereby they might recognize their true nature'.[7] But this is *not* to say that tragedy was wholly devoid of beauty – as Lacan, for instance, shows with *Antigone*, whose beauty is the very lure for us to affirm the incestuous horrors of the real[8] – or again to say that beauty is always bad in art while ugliness is always good. For Nietzsche also notes the cases where 'the ugly' is quite rightly 'excluded from art' when 'the aesthetic man reacts with his "No"' – cases where a work is, say, only the 'expression of a depression', whose *effect* is 'depressing' as it 'weighs down', 'impoverishes', and wrongly 'takes away strength' (WP, 809).

Ugliness for Nietzsche, then, is only of value when it comes from a 'master of this ugliness and awfulness', expressing a 'victorious energy' over the harsher aspects of existence (WP, 802) – not where it succumbs to them and, with 'that tyrannical will of the great sufferer', is bent only on

Figure 3.1 *The Fall of Icarus*, **Peter Paul Rubens, 1636.** Source: Royal Museums of Fine Arts of Belgium, Brussels.

'taking revenge on all things' by 'branding them with his image, the image of his torture' (WP, 846).⁹ And it is likewise for Nietzsche that beauty is only of value where it is *not* an escape but the artist's 'expression of gratitude for happiness enjoyed' (WP, 845), where the 'creativity is gratitude for their existence' (WP, 852). For this is what is bestowed in that 'making perfect, seeing as perfect, which characterizes the cerebral system bursting with sexual energy' – and which 'revives through contiguity this aphrodisiac bliss' – where here for Nietzsche, observed proto-Freudianly, 'art and beauty is an indirect demand for the ecstasies of sexuality communicated to the brain' (WP, 805).

Freud's *Civilization and its Discontents* had also marked how aesthetic beauty is 'a derivation from the field of sexual feeling' by 'an impulse inhibited in its aim' – consisting, then, of what are 'originally attributes of the sexual object' that are now attached *not* to the arousing genitals themselves, which may be too confronting or immediate, but rather, via the play of the signifier, 'to certain secondary sexual characters' (SE21, 82–3). Hence, the prized nature of the curve of a bay where the setting sun meets the sea, whose streams of light the moon will soon reflect to light up the night sky – all of which connotes, with a suitable amount of distance, indirection and mediation, the much longed for sexual relation. But again, Nietzsche warns, we must still be careful of cases where 'artists of decadence, who fundamentally have a nihilistic attitude towards life, take refuge in the beauty of form' (WP, 852). For this 'love of beauty' can also be an 'expression of the very inability' to '*see* the beautiful, *create* the beautiful', in certain situations – as opposed to the 'profundity of the tragic artists', Nietzsche again reaffirms, whose 'aesthetic instinct' mobilizes a strength of abundance that even 'affirms the large scale economy which justifies the terrifying, the evil, the questionable – and more than merely justifies them' (WP, 852).

The importance of situating Bataille's intervention into aesthetics with Nietzsche's is that we can now see why Bataille can neither be praised for justifying hatred of aesthetic beauty, nor dismissed for a morbid fixation on the ugly, low, and base. It all depends on the psychosomatic context of creation – *abundance or lack* – and analysing carefully on a case by case basis. So when in the *Documents* article, 'Formless', Bataille invokes this as what 'serves to bring things down in the world generally requiring that each thing has its form' – this is a riposte not to those who *also* appreciate form, but rather to 'those academic men' fixated on *only* 'giving a frock coat to what is, a mathematical frock coat' (VE, 31), such that they occlude key aspects, lowly *formless* aspects, of existence. This also speaks to Nietzsche's claim that it is sheer 'infamy', and one 'ought to thrash', anyone saying beauty, truth, and the good 'are one', for this elides the base roots of all three, which for Nietzsche is the sense in which 'truth is ugly' (WP, 822) – and what Bataille in *Documents* articles 'Materialism', and 'Base Materialism and Gnosticism', invokes as 'matter as an active principle' (VE, 47), as 'raw phenomena', 'excluding all idealism' through 'direct interpretation', as we get 'from Freud' (VE, 15–6).

Conversely, for those who are failed or collapsed idealists, and now seek to *only* wallow morbidly in the low and base as if nothing else matters, the formless *cannot* be automatically brought in to affirm them as great in their creative works. For when Nietzsche goes on to say that we 'possess art lest we perish of the truth' (WP, 822), or that 'nihilism counts as truth', but 'art is worth more than truth' (WP, 853) – it is because the accomplished artist is able to play with this eternal return between form and formless, beauty and ugly, or high and low, without metonymic fixation, occlusion, or spiteful *ressentiment*, by affirming the whole cycle: even though it leads to nothing permanently high and lofty, which is the truth. This is 'the "return"' that Bataille himself, in the context of Nietzsche's encounter with Heraclitus, would later connect with 'TIME' and the 'death of God', which he capitalizes as 'FINAL'.[10]

It is also true that at the earlier *Documents* point in his development, in a work only posthumously published entitled 'The "Old Mole" and the Prefix *Sur* in the Words *Surhomme* [Superman] and *Surrealist* (1929–30)', Bataille suggests even an *Icarian* part to Nietzsche's own oeuvre for his 'hatred of bourgeois spiritual elevation' *and* working-class baseness – and also for seeking something 'elevated, weightless, Hellenic', to deify his 'sense of the earth' and the 'sexual basis of higher psychic functions' (VE, 37, 39). But this is the early Bataille, and, as I will later show, his position vis-à-vis Nietzsche continually develops, where 'in the later 1930s', as Stoekl notes, Nietzsche is 'seen as a major precursor and, free of all political taint, the victim of Fascist misrepresentation'.[11] The next section will first examine Bataille's notion of the pre-historic birth of humanity with the birth of art, to further consider the critical role of *animality* for humanity *within* its aesthetic expressions. This will be to later see if, with the aid of the kindred psychoanalytic concepts of sublimation, distance, the drive and Freudian Thing (*the real*), we can develop Bataille's aesthetics to extend on the nuance and depth of the Nietzsche who came to be his most acknowledged predecessor.

3.2 LASCAUX CAVES: DIVINE ANIMALITY AS THE ORIGINARY *REAL* OF AESTHETICS

What also supports the bringing in of key psychoanalytic concepts to examine the aesthetics of Bataille is that Nietzsche was a kind of precursor to Freud – just as Bataille in the French context was to Lacan. While ffrench, again, considers 'connections' between the latter two so 'overwhelming' as to merit 'extensive consideration' – of the former Bass notes that Nietzsche had already 'understood repression' and how 'morality and ideals are defensive distortions of the drives', such that Russell can even suggest an encounter between Nietzsche and psychoanalysis 'would not seem anything new' if cast 'in light of Nietzsche's proximity to Freud'.[12] Between Nietzsche and psychoanalysis, moreover, there has been much to say about our traffic with our animal inheritance, especially concerning what Lacan calls the 'inner catastrophes' of 'neurosis and its consequences' (SVII, 319). Accordingly, this section delves further into Bataille's aesthetics by considering his notion of the birth of Palaeolithic art coinciding with the birth of humanity through the creation of internal taboos against our animality – to see if by analytic focus here on the originary instance of the aesthetic state, we can shed more light on its nature and thereby foster its optimal conditions.

Bataille became fascinated by the 1940 discovery of the Lascaux cave paintings, in the Vézère valley of southwest France. He remarks, 'Everything changes in Lascaux. The monumental frescoes that we admire so much' are 'nearly intact' (CH, 90). For these were depicting animals, primarily, and dated from the Upper Palaeolithic period as 'the birth of art, unquestionably more than forty thousand years ago' (CH, 145), with the paintings themselves dated up to '30,000 years ago' (L, 14, 27), after 'an interminable period of stagnation' (CH, 145).[13]

Bataille deemed the cave 'truly one of the wonders of the world' (CH, 156). For by no means did he find humanity emerging from animality through shame of the latter, but precisely the opposite. The animals were painted with care, accuracy, 'a sense of magnificence' (CH, 79), and 'beautiful simply because their authors loved what they depicted' (CH, 75) – whereas whenever humans were depicted, Bataille observes, 'there is some taboo affecting the accuracy' (CH, 61), with the 'nearly complete loss of the faculty of imitation' that is 'so different from the naturalistic and generally beautiful representations of animals' (CH, 67), suggesting that 'animality is designated positive, humanity negative' (CH, 74). Bataille felt the human depictions to be based on 'childish techniques' (CH, 50) that are 'even caricatural' (CH, 107): 'generally tiresome caricatures, engraved artlessly and without conviction' (CH, 168) – while also noting that it was only by hiding 'beneath animal masks' (CH, 85), or 'an animal head' (CH, 60), that men were depicted, again suggesting that each author had 'accepted, far from feeling ashamed of, as we do, the share of the animal that remained within him' (CH, 61).

Bataille, then, finds these Palaeolithic artists expressing shame at the humanity they 'would eventually become', which they 'did not prefer', while 'apologizing' nostalgically for what they felt they were betraying by prohibiting animality – so as to become instead the 'creator of a world of durable things', and later of 'an elevation of the mind linked to the feeling that durable things offered', which subsequent to the history of Platonism, especially now, 'has ordained' our 'pretension' (CH, 80). But here the aesthetic experience at its *earliest* awakening, with what Bataille notes are 'not just tools but objects in which sensibility flourishes' (CH, 58), can very much be seen as a *return* of our repressed, prohibited animality as sensually affirmed, transfigured in the imaginary, sublimated to 'the domain of divine animality' (CH, 165). For in early religions, Bataille recollects, 'the animal is closer to the world of the gods', as 'man abides by interdictions, taboos, to which the animal is never held' (CH, 165) – meaning animals were *sovereign*, and 'the first gods were certainly animals, and generally animals had to have seemed divine' (CH, 167) – even as late as 'Greek art', Bataille recalls, which linked 'Athena to the owl, Dionysos to the bull' (CH, 165).

Although this divine, aesthetic animality can be hard to see for us where 'the opposition that still prevails today' is 'between *animality* devoid of religious signification and *humanity-divinity*' – where, Bataille notes, God makes 'man in his own image' and, through taboo, is 'the divinity of understanding and work' (CH, 141–2) – Bataille suggests how early religion's aesthetics once enabled rather the *affirmation* of what was lost of our earlier, now latent animality as 'a sovereign value, refusing every subordination to interest' (CH, 141). This value pertains to what Lacan would call '*jouissance* of transgression' (SVII, 195), which, in going 'beyond the limits normally assigned to the pleasure principle in opposition to the reality principle' (SVII, 109) and its usual prohibitions, 'to trample sacred laws underfoot' (SVII, 195), must also broach what Bataille calls 'the horrible domain of death' (CH, 165). And indeed for Lacan '*jouissance* implies precisely the acceptance of death' (SVII, 189), what Bataille in *Eroticism* calls 'assenting to life up to the point of death' (E, 11) – when we open ourselves onto risk and chance in the animal *real* of the erotic sphere.

This eroticism-and-death relation stunningly emerges for Bataille in the final painting at the bottom of the Lascaux pit, 'into which it is now possible to descend with the help of a vertical iron ladder, securely affixed to the rock' (CH, 170). For here is depicted a 'human figure, who has the head of a bird', with spear in hand but drawn 'roughly, as if a child had traced its schematic silhouette' and 'sprawled-out', 'like this man is dead' before a bison struck, disembowelled, spilling its contents over the earth (CH, 170). In his final 1961 *Tears of Eros*, Bataille remarks even that 'nothing in this whole image justifies the paradoxical fact that the man's sex is erect' (TE, 51). Nothing, that is, except for the relation between eroticism and death that Bataille discloses in the correlation of taboo *and* transgression – linking us to our prohibited animality and thus, too, to the risk of death, in a cycle that is still fundamentally sexual.

We today, nevertheless, tend to express guilt for any residue of animality we fail to escape altogether: where, Bataille observes, part of us 'is revolting to the eyes of the other part' (CH, 76), and 'the component judgements are ambiguous' (CH, 73); but the paintings remind us that here we have undergone a *reversal* of our earlier shame for actually leaving animality behind. This is also for Bataille linked to the 'remorse' we had for having to kill the animals we loved in the hunt, reducing them 'to the level of a thing' in their being 'reduced to a foodstuff' (CH, 78). For really, Bataille notes, 'the thing is on the side of humanity', where the thing 'is a tool' and initially 'all that separated human beings from animals', but where we are by use of tools increasingly 'subjugated to work' (CH, 55) – and later become, 'through reason', Bataille must add, 'slaves to the work that we must pursue at any price' (CH, 85).

This lost primal shame in betraying animality, without and within, is also strikingly evident in the representations of 'female figures', which mostly belong to 'portable art', Bataille recalls, and, 'as statuettes whose characteristics are well known', will 'form a third world' apropos of animals and men because their features 'emphasize fertility – hips or breasts' – that tend 'towards deformity', towards a 'deformed idealism' (CH, 68). But in this Bataille observes that 'their human aspect is also suppressed', through the 'absence of a face' – with 'no eyes, no nose, no mouth, and no ears' (CH, 68–9). And for Bataille this lends 'little credence to the hypothesis of those who see the images of men with animal heads as depicting disguised hunters' – suggesting, rather, that 'something more general than a hunting trick' has *again* 'dictated this impetus not to represent humans in the same way as animals' (CH, 69).

Bataille will explain that this is because the reduction of female figures to the 'genetic functions', to 'characteristics that for us run counter to elegance', to 'the point of heaviness' (CH, 111), is such that 'their bodies seem monstrous to us' (CH, 168) – which he contrasts with the modern 'portrait of Mrs. Graham', which instead 'places the most value on the face' (CH, 116). This late eighteenth-century portrait by Thomas Gainsborough thereby erases all the 'accentuated secondary characteristics', where 'the breasts are hardly developed, the hips narrow' (CH, 116) – and with this desirable face, Bataille concludes, relative to the reproductive act, the most seductive emphasis is now placed on 'the part of the figure farthest from the final goal' (CH, 116, 118).[14]

Thought psychoanalytically, this means our art now tends towards a neurotic direction, where, Bataille notes, 'human beings, through work, ended up distancing themselves completely from animality', and 'in particular on the level of their sexual life' (TE, 42). Freud had suggested something of this in his 1900 *Interpretation of Dreams* in comparing Sophocles' *Oedipus* with Shakespeare's *Hamlet*, where the child's incestuous parricide wish shifts from expressed to repressed with the change of epochs, where its latent presence is now inferable only from 'its inhibiting consequences', in the transferential strangeness of 'Hamlet's hesitations' (SE4, 264). On this Lacan's *Seminar VI* on *Desire and Its Interpretation* also marks, after what Freud calls Hamlet's expressed 'distaste for sexuality' (SE4, 264), the effect on Ophelia, as compared to 'the drama of the female object' surrounding 'Helen of Troy' (SVI, 244) – where we shift between the face that launched a thousand ships, and likely not just the face, such was the desire, to the misfortune of a girl 'floating in her dress down the river into which she, in her madness, allowed herself to slip' (SVI, 244).

Lacan in fact discerns a 'horror of femininity as such' unfolding in Hamlet, as he 'throws in Ophelia's face all the degrading, fickle, and corrupting possibilities' that drag women through 'all the acts that little by little make them into mothers', by which he 'pushes Ophelia away in what seems to be a most sarcastic and cruel way' (SVI, 244–5). And this slow, 'secular advance of repression in the emotional life of mankind' (SE4, 264), as Freud termed it – where gone is any Aphrodite, Hera, Athena, or Persephone to set it straight – is to the point where Lacan can depict our entry into language as 'castration', as an operation of the binary logic of presence or absence 'introduced through the incidence of a signifier' into 'the sexual relation [*rapport du sexe*]' (SXVII, 128) – which again is what Bataille calls 'laceration' if in certain ways 'man and animality are set against one another' (AS II, 52).

But insofar as this defence breaks down, where Lacan discerns how 'not to want to desire and to desire' is finally revealed as 'the same thing' – like the 'Moebius strip that has no underside' as its twisted path comes 'back mathematically to the surface that is supposed to be its other side' (SXI, 235) – we tend towards the destructively perverse, or psychotically worse, as we lack any adequate structure of affirmation. Here our repressed animality resurfaces in disturbed form, what Lacan calls the substitutional satisfaction of the symptom we 'give satisfaction *to*' while remaining 'not content' (SXI, 166). And such are the discontents then channelled into what Bataille bemoans as our compulsive 'task of exploiting every possible resource', which in an *all-too*-human way now *inflates* 'reason as the supreme value on which to found our contempt for animals' (CH, 65) – where 'smashing, killing, massacring have always been the consolation of those who achieved nothing' (CH, 103).

With this macabre scenario, Bataille finds himself reflecting on the origins of humanity in Palaeolithic art right when 'the latest atomic experiments', and others besides, make it possible to contemplate our absolute 'extinction' – finding himself 'struck by the fact that light is being shed on our birth at the very moment when the notion of our death appears to us' (CH, 87). Brett Buchanan reads Bataille as reflecting here not just on the birth of humanity but on its 'impossibility', as the always *incomplete* transition from animal to human runs aground, again and again, on the 'formless'.[15] This is where Lacan's *Ethics* Seminar treatment of the problem of artistic *sublimation* can be of value. For not only are similarly macabre scenarios discussed, but Lacan is also keen to stress the drive's innate capacity for sublimation by virtue of its being already tangled up in signifiers. This is the primacy of the signifier that 'embodies a historical dimension', and 'refers back to something memorable because it was remembered' – meaning for Lacan that the drive is always 'remembering, historicizing' (SVII, 208), through its 'plasticity', 'drift', and 'play of substitutions' (SVII, 90–1), in its eternal emerging and eliding, and its polymorphous palpitations and oscillations, across time.

This *sovereign signifierness* of the drive is implicated in Lacan's thesis of the unconscious being 'structured like a language' – reiterated in his *Fundamental Concepts* Seminar as an unconscious 'constituted by the effects of speech on the subject', a subject that is 'determined in the development' of such effects, throughout its life (SXI, 149).[16] It means re-accessing our base or primal animal drives need not entail a blind and crude, destructive barbarism, but can rather attain, through the process of play and sublimation, an establishing of a propitious amount of *distance-and-nearness* to 'the Freudian Thing', which is Lacan's reworked meaning of the Freudian Id – '*das Es* [the It]' – that, he claims, can even 'make the Thing itself speak' (SVII, 132, 137). It means that in the interpretative play of signifying chains within – where, Lacan reminds us, 'desire, in fact, is interpretation itself' (SXI, 176) – we can *raise* our animality to the sublime in aesthetic expressions, where sublimation for Lacan 'raises an object', an earthly, *animal* object, 'to the dignity of the Thing' (SVII, 112).

Lacan also discusses how the primal *aim* of the drive is altered, 'inhibited', in sublimation, as one of its '*four* vicissitudes' that is 'nonetheless satisfaction of the drive, without repression' (SXI, 165). But lest one seeks to rationalize regressing to neurosis, Lacan must follow Freud to invoke a natural limit to plasticity in the drive that means at some point there is demand for 'a certain level of *direct* satisfaction, without which harm results, serious disturbances occur' (SVII, 91). For Freud had remarked similarly on our capacities for sublimation, in his 1908 '"Civilized" Sexual Morality', regarding the 'certain amount of direct sexual satisfaction' that 'seems to be indispensable for most organizations', suggesting even that it 'would have been more healthy' for some people 'to be less good' (SE9, 191). As Louis Rose was to later put it, this is because by sublimation 'the ego channelled early sexual strivings into non-sexual aims, and thus even the most exalted of such aims did not fail to express an original element of longing'.[17]

Viewed in terms of this delicate balance, not just the Palaeolithic art observed by Bataille, but also his creative, intellectual *response to them* as writer, philosopher and scholar in his articles, lectures and books can be seen as optimum quality sublimations. For what they enable is a new temporal unity between the indirect-*and*-direct, high-*and*-low – or human-*and*-animal – that conjoins them in a cycle that we can affirm with Nietzsche as the eternal return and *being* of becoming.[18] And this is far from the 'practical, utilitarian meaning' (CH, 83) that Bataille laments is usually imposed on Lascaux, that sees only 'an appetite for meat' (CH, 69), wishful 'magic' (CH, 78), or 'a hunting trick' (CH, 69) expressing merely the 'desire for efficacy' in aiming 'to ensure the capture of the real animal' (CH, 78). It is not for Bataille that this dimension is never there, only that 'there is another aspect to it', the failure of which to acknowledge reveals 'a certain poverty' (CH, 78) that is again 'linked to our inability to find a complete response to our desire in an animal world' – having learned, from a 'very young age', only 'to see *what is lacking* in the animal and to designate with the word "beast" those among us whose lack of reason made us ashamed' (CH, 84).

This *lack*, Bataille notes, forces us 'to see in these paintings a world of only an unfortunate sense of need', which in fact makes them 'impenetrable to us' (CH, 84), as we are told that 'in vain we sought our dreams in these figures, which were a response, as the dreams of children often are, to the cravings of hunger' (CH, 82). But even on such cravings we can add Lacan's observations on 'the dream of little Anna', the daughter of Freud whose 'hallucination of food' such as '*tart, strawberries, eggs*, and other delicacies' is 'not purely and simply the making present of a need', for 'she only hallucinates forbidden objects' (SXI, 155). Within the logic of transgression, then, this indicates for Lacan precisely 'the presence of the desiring and sexually desiring subject', as per Freud's maintenance of 'libido as the essential element of the primary process' – meaning that 'it is only on account of the sexualization of these objects that the hallucination of the dream is possible' (SXI, 154–5).

This desire for the forbidden, broaching *jouissance*, fits nicely with Bataille's discernment of how in Lascaux 'the animal, which no interdiction limited, provoked transgression' and thus seemed divine, where the death of the animal, of the being they loved, 'to which the hunter was linked through these close ties' (CH, 132–3) – 'hoping to assume the animal's ferocity as their own' and 'appropriate their courage' (CH, 74–5) – also had the sense 'of crime and transgression, which will remain fundamental in sacrifice' (CH, 171). This sacred-sacrificial dimension is what becomes so manifest in Bataille's 1955 specially dedicated work, *Lascaux; or, the Birth of Art*, where he notes that 'from the first, divine animality overshadowed all the great works of man', where still even thousands of millennia later 'animality deeply stamps the gods of ancient Egypt and Greece' – all of which *reveals* for Bataille, standing out before his animals strewn across cave walls, and 'contains the secret of Lascaux' (L, 123).

Lacan had himself observed in his *Seminar V* on *Formations of the Unconscious* how, alone and apart, 'humans are not always so easily deified' – where Daumier, for instance, was 'criticized for having given the Greek gods the rather crumpled forms of the bourgeois men and women of his time', rather than the 'beautiful and good form' of, say, 'the phallus', or a 'Venus de Milo or Aphrodite of Cnidus', and 'criticized for it as if it were a sacrilege' (SV, 352). As such, seeing then only lack and calculation at the level of need in Lascaux's manifest animality, abreast of such an originary sacred, is also what forecloses the aesthetic state from its optimum *abundance*. For Nietzsche had even described this as the 'blooming physicality' of 'animal vigour', that which 'functions through the images and desires of intensified life' as 'a stimulant to it' – and where, Nietzsche concludes, 'a blending of these very nuances of animal well-being and desires constitutes the aesthetic state' in its optimally abundant form, in 'that bestowing and overflowing of bodily vigour' (WP, 801–2).

The next section examines further this blooming state of animal abundance through the notion of *sovereignty* that Bataille connects to his later affirmation of Nietzsche as the sovereign man of art. It is what will finally enable us to solve the problem of aesthetics raised by the young Bataille, by linking it to another key concept of the mature Bataille, again assisted, wherever possible, by the psychoanalysis and philosophy of Lacan and Nietzsche.

3.3 THE *ACCURSED* SOVEREIGNTY OF ART, AND NIETZSCHE

Sovereignty was the notion Bataille explored to further open up a domain beyond the kind of 'utility' that we today have too narrowly conceived yet installed as dominant nonetheless. And in a fundamental way, art came to occupy a critical place for this via its creative sense of 'useless' play, beyond a pre-given purpose. But just what kinds of opening up, or irruptions from the Other, are thereby enabled, can still be much the open question – one where Bataille's reworked notion of sovereignty can here be brought to bear. This section examines Bataille's specific appending of his notion of sovereignty to Nietzsche's praxis as writer and thinker. The aim is to offer some final considerations for the type of art we should be encouraging.

It is in the 1953 *Sovereignty* volume III of *Accursed Share* that Bataille suggests Nietzsche's is 'the only philosophy that wrenches one away from the servitude inherent in philosophical discourse' and 'restores sovereignty to the free spirit' – noting that here for Nietzsche it was 'crucial to deny Christian morality, which utterly condemns the animal play of strength' (AS III, 401). Coming as it does in a chapter entitled 'Nietzsche and the Transgression of Prohibitions', Bataille must soon add to this pronouncement a counter-affirmation of the 'need for prohibitions' on 'sexuality and death', that found the 'difference between man and animals', without which the '*possibility* of life as we know it is not given' (AS III, 403). But this is not without also restressing that none of us would ever have a 'sovereign attitude' if we 'sometimes did not lift those prohibitions' – *in the real of transgression* – and thus attain, 'beyond the rules' one 'observes and even reveres', the 'sovereign moment of being within' (AS III, 403).

This *sovereign* moment is what Bataille distinctly interpolates to Nietzsche's experience of the 'certainty of the death of God' (AS III, 405).

This, of course, is the god of the Judaeo-Christian-Platonic metaphysical traditions that Bataille astutely notes is 'represented by Socrates and morals, Christianity and God', that tried to *double-up* on our initial negation of animality during our Palaeolithic transition to humanity, by placing prohibitions also on our periodic need to *return* – that thereby 'attempted to organize into a single block all the conflicting possibilities of the human being' (AS III, 410). This block is again the Sovereign Good that Lacan also discerns is 'the philosopher's stone of all the moralists' from Plato, Aristotle, the Stoics and Epicureans down to the Christian tradition in Augustine and Aquinas (SVII, 96, 221) – which, in effect, as Bataille puts it in *Eroticism*, leaves 'transgression condemned' as 'sin' (E, 127, 262).[19]

Through Nietzschean sovereignty, however, this subordination beneath a Sovereign Good, enshrined as God, in a single block as philosopher's stone, is no longer possible without deception and trickery. And Bataille cites how the latter for Nietzsche now amounts to 'a gross prohibition' in the form of 'thou shalt not think!' – with the hypothesis 'God' itself being merely a 'gross answer, an indelicacy against us thinkers' (AS III, 376).[20] But what Bataille marks Nietzsche to expressly oppose to this gross indelicacy, when he 'sets himself against Jesus', is *Dionysos*: where the 'seduction of Dionysos is a prelude to tragedy' – as opposed to the lure of Jesus, Bataille suggests, in the *Sovereignty* chapter entitled 'Nietzsche and Jesus', which is linked rather to an 'arranged marriage', in a 'match dictated by utility' (AS III, 378), and faith in a narrowed notion of moral reason. This opposition is such for Bataille that he will discern how God's 'believer *withdraws from the game*', the game of life, whereas 'the disciple of Nietzsche *throws himself into it*' (AS III, 378).

What Nietzsche compels us to be thrown into is specifically the sovereign moment, which, beyond what Bataille calls our 'general submission to the concern for the future' (AS II, 379) – our concern for consequences, safety and utility, governed by taboo – is indeed potentially tragic. But this is why the invocation of Dionysos is so important, for it allows for affirmation of this sovereign space where, Bataille cites Nietzsche proclaiming: 'Only Dionysian joy is sufficient'; and adding, '*I have been the first to discover the tragic!*' – especially insofar as a 'tragic wisdom' emerges that is the opposite of a simple 'yearning for nothingness' (AS III, 381).

This yearning for nothing is what Nietzsche deemed was Jesus's true message and disposition, that of a thinly veiled *nihilism:* likening his completely desexualized, denaturalized notions of love and praxis to 'childishness', 'idiocy', 'decadence', and 'infamy' (AS III, 392) – even referring to it in *The Anti-Christ* as a case of 'retarded puberty' (AC, 32). For this perpetual cutting away from nature, animality, earth and body is, for Nietzsche, nothing but the 'vivisection and self-torture of millennia' that conjoined an 'evil eye' and 'bad conscience' with our 'natural inclinations', and what we ought now to 'reverse' (GM II, 24) (WP, 295).[21] And what Bataille wants to emphasize here is that the *sovereignty* of this gesture of reversal today also means going beyond the said utility of forever increasing production and accumulation in the field of labour and work. For with the capitalist-or-communist dichotomy of today, along with the ever-looming threat of fascism of the far-right, it seemed to Bataille that 'no one can escape from the Christian system without being immediately obliged to adopt a system that is just as closed (or more so)' (AS III, 380).

The way out of such closures for Bataille, 'reducing each man to the object', is precisely now 'the attitude of Nietzsche', which can 'free the subject' with the 'refusal to serve (to be useful)' – being to Bataille's mind fundamentally 'the principle of Nietzsche's thought, as it is of his work' (AS III, 368). For this refusal is forever 'positing a sovereignty independent of its mired forms', and especially from the 'moralizing (enslaving) sovereignty mired in Christianity' (AS III, 368) – such that for Bataille it also 'refused the reign of things' when subsequently 'science' and objectivity in the Enlightenment are posed as 'mankind's limit and end, since, assumed as such, it ensures the mind's subordination to the object' (AS III, 367). This is how Bataille finds that 'Nietzsche's gift is the gift that nothing limits' – as 'the sovereign gift, that of subjectivity' (AS III, 371) – which, for Bataille, is primed 'to rediscover the lost sovereignty' on which his three volumed *The Accursed Share* perceives a basis for starting anew' (AS III, 367). For as stated right from the start in the work's 'Preface', the hope for Bataille in this is very much 'to lift the curse that this title calls into question' (AS I, 9) – namely that appended by the history of Western metaphysics to that part of us we *share* with other animals and the rest of nature, *in* the real.

The way out of our subordination to the closure of this curse is further for Bataille now 'the opening of art', which unlike the constructions of metaphysics, 'lies without deceiving those whom it seduces' – but only insofar as a 'sovereign thought', here, 'corresponds to the "man of sovereign art", who first expressed himself in the work of Nietzsche' (AS III, 428). For art can only function in this sovereign way for Bataille if the aesthetic is kept separate from the political, a political realm that is thereby kept calm, lucid, rational, and objective 'with a view to a less unequal distribution of resources in the world' (AS III, 429) – 'whence the ambiguity of this work', Bataille self-reflects, 'which, wanting to reach the sovereign moment, considers practical questions so as to separate them from it, *and conversely*' (AS III, 428).

This is where Bataille's Nietzscheanism can approximate something of a kindred psychoanalytic ethics, as Bataille then expresses the desire for a more '*conscious* subjectivity' to spread, and have primacy, in the world – which, he concludes, would mean 'the world of things would escape the irrational government of an objective thought that is constantly distorted by the action of an unconscious subjectivity' (AS III, 429).

Here Lacan's deflationary tripartite ontology can be of value vis-à-vis Bataille's desire for a *more conscious* subjectivity, which is akin to what Lacan calls 'the analyst's desire' (SXI, 274) – where the 'desire of the analyst' is that through which, in the streaming signifiers within, we encounter precisely our 'sexual reality' (SXI, 156), and are 'brought back to the plane at which, from the reality of the unconscious, the drive may be made present' (SXI, 274). For right from his first Seminar Lacan declares that 'it is within the dimension of being that the tripartition of the symbolic, the imaginary and the real is to be found', calling them 'those elementary categories without which we would be incapable of distinguishing anything within our experience' (SI, 271).

With the symbolic broadly representing work and reason, and the imaginary play and fiction, we can find in this distinction, then, two distinct modes of traffic with the real that are equally important, but should also in no way be confused such that disturbances occur, as crippling symptoms or destructive acting-outs, based on some illusion *mistaken* as real. Lacan even describes the junction of these three orders as ever confused in our 'fundamental passions' of 'love', 'hate', and 'ignorance' (SI, 271). And this is such that he must confess that a 'path for the race towards destruction' becomes 'exactly' the hallmark of '*Western moralism*' – one that is secretly 'clothed in our everyday discourses under many guises', which 'meets with extraordinarily easy rationalizations', and 'diffuse flocculations of hatred which saturates the call for the destruction of being in us' (SI, 277).

Thought further in a Bataillean way, in the sense of the question of aesthetics being examined here – aimed at the *real* at the base of it all – the imaginary corresponds to the aesthetic sphere, searching for sovereign moments *beyond* the realm of things, purposes, and utility in the accumulation of resources. For the latter is rather the symbolic, which should, if kept free of the aesthetic-imaginary, correspond to our entry into clear, conceptual language that is rational and mathematized, logical, and empirical, in calculations concerning the politically fair-minded production and distribution of resources.

And with this separation, which is also a *coordination* in what Bataille knows is a 'precarious equilibrium' – given the 'contradictory impulses' we inherit of the transition from animal to human that 'never denotes, as simpleminded people imagine, a stabilized position' (AS III, 342) – we arrive at another distinctive aspect of the taboo–transgression interrelation definitively articulated through Bataille's work. This is where the taboos placed on certain animal aspects of the real, pertaining to sexuality and death, govern the world of work, labour, calculation, politics, and reason (the *symbolic*), a world counterbalanced by the periodically organized transgression of such taboos, governing now the sovereign realm of *non*-productive expenditure, the sacred aesthetic and erotic (the *imaginary*). The latter is also where again Bataille will stress that 'not only does the return to animality that we perceive in sovereignty – and in eroticism – differ radically from the animal starting point', it is also what, within its *being in the real*, melds into the human world it opposes, as 'a hybrid of transgression and prohibition' (AS III, 342).

Here, then, in this hybrid transgression, we temporarily experience the returned prohibited aspects of the real *post-symbolically* – as transfigured in the divine imaginary – and thus attain by the sublimated drive in *its* returning a final affirmation of the *real* and its place in the totality of being: An affirmation that defeats nihilism once and for all as it is an affirmation of our 'low' roots that does not reduce to them, and no less succumbs to the fundamental fantasy of metaphysics of escaping them for good. No more significant criteria for aesthetics can be imagined.

Before the next chapter presses on to consider Nietzsche's affirming influence on psychoanalysis itself – and how this specifically impacts Bataille and the surrealist modernist movements in the arts: here we can once again, in conclusion, take up Lacan's distinction between the imaginary and the symbolic, and through its lenses throw a light more focussed in support of Bataille's final aim to keep the political realm conceptually clear, objective, and rational in its pursuit of greater equity – free of the distorting effects of an unconscious subjectivity, caught in the imaginary, which is best expressed, made manifest, and enjoyed as a *jouissance* of transgression, in an aesthetic realm now properly restored, and *rendered sovereign*, beyond but alongside the realm of things.

> I don't want to lose sight of the main thing. The main thing is always the same: sovereignty is NOTHING.
>
> —Bataille, *Sovereignty*, in *The Accursed Share* III, 30

NOTES

1. Richardson notes that Bataille's *Documents* journal gathered 'most of the surrealists with whom Breton had fallen out with in 1929', which is why Breton 'regarded this as a provocation and concluded that Bataille was set upon undermining his own authority within surrealism', launching thus a 'pre-emptive strike' in his *Second Manifesto* 'of such violence that it still shocks today' – but as too, Richardson adds, does Bataille's reply in 'The Castrated Lion', which dubs Breton an 'old religious windbag' and 'priest' of 'police reports' that are 'fine for little castratos' (WS, 28–9). Allan Stoekl suggests that Bataille deemed Breton caught in 'an affirmation

of aestheticism and idealism tinged with religion' – such that by extension, as Simonetta Falasca-Zamponi puts it, *Documents* became for Bataille 'the forum from which to launch an evaluative analysis' and 'prosecutorial trial against aesthetics'. Nevertheless, Kevin Kennedy suggests that while much commentary views Bataille as 'constituting a kind of anti-aesthetics or a hatred of aesthetics', such as the paradigmatic work of Yve-Alain Bois, Rosalind Krauss, and Allen Weiss, still a 'systematic aesthetics may in fact be derived from his work'. Richardson, "Introduction," in Bataille, WS, 4–5. Stoekl, "Introduction," in Bataille, VE, xi. Falasca-Zamponi, *Rethinking the Political: The Sacred, Aesthetic Politics and the Collège de Sociologie* (Montréal: McGill-Queens, 2011), 97–8. Kennedy, *Towards an Aesthetics of Sovereignty: Georges Bataille's Theory of Art and Literature* (Bethesda: Academica Press, 2014), 3–4. Bois and Krauss, *Formless: A User's Guide* (New York: Zone Books, 1997). Weiss, *Perverse Desire and the Ambiguous Icon* (Albany: SUNY Press, 1994).

2. Further formulations of this central distinction are in Nietzsche's *Twilight of the Idols*, IX, 8–9; *Genealogy of Morals*, P, 3, and I, 2; *The Case of Wagner*, E; and *The Will to Power*, 48, 59, 845–6, 1009.

3. Falasca-Zamponi, *Rethinking the Political*, 98.

4. Stoekl, "Introduction," in Bataille, VE, xi. Breton, *Manifestoes of Surrealism*, trans. H. R. Lane (AnnArbor: Michigan, 1969), 184.

5. See Freud, "Repression (1915)," in SE14, 149.

6. Volume one of Heidegger's Nietzsche lectures is dedicated to this selection. Volume two is on 'The Eternal Recurrence of the Same'. Nietzsche, "The Will to Power as Art," in WP, 794–853. Heidegger, "Volume I: The Will to Power as Art," in *Nietzsche: Volumes One and Two*, 1–263.

7. Bataille, "The Obelisk (1938)," in VE, 218.

8. For detailed discussion of Lacan's *Ethics* seminar analysis of the beauty effect in Sophocles' *Antigone* – whose key 'moment of transgression' or 'crossing over' (SVII, 281) begins with the invocation by the Chorus of the *crime* of Oedipus, Antigone's Father – see Themi, *Lacan's Ethics and Nietzsche's Critique of Platonism*, 50–4.

9. As I will discuss in sections 4.1 and 4.2, this branding at large of one's own torture is actually what Nietzsche diagnosed in Schopenhauer's excessive pessimism about sexual life in general.

10. Bataille, "The Obelisk," in VE, 220.

11. Richardson does not set much store on this early critique beyond rhetorical polemic, suggesting what Bataille critiques in Nietzsche and surrealism here can seem close to where his own oeuvre culminates thirty years later. Even so, in his postwar volume III of *Accursed Share*, Bataille suggests Nietzsche sometimes 'fell into the impasse of power', by neglecting 'the concordant demands of prohibition' in his transgression of Christian taboo on 'the animal play of strength' (AS III, 401). Stoekl, "Introduction," in Bataille, VE, xiv. Richardson, "Introduction," in Bataille, WS, 7.

12. Roudinesco records that Borel, Bataille's analyst of the late 1920s, 'enjoyed having artists and other creative people as his patients' and in 1926 was 'one of the founders of the SSP', the Freud affiliated Paris Psychoanalytical Society. She also

cites how Lacan 'borrowed Bataille's ideas on the impossible and heterology', as the 'science of the unassimilable, of the irrecoverable, of ordure and "remains"' – 'deriving from them a concept of the "real" seen first as "residue" and then as "impossible"'. Nevertheless, although Noys suggests Bataille's 'contribution to Lacan's thought' was 'erased' and that 'Lacan's success in Anglo-American academia would need its own history of the misreading and misappropriations he has been subject to, which has yet to be written' – I have already suggested how Noys's refusal of any assimilation between Bataille and Lacan on the real may serve as an example of one of these misreadings. Ffrench, *After Bataille*, 8–9. Bass, *Interpretation and Difference*, 1–2. Russell, "*L'effet c'est toi*: Projective Identification from Nietzsche to Klein," *American Imago* 70.4 (2013): 563. Roudinesco, *Jacques Lacan*, 134, 121, 135–6. Noys, *Georges Bataille*, 3, 31.

13. Kendall notes that although Bataille was already writing on pre-history in his 1930 *Documents* critique of aesthetics, 'cave painting did not surface as a vehicle of his primary concerns until the early 1950s'. Bataille returns to these paintings in his 1957 *Eroticism* and final 1961 *Tears of Eros*, following his specially dedicated 1955 work *Lascaux; or, the Birth of Art* – with his other specialist lectures and articles on the topic more recently collected posthumously in *The Cradle of Humanity: Prehistoric Art and Culture*. Kendall, "Editor's Introduction," in Bataille, CH, 11.

14. Horbury marks where certain parts of contemporary feminisms demand the abolishing of facial seductive emphasis as well, as if to mask even further the unconscious desire of our inherited animality – increasingly in the name of a ~~Woman~~ that, in Lacanian terms, because of an increasingly puritan structure, 'doesn't exist' (SXX, 57, 72). Horbury, "What does Feminism Want?" 575, 578–9, 582, 580, 588.

15. Buchanan, "Painting the Prehuman: Bataille, Merleau-Ponty, and the Aesthetic Origins of Humanity," *Journal for Critical Animal Studies* IX.1/2 (2011): 14–5.

16. Ross Skelton suggests this thesis is 'Lacan's adjustment of Freud', which by linguistically reconceiving Freud's condensation as metaphor and displacement as metonymy, 'moves the emphasis from images to sounds, from sight to hearing and therefore towards the *listening* of the analyst'. He also notes where overreach in this can occur to conceal the Hegelian view that the 'whole process of the animate and inanimate world we inhabit is nothing other than the embodiment of an Absolute mind that thinks us' – which would be to return to a version of the inflationary religious metaphysics familiar to us from the history of Judaeo/Christian-Platonism. For a deflationary analysis of the ontology implicit in Lacan, see Themi, *Lacan's Ethics and Nietzsche's Critique of Platonism*, 7–22, 35–7, 119. Skelton, "Is the Unconscious Structured like a Language?" *International Forum of Psychoanalysis* 4.3 (1995): 168, 174, 178.

17. For Lacan's solution to Freud's problem of sublimation, ultimately augmented through a Nietzschean prism, see chapter 2 of Themi, *Lacan's Ethics and Nietzsche's Critique of Platonism*, 23–40. Rose, *The Freudian Calling: Early Viennese Psychoanalysis and the Pursuit of Cultural Science* (Detroit: WSU, 1998), 17.

18. Russell records how in the early 1960s 'Deleuze and Derrida foregrounded Nietzsche's thinking about energetics as the antidote to what had become stagnant

in the academic schools of phenomenology and structuralism', saying 'metaphors of energy were precisely what was needed to shake up and destabilize efforts to establish the priority of the metaphysical concept of "structure", and to invent new ways of thinking the border between psychology and ontology' – citing Derrida who writes: '*Form* fascinates when one no longer has the force to understand force from within itself. That is, to create'. Russell, *Nietzsche and the Clinic* (London: Karnac, 2017), 22.

19. Brady Bower also notes that Bataille's 1928 *Story of the Eye* 'repetitively returns to the figuration of prohibition in order to reconstruct the framework within which desiring and enjoyment are possible', linking it to Lacan's *Ethics* Seminar injunction to act 'in conformity' (SVII, 314) with desire as a duty to find 'structures that render desire liveable'. Just how the violence, 'urethral erotism', and priest's enucleation metaphorize Bataille's 'ambition' to annul Christian authority specifically, so as to recalibrate the taboo–transgression structure and make desire more liveable, was discussed here in chapter 2, the earlier version of which can be found in Themi, "Lacan, Barthes, Bataille, and the Meaning of the Eye—or Gaze," *The Undecidable Unconscious: A Journal of Deconstruction and Psychoanalysis* 3 (2016): 104–7, 109–10, 113–4, 119. Bower, "Story of the Eye: Fantasy of the Orgy and Its Limit," *American Imago* 59.1 (2002): 76, 87.

20. Bataille is quoting from the 'Why I Am So Clever' chapter of Nietzsche's 1888 *Ecce Homo*.

21. For thorough analysis of Nietzsche's ever pertinent critique of the Christian denaturalizing of our more animal, bodily values, see also Themi, *Lacan's Ethics and Nietzsche's Critique of Platonism*, 99–102.

Chapter 4

Nietzsche's Affirming Psychoanalysis in Freud, Surrealist Modernism, Bataille, and Lacan

The previous chapter saw how Bataille's early critique of surrealism could be further grasped and developed in light of his later engagement with Palaeolithic art, Nietzsche, and proximity to psychoanalysis – enabling a criterion of aesthetics to be drawn which enacted *not* so much a distinction but rather an affirming cycle of return between such predicates as 'high' and 'low'. Now I wish to examine the affirming influence of Nietzsche on psychoanalysis itself, and how this might again support Bataille's notion of aesthetics as a privileged space for an erotics. The aim will also be to see how all this was at play in Bataille's encounter with the modernist movements in the arts, of which surrealism formed a distinctive branch, in a milieu that was increasingly dominated over time by Lacan.

Nietzsche *and* Freud, moreover, were both important influences in the development of cultural modernism, as part of a crisis of reason where irrationality, instinctual violence, exploitation, and purposeless chance are discovered to have much more prevalence than previously hoped.[1] But Bataille is perhaps the most perspicuous example of this combined Nietzsche–Freud influence with his dissident brand of surrealism, as one of the first interwar French authors to undergo his own analysis – 'with Dr. Borel' in 1927 – who even applied its results to the end of his erotic novella *Story of the Eye* (1928), before going on to found French Nietzscheanism through the journal and secret society *Acéphale* and the College of Sociology (1936–39), having earlier found that his 'reading of Nietzsche in 1923 is decisive' (AN, 106–8).[2] Further to this is Bataille's subterranean influence on his friend Lacan, the famous French Freudian, with Bataille's notion of heterology as a science of the heterogeneous defined 'outside the reach of scientific knowledge' (VE, 97), becoming, in Lacan's hands, a psychoanalytic science of the real defined as being behind a barrier 'to the point of inaccessibility' (SVII, 209), as impossible to assimilate to our socio-symbolic constructs – not without a '*jouissance* [enjoyment] of transgression' (SVII, 195) that links up in an erotics our sexuality with death.³

What this chapter will first discuss is the prior influence of Nietzsche's philosophy on the founders of psychoanalysis themselves, namely Freud and his earliest collaborators in the Germanophone context, east of the Rhine. By discussing Nietzsche's initial relation with, and influence on, psychoanalysis itself, the aim then is to throw more light on how their combined influence impacts the cultural modernism of which surrealism was part, which Bataille was engaged with as a kind of Freudo-Nietzschean practitioner and critic, whose consequence was in a sense the discourse of Lacan: the analyst initially no stranger to surrealism itself, just as surrealism was equally no stranger to Freud.⁴

4.1 GERMANOPHONE CONTEXT: NIETZSCHE AND FREUD

In his 1980 study on *Freud and Nietzsche*, Paul-Laurent Assoun observes 'a strange contemporaneity' between them – only twelve years apart in age – where Nietzsche publishes his greatest works and achieves a belated recognition at 'the end of the 1880s, at the moment of the birth of psychoanalysis'.⁵ But the strangeness comes from the seeming ambivalence Freud has towards reading Nietzsche: at times expressing 'an excess of interest' in the philosopher who 'represents a nobility inaccessible' to him, who might nevertheless 'find the words for many things which remain mute within'; while at other times expressing a defensive resistance to where Nietzsche had 'intuitively anticipated' psychoanalytic findings, but being later prepared 'to forgo all claims to priority in the many instances'.⁶

Part of what Assoun suggests is at stake in this cautious distance, mixed with admiration, is Freud's ambition to found psychoanalysis as a *science*, rather than appear as a kind of clinically applied philosophy, associated here with a 'world-view (*weltanschauung*)' that leaps from facts to values. This is such that what Freud takes to be Nietzsche's 'anticipatory divinations', stemming from insights into his own pathology projected out as a new set of values into the world, would stand opposed to any scientific project which sticks to matters of fact – which, Assoun concludes, means that Freud does not want to sacrifice 'the "pain" of scientific labour, which has authenticated Nietzsche's intuitions'.⁷

This wording indeed echoes Freud's sentiment in his 1925 article, 'An Autobiographical Study', which calls Nietzsche, after Schopenhauer, 'another philosopher whose guesses and intuitions often agree in the most astonishing way with the labourious findings of psychoanalysis' (SE20, 59–60). Bass, however, suggests that the idea that Nietzsche's project came from insight into his own pathology, projected out as ideology from the personal to the political through 'guesses and intuitions', overlooks how Nietzsche's insights stem from 'his critique of metaphysics'. Bass in fact cites Paul Ricoeur's study which famously conjoined Nietzsche, Freud, and Marx as the three 'masters of suspicion', to affirm that Nietzsche's results also stem from his beginning 'as a philologist who then extended the method of historical, linguistic interpretation over the whole of philosophy' – to make of 'interpretation a manifestation of the will to power'.[8]

Freud's distancing comments towards Nietzsche, moreover, can even appear as self-reflexive in that they tend to overlook his own need for introspection when it came to his clinic. This is where Lacan's first seminar, on *Freud's Paper's on Technique*, describes him as daring initially 'to attach importance to what was happening to him, to the antinomies of his childhood, to his neurotic problems, to his dreams', when he came by such contingencies as 'death, woman, father', – willing to engage here in a 'return to origins' that Lacan concedes 'barely warrants being called science' – from knowing 'he would only make progress in the analysis of the neuroses if he analysed himself' (SI, 2).

In this, then, Freud's distancing can also seem to overlook the perpetual incompleteness of his own ambition to establish his findings on the slippery-slopes of the unconscious as a hard-science. And this is despite having also submitted himself to what Lacan notes as 'the discipline of the facts, of the laboratory', in distancing himself from 'the wrong language', along with a tendency for 'dabbling in speculation' – insofar as with Freud's 1900 *The Interpretation of Dreams*, Lacan concludes, 'something of a different essence' is reintroduced, 'namely, meaning' (SI, 2).[9]

The difference as resistance Freud keeps between himself and Nietzsche, however, further comes out in moments with a more *passive* relation to the moral Law, with its Judaeo-Christian origins, maintained by Freud – especially as compared to the transformative incitements of Nietzsche's ethics, calling for nothing less than a *'revaluation of all values'* (EH IV, 1). For Nietzsche based the latter on a genealogical critique of Christianity that traces it back to its *Hebraic*, as well as Hellenic, roots – having felt so keenly that the Sovereign Good of Plato's metaphysics, and the Law it enshrined, when combined with late Judaism to form Christianity, was merely a diluted down 'Platonism for the masses' (BGE, P), and a wrong turn in history that left us alienated from our more natural drives and instincts.

This historical process was what Nietzsche in his 1888 *The Anti-Christ* termed 'the denaturalizing of natural values' (AC, 25), that which involved the excessive rejection of our biologically inherited instincts for the sexual, aggression, and will to power – through an 'ascetic ideal' made Sovereign as if an end in itself, that in its puritan excess would discourage the proper flourishing of culture by barring so much of ourselves from its active potential for sublimation.[10] This was such that paradoxically instead, from its crude negations and overwrought *denials* of natural enjoyments, Nietzsche will discern in his 1887 *Genealogy of Morals* how here 'pleasure is felt and *sought* in ill-constitutedness, decay, pain, mischance' (GM III, 11) – according to the formula that 'instincts that do not discharge themselves outwardly *turn* inward', where we get what Nietzsche calls 'the *internalization* of man', of which the dubious, mixed results were later dubbed the 'soul' (GM II, 16).

But whether this internalized aggression as *jouissance* is through the demand for confession, renunciation, or even 'self-flagellation' (GM III, 11) of late-Judaism and the Christian middle-ages, symbolic residues of which could remain in Freud's clinic – or, now, the reversed externalized 'late-capitalist' imperative to *enjoy* consumerism blindly, perversely, until it hurts – here is the ascetic ideal that nevertheless links the Freudian *superego*, of the 'internalization or turning inwards' of violence (SE23, 244), to the Nietzschean 'bad conscience' (GM II, 16). And this is what is linked by Zupančič to 'Lacan's reading of the superego law in terms of the "imperative of enjoyment"' – and to how already, 'of course, Nietzsche recognizes this mode of enjoyment in the whole history of Christianity'.[11]

When it comes to this dialectic of enjoyment between 'perversion and asceticism', Silvia Ons will corroborate that 'Nietzsche anticipated psychoanalysis when he pointed out the connection between the two' – in speaking of 'ascetic voluptuousness', and the 'lascivious nature of asceticism' – as if 'the operation performed by Freud in the clinic were parallel and related to that performed by Nietzsche in philosophy'.[12] But still there are the moments alluded to where Freud seemingly halts before tracking his own critique of superegoic Christianity back to the denaturalizing Judaic Law, where Assoun records him even protesting at one point that a simple 'head cold' suffices to cure him 'of such desires' for any concomitant Nietzschean intoxication. Here perhaps is where Freud sees only 'death-wish', which, for Assoun, 'is what stops Freud at the gates of the temple of Dionysos', as the 'Jewish atheist' who resists the genealogical affirmation that with the Church in Greece and Rome, 'Israel triumphed with its vengeance over all the most noble ideals'; and this is such that while 'every return to Nietzsche' is 'replacing a repressive Superego' with a *will to power*, 'drunk with innocence', instead, Assoun concludes, 'psychoanalysis obstinately summons back the condition of desire from the side of the [Judaic] Law'.[13]

While acknowledging the moments where this *difference* between Freud and Nietzsche comes to the fore, it nevertheless remains of interest to look for moments of the opposite effect taking place – where, perhaps, the *influence* of Nietzsche seems to encourage Freud to take a more active stance in his appraisal of the *status quo ante* of the general field of ethics. There is, for instance, the Vienna Wednesday Seminars of 1908, where Nietzsche's thought is actively discussed and presented on – although here Freud is found responding with his usual admixtures of praise and resistance, and even perhaps some wild analysis, in speculating of Nietzsche about 'maternal fixation', a 'paternal complex', 'Christ as an adolescent fantasy', and 'narcissism' linked to 'homosexual tendencies'.[14]

This again invokes Freud's idea that Nietzsche's findings were the result of introspection universalized out onto the world, transforming thus an 'is' into an 'ought' which for Freud disqualifies his psychology from the status of science and renders him, of all things, unable shed the will to play theologian: simply by intervening philosophically into the moral sphere![15] But where if not from facts should our thinkers base their values on? – Errors? This Nietzsche saw as the great blunder of Western religious metaphysics, with its imaginarized idea of the Good *mistaken* as real amounting to what in his 1888 *Twilight of the Idols* he duly calls 'a level of ignorance at which even the concept of the real, the distinction between the real and the imaginary, is lacking' – where, Nietzsche concludes, 'at such a level "truth" denotes nothing but things which we today call "imaginings"' (TI VII, 1). It can even strike one as a bit of amateur Humean philosophy for Freud to suggest it follows from the fact that an 'ought' cannot be *deductively* inferred from an 'is' that one ought not infer one's 'oughts' in some other viable way from appraisals of facts, lest they fall prey to theology.[16]

Freud himself later acknowledged in his 1933 'Weltanschauung' lecture that while, unlike religion, science is content to focus on facts, nevertheless, 'it is true that from its application rules and advice are derived on the conduct of life' – where thankfully, Freud must add, it is not by necessity that these be the same as those offered by religion, and where if they are 'the reasons for them are different' (SE22, 162). Zupančič in fact marks the positivist tendency to avoid questions of value entirely as stemming from the imposition of Calvinist-capitalism, where science again can only keep its respectability, and preferred terrain of facts, as long as it does not compete with religion and 'becomes a profession', according to the Protestant work ethic, by 'renouncing (often with pride) the temptation to formulate any kind of proposition within the ideological field' – namely that of capitalism itself, as structured now like a religion.[17]

Nietzsche actually saw the positivist *reduction* of values to facts as an 'overestimation of truth' (GM III, 25), as itself continuing the theological 'Christian faith which was also Plato's, that God is truth, that truth is *divine*' (GM III, 24) – that is, as not the overcoming but merely the *altered expression* of the ascetic ideal which only now, ascetically again, denies itself of its inflated metaphysical religious 'exteriors' (GM III, 25, 27). For sensing that science itself 'never creates values' (GM III, 25), Nietzsche reserves this vital task for the *'genuine philosophers'*, acting as *'commanders and legislators'* (BGE, 211) – and who are in this, by drawing also on the sciences as a scholarly base, from the 'honesty' motto of 'long live physics' (GS, 335), far from the countenance of any priest-idealist or theologian of the hitherto Sovereign Good.[18]

Back in 1908, however, despite such positivist quibbles about sticking to facts instead of judgements of value, Freud comes out with his article '"Civilized" Sexual Morality and Modern Nervous Illness', where he is found *actively condemning* the intimidating effect of inherited religious mores on our libidinal development. Here he bewails 'the harmful suppression of the sexual life of civilized peoples (or classes) through the "civilized" sexual morality prevalent in them' – such that when libido did emerge it was irreparably damaged, with many who would have been healthier being 'less good' falling now as 'victims to neurosis', as the 'well-behaved weaklings who later become lost in the great mass of people that tends to follow, unwittingly' (SE9, 185, 191, 197). This invokes Nietzsche's lament in *Beyond Good and Evil* that 'Christianity gave Eros poison to drink', such that 'he did not die of it but degenerated – into a vice' (BGE, 168) – a move Nietzsche saw was determined not only by the later Judaic priests, who provided the soil whence Christianity could grow, but also by the later intervention of Plato's Socrates into the *original* flourishing of *Hellenismos*. This original flourishing was what Lacan himself in his *Transference* seminar called the 'fertile period' of the 'sixth and fifth centuries', those that were 'overflowing with intellectual creativity', where 'we find ourselves at the historic climax of a particularly active era' (SVIII, 70).

Here, then, in our philosophical prime, in what for Nietzsche was *not* a coincidence, 'the symbols of sex' were also 'venerable as such' (WP, 148; TI X, 4) – which also accords with Freud's idea that it is our relation to libido that *'lays down the pattern'* for our 'other modes of reacting to life' (SE9, 198). Freud restates this finding in his *Leonardo da Vinci* essay two years later in noting how, in the midst of the Renaissance's attempt to retrieve Antiquity's values, the earlier repression of his sexual life does not favour its later sublimation: where again such a 'pattern imposed' meant 'his activity and ability to form quick decisions began to fail', where the 'tendency towards deliberation and delay' was disturbingly noticeable, and comparable to 'the regressions in neurotics' (SE11, 133).

In tracing back such regressions to their historical origins, Nietzsche suggests that whereas 'the Sophists were Greeks', conversely, 'when Socrates and Plato took up the cause of virtue and justice, they were *Jews* or I know not what' (WP, 429) – speaking again to their combined *denaturalizing* intervention that in terms of libido meant a demonizing ignorance of the most basic 'prerequisite of our life', which in calumniating the sexual 'threw *filth* on the beginning' (TI X, 4). With such a pattern laid down, Nietzsche here will bemoan the ensuing, concomitant loss of 'all the scientific methods', of 'natural science in concert with mathematics and mechanics', along with 'the *sense for facts*' and 'art of reading well' – all of them replaced by the Hebraic 'art of holy lying' which again, Nietzsche must stress, already 'is not lacking in Plato' (AC, 59, 44, 55).

Such passages also serve to clarify that there is *no* prescription in Nietzsche of a return to any pre-Socratic, pre-scientific, mystical cosmology which maintains, as Lacan puts it, 'that Being thinks', and 'by speaking, enjoys', as if 'what is thought of is in the image of thought' (SXX, 105). 'Parmenides was wrong and Heraclitus was right' (SXX, 114), Lacan himself will conclude, in locating the source of this onto-theological tradition in the Parmenides who, unlike Heraclitus, is omitted from Nietzsche's praise of the best Hellenic instincts. For these Nietzsche took to be typified in the '*Sophist culture*' or '*realist-culture*' of those such as Thucydides with their 'strong, stern, hard matter-of-factness' – where, Nietzsche must stress, 'the high culture of Thucydides', 'as necessarily as Plato's does *not*', belongs to 'the Periclean age' which 'has its predecessors in Heraclitus, in Democritus, in the scientific types of the old philosophy', where even today 'every advance in epistemological and moral knowledge has reinstated the Sophists' (WP, 428).[19]

We can see Freud also take up this countenance of lament and reform again in his 1925 article 'Resistances to Psychoanalysis', where, without referencing Judaism, but for noting anti-Semitism as readying him for the isolating resistances psychoanalysis faced, he *recommends* 'more play given to truthfulness' in our relation to libido, with repression 'replaced by a better and securer procedure', and a 'reduction in strictness' relative to our inherited moral codes (SE19, 220, 222) – a recommendation that can be indeed be read as a call for a *revaluation* of values. Later in 1925, Freud even pens a letter to the *Jewish Press Centre in Zurich* where he professes to standing 'as far apart from the Jewish religion as from all other religions', as having 'no part in them emotionally' except as a 'a subject of scientific interest' – although not without adding that, nevertheless, he 'always had a strong feeling of solidarity' with his fellow Jewish people which he encouraged in his children, having 'all remained in the Jewish denomination' (SE19, 291).

But perhaps the most revealing place where what is at stake in this repetition of difference *within* the influence of the philhellenic Nietzsche on the Hebraic Freud is where Lacan discerns a 'strange Christocentrism' in Freud's treatment of the Judaeo-Christian thematic that is, 'needless to say, odd to find' (SXVII, 176). This is where Freud posits two Moseses, the first of whom was allegedly murdered by his followers, which hearkened back to the murder of the primal father-ruler of the Palaeolithic hordes we are said by Freud to have lived in – but also echoes forward to the murder of Jesus alleged by Freud to bring this whole complex to light to redeem us of the repressed guilt, enabling us to better accede now to the renunciation demanded by his Law. Lacan finds this odd not just because of the scant evidence, finding the primal Father to be a symptomatic 'fantasy' of omnipotence 'caused' by the repressive operation of the Law (SXVII, 129), but also because of Freud's usual condemnation of the unrealistic nature of Christian Law. For Freud in fact had rebuked the demand to 'love thy neighbour as thyself' in correctly finding that 'the historical spectacle of a humanity that chose it as its ideal is quite unconvincing, when that ideal is measured against actual accomplishments' (SVII, 193).

Later Lacan calls Freud's broadly Oedipal primal father and dual Moses and Jesus murder repetition thesis a 'cock-and-bull story' making 'absolutely no sense' – a 'Darwinian buffoonery' and Lamarckian fancy of repressed murder returning 'via mnesic transmission through chromosomes' (SXVII, 111, 114, 112, 115). In even less flattering terms, Lacan even refers to Freud as trying to save the Father in this, as playing Jesus like 'a good Jew who was not entirely up-to-date' (SXX, 108–9).[20] But armed with his questionable primal-father thesis, Freud had proceeded in his 1921 *Group Psychology and the Analysis of the Ego* to make the further striking claim that Nietzsche's *übermensch* [overman] was not a transformative figure 'from the future', as Nietzsche hoped, but rather a projected fantasy of this primal Father figure 'at the very beginning of the history of mankind' (SE18, 123). This is especially odd because Nietzsche's model for the *übermensch* is often the *really-existing* hyper-educated Greek and Roman nobles of Antiquity, along with figures like Goethe and Beethoven closer to Nietzsche's present – as has been pointed out, for instance, by Brian Leiter.[21]

Nevertheless, there is again a moment where Freud could almost be read as acknowledging the full force of Nietzsche's critique of the whole trajectory of Judaeo-Christian *and Monotheism*, he notes that the 'harmony in the cultivation of intellectual and physical activity' that was 'achieved by the Greek' was 'denied to the Jews' – although not without adding that in choosing to value the spiritual over-against the physical, the Jewish peoples at least chose 'the worthier alternative' (SE23, 115). But Freud must then immediately concede to being at a loss to explain why in this alleged 'advance in intellectuality [*Geistigkeit*]' – or *spirituality* – the people 'clung more and more submissively to their God the worse they were treated by him' (SE23, 115), which, conversely, is something Nietzsche himself can explain in marking this submission as being to an ever-*denaturalizing* God-Father figure: where a *lack* of denaturalizing was blamed for each misfortune only so as to justify ever more – according to what for Nietzsche amounted to an 'idiotic formula', of 'obedience', concocted 'for preserving the power of the priest' (AC, 26).

Nietzsche actually discerned the Platonists to do the same after the Golden Age of Greece, where, in the *fourth* century BC – subsequent to the disaster of the Peloponnesian War that Thucydides founded history as a discipline to record so well – 'gradually everything Hellenic is made responsible for the state of decay, and Plato is just as ungrateful to Pericles, Homer, tragedy, rhetoric, as the prophets were to David and Saul' (WP 427).[22] And it is precisely in this sense that Nietzsche remarks, 'The Sophists were Greeks: when Socrates and Plato took up the cause of virtue and justice, they were *Jews* or I know not what' (WP 429).

Thus, Nietzsche would disagree with Freud's claim that to value spirit over body is to choose the best of the two: finding this the kind of impossible choice that leads precisely to our civilization's discontents, as the intellect becomes infused, overwhelmed, with symptoms of repression and continually distorted in its cognitive claims. In any case, here we can see where there is the potential *influence* of Nietzsche on psychoanalysis, and where there is a residue of *resistance that leads to a difference*: Nietzsche's project demands intellectual affirmation of the real of the bodily drives and a transformation of the alienating Law that unduly prohibits it; whereas Freud at times, by comparison, seems locked in the Schopenhauerian pessimism of *eschewing* the desiring will from fear that it entails much risk and leads to no good, staying closer to the Hebraic Law of confession, castration, and renunciation. This is also evident in the response to Freud of those of his collaborators such as Otto Rank, who, Assoun notes, saw himself being to Freud what Nietzsche was to Schopenhauer regarding negation versus affirmation of the will – with Otto Gross, Alfred Adler, Carl Jung, and Wilhelm Reich additionally coming to use what Assoun calls Nietzsche as 'a referent in the disagreement' that they had with some of Freud's views.[23]

Perhaps tellingly for this referent is that what Nietzsche expressly notes of Schopenhauer is that 'as soon as the thing-in-itself was no longer "God" for him, he had to see it as bad, stupid, and absolutely reprehensible' (WP, 1005) – such that he 'treated sexuality as a personal enemy' (GM III, 7) and thence, traversing from the personal *is* to the political *ought*, 'revenges himself on all things' by 'branding them' with his own image, 'the image of his torture' (GS, 370). But it is of interest also to track this oscillation of influence-*and*-difference forward in time, and west of the Rhine – into the milieu of the cultural modernism that the Freudian Lacan shared with the more Nietzschean Bataille: whose valuable participation in *and* confrontation with the modernist *surrealist* art indebted to the techniques of Freud will come, I suggest, from being embedded with the influence of *both* Nietzsche and Freud.[24]

4.2 FRANCOPHONE CONTEXT: BATAILLE, SURREALISM, MODERNISM, LACAN

In 2003, in one of the first works, if not *the* first, to begin the task of reading Nietzsche and Lacan in light of each other, Zupančič suggests that Nietzsche himself is modernist when claiming 'to break the history of mankind in two' – remaking 1888 as 'year I' for the 'new calendar' demanded by the completion of his *Anti-Christ:* 'the first book of the *Revaluation of all Values*' (TI, P). Together with his 'bombastic' style which can also strike one 'as quite modernistic or, rather, as avant-garde', Zupančič compares him here to the painter Kazimir Malevich, who, with his work *Black Square*, claimed to have introduced 'the first new form that was ever created', 'a new object in reality', with the 'painting-surface as object'.[25]

Although Zupančič then concedes that Nietzsche's own tastes in art can still seem 'conservative' from this perspective, I suggest this feeling falls away upon a full consideration of how his revaluation entails a radical *re*-naturalizing of our drives and instincts in a manner akin to *pre*-Platonic cultures – which is something he already saw threatening to *re*-emerge in the various historical figures of the past he endorsed to finally overturn the spiritual dictatorship of the Christian-Platonic Sovereign Good that lasted 'nigh two millennia' with, figuratively speaking, 'not a single new god' (AC, 19). And it is here that we can form a comparison with Bataille's radical surrealism, which even points to an analogy with the Renaissance project that Nietzsche so admired and wanted to extend, but does so in an expressly *Freudo*-Nietzschean way, as I will show, that again conjoins surrealism with the incitements of modernism to forever start over, again and anew.

With respect to how going back into the past, to retrieve something of value that was lost, can still be part of modernism – Robert Gooding-Williams for one observes that modernism is 'not simply a period concept' but rather 'a break in an otherwise continuous sequence', which thus includes projects such as Nietzsche's for the creation of '*new* values' from the death of God and the notion of morality implied, by connecting new values to the 'revaluation of those Christian-platonic values'. Gooding-Williams also notes in this how Habermas links Nietzsche to 'aesthetic modernism', as 'a precursor to surrealism', *and* to postmodernism's rejection of 'the Enlightenment'.[26] However, while Nietzsche is no relativist in any nihilistic anti-science sense, he indeed deems not the Enlightenment but the Renaissance as 'the last great cultural harvest Europe had to bring home', from its restoring of 'noble values' through the '*revaluation of Christian values*', which alas was destroyed by the Reformation when 'a German monk, Luther, went to Rome' (AC, 61). The Enlightenment that followed Nietzsche thence saw as still unconsciously infused with an expressly Christocentric or Platonic moralism – and Bataille's will to go back even further from the Platonists, to primitive culture, can be fruitfully read here as a new modernist way to leap beyond and behind the Christian-Platonism that Nietzsche so deplored, even further still.[27]

It is in his 1948 Club Maintenant presentation, 'The Surrealist Religion', where Bataille suggests that just as the Renaissance involved the later Middle Ages feeling they had strayed too far from antiquity, seeking then 'to find again in Greece and Rome a mode of existence that had been lost' – surrealism likewise seeks to revitalize by going back to 'primitive society', where for Bataille 'the quest for primitive culture represents the principal, most decisive and vital, aspect and meaning of surrealism, if not its precise definition' (WS, 71). But surrealism's method for this is also what Bataille's earlier 1945 article 'Surrealism and How It Differs from Existentialism', reviewing the *Arcane 17* work of Breton, notes to be a *Freudian* investment of dreams and encouragement to *'automatic writing'* – described here as a 'type of thought, analogous to dream, which is not subordinated to the control of reason' but rather governed by 'chance' (WS, 57, 62).

This is basically the technique that Freud called 'the fundamental rule of psycho-analysis' in his 1912 article on 'The Dynamics of Transference' – namely that of *free-association*, 'which lays it down that whatever comes into one's head must be reported without criticizing it' (SE12, 107). It is also what he had earlier depicted, via Schiller, in his 1900 *The Interpretation of Dreams*, as a 'relaxation of the watch upon the gates of reason', by the 'adoption of an attitude of uncritical self-observation' – to which, Freud adds, bringing in more definitively the domain of letters: 'I myself can do so very completely, by the help of *writing* down my ideas as they occur to me' (SE4, 103).

In another 1948 article on 'Surrealism', Bataille even quotes Breton in similar terms describing 'automatism' as the 'real functioning' and 'dictation of thought' that emerges in 'the absence of all control exercised by reason and outside all aesthetic or moral considerations' (WS, 55). But it is precisely within this 'free poetic release', as Bataille had marked in his 'Surrealism and How It Differs from Existentialism', that what emerges now is 'as difficult to bear as it is decisive and virilely sovereign' (WS, 65) And so, then, to Bataille's way of thinking in particular, 'the difficulty which remained was to *affirm* the value of what was finally released within the shadow' (WS, 65).

Here it is Bataille's expressly Nietzschean current that comes to the fore, in seeking to revitalize the present through the *affirmation* of the real of the drive in its own archaic sovereignty, by overcoming what he condemned as 'the dualist evolution' in his 1948 *Theory of Religion* text. This was where the sacred or divine suddenly 'appears linked to purity', and purity only, cleansed of any 'animal intimacy' and re-defined as *opposite* to anything earthly, bodily, sensuous (TR, 69, 71–2) – with the latter relegated to the fallen status of evil, sin, or hell. Such a declension of the *original* notion of the sacred to 'sin' and 'evil' is also what Bataille exposed in his 1957 *Eroticism* as built up on an underlying 'contempt for animals', which for the prejudiced mind of dualist psychology 'are now disgusting' (E, 126–7, 136–7).

Bataille will intervene on such a puritanism with a Nietzschean return of Dionysos, our knowledge of which is no doubt extended from Freud's focus on the infantile emergence and subsistence of the polymorphous libido's partial drives – from the oral to the anal and into the genital in its active-passive palpitations and regressive pulls – but not by also losing the demand for a *positive* affirmation of this normally unconscious terrain. Such an affirmation again comes of Nietzsche's preference for Dionysos to the oppositional countenance of '*the Crucified*' (EH IV, 9; WP, 1052): that is, from being *pro* instead of 'anti-nature' to the point of 'castration' in morality (TI V, 1–2) – preventing thus the analysis from regressing to a Christian confessional praxis of renunciation and negation for adaptation to the status quo.[28]

This more positive stance is what can enable the restoration, and even *renaissance*, of the *erotic* aspect of religious being – of the divine animality originally implicit of all the sacred – where as Bataille recalled in his 1955 *Lascaux; or, the Birth of Art*, even as late as Ancient Greece 'animality deeply stamps the gods' (L, 123). It is what can enable the *communication* of an experience through the rituals of myth that form the bonds for a community – *a community of the real* – where finally, Bataille hopes, with his 1948 intervention into 'The Surrealist Religion', that 'state of passion, the state of unleashing which was unconscious in the primitive mind, can become lucid' (WS, 81).

Armed, then, with this new lucidity, stemming from renewed openness to our animal immediacy, here is where we can imagine a modernist reconfiguring of the usual relations of taboo-*and*-transgression, beyond the Western metaphysical tradition of the dualist Good – which ever since Socrates and Plato, as Nietzsche first saw, sets up the spirit as a pure space from which to nigh prohibit outright our earthly, bodily animality and condemn it as 'false', precisely on account of what makes it *real*: namely 'death, change, age, as well as procreation and growth' (TI III, 1). But we can see the influence to *re*-structure prohibition also in the more Freudian Lacan, who was 'a silent presence', as Roudinesco records, 'at the secret activities of *Acéphale*' – the secret Nietzschean society founded by Bataille – with the early gatherings of Bataille's other prewar groups such as *Contre-Attaque* and the College of Sociology also 'held in his [Lacan's] apartment'.[29] For Lacan's *Ethics* seminar told of those societies that 'live very well' with transgression built *into* laws, who rather than 'promoting their universal application' can also 'prosper as a result of the transgression of these maxims', so as to allow periodic outlets for primitive drive (SVII, 77–8). And all this Lacan could contrast with the ruminations of St Paul, who feels an 'excessive, hyperbolic', 'desire for death' (SVII, 84) as a result of his universal taboo on animality: creating precisely 'the Law which causes sin' (SVII, 170) that is paradoxically built up by the demand to always repress, without respite.[30]

Lacan could then observe more ominously how our own societies still do not know what to do with their *jouissance*, as the destructive aspect of the drive tends to explode blindly in what only 'seems to us to be an inexplicable accident', or sudden 'resurgence of savagery', through such horrors as mass-marketed industrialized war (SVII, 235) – leading us down the path of a 'race to destruction' ironically forged by '*Western moralism*' itself (SI, 277). But here again we can see the influence of Bataille's notion of a ruinous, non-productive, or non-utilitarian *expenditure* in *The Accursed Share*, a work which seeks to 'lift the curse' (AS I, 9) placed on the *gift* of the drive by capitalist society, emerging from Christianity without knowing how to structure its waste, hellbent only on the blind *accumulation* of ever more Calvinist-Capitalist profits, as the latest version of the Good.

The aim now is to *lift the curse* by reconfiguring a space where this wasteful, destructive aspect of the drive can be affirmed in a sublimated manner: through what Lacan calls a 'retreat from goods' and the 'competition for goods' via an 'open destruction of goods' – like in the 'ritual ceremonies' of 'potlatch' of primitive societies past – enabling thus a 'maintenance and discipline of desire' by the *transgression* of taboos normally governing the workaday 'ethical register of utilitarianism', but done 'consciously and in a controlled way' (SVII, 235, 216). In this Lacan, here, can be read as building on Bataille's tracing of this *correlation* of 'organized transgression together with the taboo' to the 'oral teaching' of the anthropologist Mauss: with Bataille noting his fellow surrealist and cofounder of the College of Sociology, Caillois, to have definitively taken this insight up (E, 65) – with Caillois in turn describing with Bataille an 'intellectual osmosis' that made it difficult to distinguish their respective contributions to the work they 'pursued in common'.[31]

Part of what Bataille also wants to do now with this reorganized transgression, in his 1945 'Surrealism and How It Differs from Existentialism', is make *surrealism* an exemplary modernist practice to enable our drive's propitious release, by *not* 'subordinating it to anything', or forcing 'a superior end to it' (WS, 65). This is where for Bataille it is 'the prerogative of surrealism to free the activity of the mind from such servitude', by periodically liberating the drives from 'rationalism', through the 'poetic liberty' traditionally linked to 'myths and the rituals connected to them' (WS, 65). For Bataille sees surrealism restoring such *sovereignty* when its 'words, no longer striving to serve some useful purpose, set themselves free and so unleash the image of *free existence' – bestowed* 'in the instant' – the seizure of which to Bataille's mind 'cannot differ from ecstasy', just as 'reciprocally one must define ecstasy as the seizure of the instant' (WS, 66–7).

Bataille again then cites Breton's depicting of this process as 'a vertiginous descent into ourselves', and a 'perpetual promenading across forbidden zones' (WS, 66–7). And so, it is through these forbidden zones we are led by this surrealism, accented by Bataille, *beyond* the narrowed realms of utilitarian accumulation and production, to enable the ruinous expenditure that also defines for Lacan the death-drive as a *'jouissance* of transgression' (SVII, 195). No more significant criteria for the arts can be imagined: For by enabling the space for this *jouissance*, the death-drive is less the death-wish Freud feared and more a sublimated *jouissance* of the real that gives us the communal release we need to sustain our precarious psycho-sexual balance – gifting us access to the primitive animality left behind through human taboos purposed for work: granting poetic space for the transgression of these taboos to place us momentarily in the more primitive, archaic realm of myth.

A Classical example of this Lacan himself gives is in his *Seminar V* on *Formations of the Unconscious*, where he cites the comedic works of Aristophanes for where 'the id gets the upper hand, pulls on the boots of language' for the expression of 'sexual needs most especially', which is 'powerful stuff' – as in *'The Clouds'*, Lacan notes, where in response to the hyper-rational-moralist position, *it* 'makes fun of Euripides and Socrates' (SV, 122). But the high value Bataille came to bestow on surrealism for this transgressive liberty can still come as quite a shock, given the very public falling out he initially had with Breton.

Bataille's dispute with Breton and surrealism, however, was in some ways short lived, and as Richardson suggests, more 'emphasized by writers associated with post-structuralism', who sought to see Bataille 'as a precursor of "postmodernism"' by dissociating him 'from contamination with surrealism'.[32] Bataille's postwar *Writings on Surrealism*, moreover – in the collection translated by Richardson we have here been discussing – do seem to demonstrate a kind of rapprochement forming particularly after the war, with Bataille even noting in his 'Surrealism from Day to Day', which is the surviving chapter of a book on surrealism he intended to write, how 'Breton later wrote (in 1947) that I was "one of the few men in life I have found worth taking the trouble of getting to know"' (WS, 41). And all this is despite the fact that before the war, as Richardson puts it, Bataille had put together the *Documents* journal with contributions from 'most of the surrealists with whom Breton had fallen out in 1929'.[33]

As one of the latter, in his 'Notes on the Publishing of "Un Cadavre"', Bataille came to express regret, upon reflection, for the polemics with Breton which he had in the past committed to print – seeing such 'immediate accusations' as a case of mutual misrecognition coming from 'facility and premature annoyance', and lamenting 'how much better silence on both sides would have been' (WS, 32). Nevertheless, what was at stake for Bataille at the time can very much be seen as a Freudo-*Nietzschean* critique of any residue of idealism still discernible in the surrealist branch of modernism, preferring here instead the *counter*-idealist move of *de*-sublimation – what Hollier calls the 'inscription of perversion' as *truth* – to the Icarian flight or *transposition* towards the light he initially took to constitute 'the idealist plot' of Breton, who in turn dismissed Bataille as an 'obsessive', as an 'excremental philosopher'.[34]

We can see how Bataille's critique of Icarian idealism bears the classic trace of Nietzsche's influence from, for instance, Nietzsche's critique of Plato's idea of the Good placed 'as the supreme concept' for representing, rather, the 'higher swindle' and ideal of 'a coward in the face of reality' (TI X, 2). Nietzsche famously contrasts Plato's idealism with Thucydides' 'realist culture', with his 'strong, stern, hard matter-of-factness' (TI X, 2) – and we can sense a similar countenance in Bataille's contrasting of the 'formless', 'heterogeneous', and 'base materialism' with the idealism he thought he found in Breton, while taking a cue also 'from Freud' to extract 'raw phenomena', 'excluding all idealism', through 'direct interpretation'.[35]

But in tackling here the question of Bataille's modernism, Raymond Spiteri also notes how it entails the critique of 'idealism implicit in conventional accounts of modernism', but then suggests an ambivalence in Bataille's own literature where 'transposition' again is used as a defensive escape from the 'base material' of the real: such as when he sees the priest's eye, or eye of the pure and frigid Marcel, in the sex of the licentious Simone; or 'God' in that of the prostitute *Madame Edwarda*.[36] These *surreal* manifestations, however, can also be viewed to traverse the other way, as I already demonstrated concerning *Story of the Eye*, where 'God' or its corollary of the internalized puritan 'super-ego' (super-*I-eye*) – 'the eye of the conscience', as Bataille calls it, which Nietzsche calls 'bad' as an 'evil eye' for our 'natural inclinations' (GM II, 24) – is, rather, *lowered* into the base materialism of the formless, placed in the heterogeneous orifice of the transgressive 'whore', as a way to reopen the closed, narrowly fixated taboo-structure idealized by Christianity.[37]

The further evidence of this lowering is also in the immolation of all the metaphoric *substitutes* for the eye in the novella, often with beams of cum or floods of urine, particularly 'the eggs'. But we can find, moreover, this 'back and forth movement' of high-*and*-low, 'from refuse to ideal, and from ideal to refuse', affirmed as a whole already in *Documents*, in entries such as 'Rotten Sun' (VE, 20–1) – where Bataille shows he seeks neither to escape from the lows nor privilege them to the exclusion of highs, but rather to affirm the whole cycle between them as an eternal return. And this is what also speaks to Nietzsche's critique of the alleged eternal Good as being part of his *active* will to affirm, rather, the eternal return as the *being* of becoming, and as becoming of being, as both the same and a repetition of difference.[38]

This return of difference is what might normally be a return of the repressed death-wish, monstrous perversion, or crippling symptom, if viewed from a narrowing Freudian lens devoid of any Nietzsche, halting at the Schopenhauerian stage of pessimism about the will – preferring through renunciation and resignation the risk of neurosis and nihilism to the chance entailed of affirming the drive *in* the real.[39] But what Bataille ultimately wants to do here is refocus the eternal return of Nietzsche, and the return of the repressed of Freud, onto a periodic cycle between high-*and*-low reconstituted as between the human-*and*-animal side of us – as carefully coordinated between the times for human taboos placed on animality, for purposes of work and accumulation, and the times for the transgression of these normally operating taboos, so as to re-access our 'low' animality and discharge or expend our energies.

So, whatever the initial misrecognition in placing Breton as fixated on the 'high' in this cycle, who in turn misplaced Bataille as fixated on 'lows', Breton's rapprochement with Bataille, after *Documents* (1929–31), began in the *Contre-Attaque* group founded by Caillois (1935), to reconcile surrealism with activism in response to the rise of fascism and betrayal of the revolution by communism – subsequent to the collapse of the bourgeois centre, exposed as the corruption which could not hold. But so as to outdo fascism's reclaiming of the power of *affect* – something which led to accusations of 'sur-fascism' and the splitting of the surrealists from *Contre-Attaque* in 1936[40] – Bataille and Caillois then took their more directly Nietzschean inspiration to found the journal (and secret society) *Acéphale* and the College of Sociology, to further explore the sacred (1936–39).

Here is where they begin referring to themselves as 'ferociously religious', in line with Nietzsche's declaration of being the 'last disciple of the philosopher Dionysos' – with his vision for 'eternal recurrence', saying 'Yes to life beyond death and change' (TI X, 4–5), acting as inspiration for their symbolic *acephalic* ('headless') figure, illustrated by fellow (ex)-surrealist André Masson. Of this, Bataille will proclaim, as standing outside himself in a kind of *ecstasis* (ἔκστασις): 'superman and *acephalic* man are bound with a brilliance equal to the position of time as imperative object and explosive liberty of life'; where Dionysos is the 'symbol of the will to power', and 'the destructive exuberance of life' – and 'time becomes the object of ecstasy', which 'appears as the "eternal return"'.[41]

With the collapse of these movements in the onset of war, Bataille was the one now accused of a mystical idealism – echoing his earlier naming of

Breton a religious windbag – by the wartime surrealist group during Breton's exile, in response to Bataille's *atheological* works founded on the sovereign *jouissance* of Nietzsche's word: 'God is dead'. Richardson, however, marks this attack on Bataille to have occurred in a rather 'childish tract, *Nom de Dieu*' – with Kendall concurring that the *Nom de Dieu* attack on Bataille for an alleged 'idealism' was a 'misguided pamphlet' – following publication of Bataille's 1943 *Inner-Experience*.[42] In the section of the latter entitled 'Critique of Dogmatic Servitude (and of Mysticism)', moreover, Bataille himself in fact states: 'God, even without a form or mode [. . .] is a stop in the movement that brings us to the most obscure apprehension of the *unknown*' – adding that by freeing this apprehension from 'confession', he is justified in abandoning 'the word "mystical"' (IE, 10, 215–6n).

But Breton's return at the cessation of war, and Bataille's *Writings on Surrealism* between 1945 and 1951 here discussed, confirms the thesis of their eventually being not so much vast distance between the two, with Bataille referring to himself, in his 1946 'On the Subject of Slumbers', as surrealism's 'old enemy *from within*' in light of past polemics (WS, 49). And subsequently they collaborated on surrealist publications, with Bataille providing the positive analyses here discussed, and on a surrealist exhibition on the topic of 'Myth', with Bataille contributing his important text on 'The Absence of Myth' (WS, 48).

4.3 DIONYSIAN CONTEXT: PRESENCE OF MYTH IN ABSENCE

Kendall actually suspects something disingenuous in Bataille's self-nomination as surrealism's enemy *from within*, suggesting his description in *Unfinished System of Non-Knowledge,* as being 'beyond but alongside surrealism' (US, 77), is more accurate, and that 'writing in defence of the surrealists was one way that Bataille could counter the Existentialists', who were a rising trend after the war, while 'still smarting from Sartre's negative review of *Inner Experience*'. For Sartre had also labelled this work a 'new mysticism [*nouveau mystique*]', and 'bad faith' even in regretting the death of God in tone while celebrating the ecstasies of inner-experience such a death enabled, with Kendall noting another key sticking point was that 'where Sartre saw contingency, the Surrealists – or rather Bataille on their behalf – proposed a will to chance and limitless revolt'.[43]

But it is within this transgressive space of chance that Bataille's 1947 'The Absence of Myth' can be of value for understanding the modernism implicit of surrealism, and Bataille's specific intervention into it as a *Freudo-Nietzschean* practitioner and critic – which again throws light on the initial relation between Nietzsche and psychoanalysis, and its effects on aesthetics, as has been the aim of this chapter.

In this concluding section, then, here we can recapitulate beginning from Bataille's 'Absence of Myth' on how in order to revitalize our profane world in the order of things, which for Bataille has been 'reduced to the nothingness of things', and thereby strangled by the myth that it is *absent* of myth – which today he calls the 'coldest, the purest, the only *true* myth' (WS, 48) – Bataille hoped rather with surrealist art to go back into our more natural-animal, primitive-archaic roots, with its mytho-poetic re-connections to nature, so as to leap forward and begin again in the present with something radically *new*. And this is a project we can more fully grasp here, in conclusion, by enumerating some of its key consequences not just for a new aesthetics, but also for a new ethics of culture that entails both a new erotics and a new ontology – all along the path of forging this new, potentially ameliorated, society.

We know Bataille wanted to positively re-invest surrealist mytho-poetics in this transformative revolutionary way from his 1948 article on 'Surrealist Religion', where he suggests that when surrealism 'has an influence over industry and over the whole of human activities, these human activities will have been profoundly changed', and in ways 'we could not have predicted' (WS, 88). There was also his 1948 article 'Surrealism and God', where he overtly states that he does 'not mean to condemn the surrealists, but to point out a profound difficulty', pertaining to the myth that enforces the absence of myth by reducing our works and movements alike to things, which, for Bataille, is 'not in any way a critique, but an apology for surrealism' – concluding: 'I do not believe anyone has esteemed it more highly' (WS, 183–4). Then there was his 1946 'Subject of Slumbers' for the surrealist journal *Troisième Convoi*, where he again invokes this 'affirmation of the hope of breaking the solitude' – suggesting that while its 'books are in order on the shelves' and its 'paintings adorn the walls', still as yet 'the *great surrealism* is beginning' (WS, 49).

The consequences of Bataille's more expansive surrealism, then, for a new *aesthetics*, would be that certain taboos usually placed on inner-animality can give way in the arts to a structured transgression: enabling us to *enjoy* our lost, animal-sensual side – in a sublimated space for what Lacan calls 'the *jouissance* of transgression' (SVII, 195), or '*jouissance* of the real' (SXXIII, 63). The resistance, hitherto, to adequately constructing this space is also what is indicated in Lacan's *Anxiety* seminar observation that what normally 'separates out *jouissance* and desire' is precisely the 'fault-line where anxiety is produced' (SX, 182). But rather than this *jouissance* being the angst ridden and provoking sado-masochistic crippling or impoverishing of the organism alluded to by Lacan when following Freud (SXXIII, 63), it is through a renewed mytho-poetics now something much closer to the experience of 'Dionysian ecstasy' first discerned in Nietzsche's *Birth of Tragedy* – which celebrated how the early Greeks could overcome the mental restrictions of 'fear and pity' (BT, 17), to experience tragic wisdom in a cathartic, orgiastic release. To go here *'beyond* pity and terror', as Nietzsche cries out in concluding his 1888 *Twilight of the Idols*, and *'realize in oneself* the eternal joy of becoming', 'which also encompasses *joy in destruction*' (TI X, 5).

This *joy*, as Boothby couches in Lacanian terms, is the death-drive *unbinding* us from 'the ego' – from what Lacan even calls a 'resistance to the elusive process of becoming, to the variations of desire' – and is why, beyond the weight of ego-resistance, Boothby can point to 'a paradoxical identity between the death drive and the realization of a fuller vitality'.[44] It is also why Nietzsche's 1888 concluding of *Twilight of the Idols* above can repeat his earliest conviction of his 1872 *Birth of Tragedy*, of tragic catharsis being a joyous, sensuous, Dionysian affirmation – much to the contrary of Aristotle's notion of a 'medical or moral', 'pathological discharge' of nothing other than 'pity and fear' (BT 22).

This is because it is the *beauty* effect implicit in Nietzsche's returned-as-affirmed sensuality, here, that acts as lure for us to face and even affirm the harshest, most amoral and difficult truths of the real – a premise also of Lacan's esteem of *pre*-Platonic tragic art, and discernment of a limit to Aristotle's 'moral catharsis', which, for Lacan, 'we always think we have to defer to', but only to end up falling short (SVII, 287). For given how Aristotle was a pupil of Plato's, this deference is entangled in what Lacan points out initially 'Nietzsche put his finger on' with 'Socrates' profound incompetence every time he broaches the topic of tragedy (SVIII, 81–2) – which, with Plato's *enthusiasm* for Socrates, and forging of the Academy on this basis, creates what Lacan calls 'the longest transference, giving this expression its fullest import, that history has ever known' (SVIII, 7).[45]

Overcoming this transference of authority for thinking to a profound historical incompetence, by recovering tragic beauty as the lure to affirmation, is what makes possible now a *new ethics* – one that is built on the increasing lucidity of how our normally unconscious, animal-desiring drives manifest in us, which means we can ethically respond more appropriately, on balance, as we learn ever more about the difficulties, origins, and conditions of our *jouissance in the real*. For as Lacan even put it, 'insofar as Freud's position constitutes progress here, the question of ethics is to be articulated', henceforth, from our 'relation to the real' – where 'to appreciate this', Lacan infers, we also have to consider 'what occurred in the interval between Aristotle and Freud' (SVII, 11).

We have seen that what occurred in between was Nietzsche's pointing to how the ethical space to affirm and knowingly *sublimate* the real, instead of repress it, was gradually foreclosed by the denaturalized unfolding of Christian-Platonism. But we have also seen that this space can be restored through art when it is augmented by a philosophy and psychoanalysis revitalized with the *combined* Nietzsche–Freud influence – *reaching across to Bataille and Lacan* – teaching us to privilege the types of art that can facilitate this affirming ethical process, based not just on a knowledge of the drives, but also on a more active, positive, self-relation to them, that does not at all eschew *experience*.

In order for this ethics to be sustainable, then, which can still demand the task of understanding a work of art – as well as the many oddities and complexities of the mind – what is required also is the preservation of a space for a new *erotics*. This would mean that fewer motivational deficits would occur because the libidinal demand, once it is no longer artificially resisted, is an implacably constant energy source, fuelling our thoughts and acts whether we acknowledge *it* or not. Staged more in Nietzschean terms: Dionysos, in the sexual sense of 'the psychology of the orgy' Nietzsche uncovers, must remain as the prerequisite for Apollo, as set out in his first born *'Birth of Tragedy'*, which he later dubbed, in *Twilight of the Idols*: 'my first revaluation of values' (TI X, 5). For without Dionysos as premise we get not the lucid, formal clarity of Apollo but just the hyper-moral rationalism of the Platonic Socratism that Nietzsche foresaw as *hostile* to 'the instincts' (TI II, 11) (BT 13) – leading to the denaturing neuroses of Judaeo-Christianity and the monstrous perversions, or mediocre nihilisms, of our various forms of capitalism today.[46]

Dionysos here instead means we are not just producing 'knowledge' of the real, or applying such knowledge to mass-produce the facile consumer goods that tap the real while denying it, which is what Lacan calls 'the service of goods' of our today that must forever 'colonize' the Freudian Thing with delusional 'imaginary schemes', or the 'fantasm' of object *a* (SVII, 303, 324, 99; SXVII, 50). For Lacan notes that here the 'small *a*' (*autre*-other), which is there to be 'substitute for big A' – which 'is the real Other' that is 'involved in *jouissance*' – is nothing but an *objectified* desire, which, through mass commodification, only concerns the subject 'elliptically and off to one side' (SX, 182, 160–1). But what Dionysos enables instead is a deepest satisfaction of the drives, beyond normal mores and commercial interests, through the periodic rotations enjoining taboo-*with*-transgression, and rational accumulation *with* the many *gifts* entailed of a knowing potlatch-type expenditure.

Such a properly coordinated rotation between taboos that enable rational accumulation, and transgressions that enable genuine potlatch-type expenditure as a subsequent release, is what is absent from our 'modern' today, always on the hunt for more commercial profits wherever any expenditure takes place. Its emphasis thus is *still* on accumulation, rather than the drive in its glorious destruction and waste as *gift*, when it is sublimated into something divine *beyond* any reductively narrowed and ideologically pre-determined utilitarian purpose. Attic tragedy provides the superlative example of this, in transferring unwanted and uncontrolled physical destructions to psychological simulation, which can indeed have positive physical consequences as we return to the world, renewed with the Dionysian wisdom, deftly veiled in an alluring way through the beautifying formal function of Apollo. In this way a culture of modernism can create new structured transitions between a politics of taboo, and an aesthetics of transgression, in a philosophically guided way that minimizes excessive disturbances in either domains – whether in the form of a neurotics of ossified-fixated taboo, or a perversion of a too wild and wayward transgression, which ultimately stem from the same lack *in* the real.[47]

And so, lastly, to stabilize this structure, what is also required, as well as entailed, is a new *ontology*: one that protects the imaginary by safely deflating it, to preserve a clear distinction between the time for work governed by taboo – by the *symbolic* relation to the real of equitable politics and rational conceptual clarity – and the time for aesthetics which then returns us to the *imaginary* manifestations of the real, but consciously through transgression in the erotic return of animality, which Bataille saw as 'poetic and divine though animal' (E, 153). But this ontology is tripartite and deflationary so as to never again allow for the formation of an Icarian *dualist* religion, caught in the bellows of an imaginary of the Good, *mislabelled* as real in a way that religiously distorts the symbolic again into an absurd, intellectually humiliating, disfunction.[48]

This ontology of 'the imaginary, the symbolic, and the real', moreover, extracted from Lacan and applied to the work of Bataille, Freud and Nietzsche, is also what Louis Saas calls one of the 'expressions of an essentially modernist sensibility' of Lacan's own, which should come as no surprise given how 'in Paris', Saas notes, 'Lacan frequented the surrealists and other avant-garde groups' with a 'lively interest in the latest developments in philosophy, literature, and the human sciences' – while his second marriage was to actress 'Sylvia Maklès, estranged wife of his friend Georges Bataille, infamous for his writings on the necessity of transgression in both sexuality and religion'. Saas in fact follows Clement Greenberg here to define modernism post-Kantianly, as the questioning of internal forms of time and space and thus 'the very structure of reality', suggesting Lacan was able to 'supplement Freud's concepts' to 'bring them into conformity with these modernist concerns, while at the same time enriching modernism'.[49] With addition of Nietzsche's *Dionysian* naturalism and Bataille's *base*-surrealism, however, I suggest we have doubly ensured that this creative enriching also remains both firmly grounded – and deeply rooted – *in* the earthly real.

The next chapter will consider the expressly paradoxical relation of literature to both happiness *and* evil that Bataille focuses on in his later years, to see how it builds on the aesthetic criteria we have been developing and extracting from him and his key intellectual sources. While finally, here, we find in the act the restored Nietzsche–Freud relation that is especially important for this project, insofar as the motivation is what Lacan calls a 'love of truth' as well as a 'recognition of realities', following the later Freud's defining of 'the analytic relation' as such (SXVII, 165)[50] – enabling *affirmation* where the aim is to better navigate the straights of *jouissance*, through a properly structured relation to the drive in the relation of culture to nature, and art to work. To continually begin again and anew until resistance to the whole eternal cycle of return between human and animal, or 'high and low', is truly minimized such that disturbances are contained, as we improve in our trained abilities to stay with the venture of *revaluation* – out of the residual Dark of Christendom and onwards and further into the *new*.

> I call Christianity the *one* great curse...the *one* immortal blemish of mankind. . . . And one calculates *time* from the *dies nefastus* [unlucky day] on which this fatality arose – from the *first* day of Christianity! – *Why not rather from its last? – From today?* – Revaluation of all values!
>
> —Nietzsche, *The Antichrist* (62), 30 September, 1888

NOTES

1. See Laura Winkiel, *Modernism: The Basics* (New York: Routledge, 2017), 65–6.

2. For Bataille as one of the first 'French Nietzscheans' and authors with 'experience of the analyst's couch', see Roudinesco, *Jacques Lacan*, 132–4, 131, 121.

3. Bataille is discussing Sade when paradoxically calling heterology a science of a heterogeneous 'outside the reach of scientific knowledge, which by definition is only applicable to homogeneous elements'. Lacan depicts the *jouissance* of transgression in terms of Sade in *Seminar VII* as to 'trample sacred laws underfoot' (SVII, 195), but also in terms of masochism in his *Seminar XXIII* on James Joyce, noting that '*jouissance* of the real includes masochism' as 'the main share of the *jouissance* endued by the real' (SXXIII, 63). For Bataille's familial links with Lacan see Roudinesco, *Jacques Lacan*, 135–8. Bataille, "The Use Value of D.A.F. de Sade," in VE, 97.

4. Roudinesco documents how Lacan contributed to the surrealist journal *Minotaure* and that 'his doctoral dissertation was greeted by them as an event'. Hal Foster notes that Lacan 'was a young associate of the surrealists in the early 1930s', who referred to them 'in the unveiling of man's relationship with the symbolic', but also stresses that while 'surrealism appears to be illustrative of Freudian notions', it can also 'anticipate' or 'contradict them', like 'actual instances of "objective chance"

(to use the surrealist term)'. Roudinesco, *Jacques Lacan*, 136. Foster, *Prosthetic Gods* (Cambridge, MA: The MIT Press, 2004), 246, 419, 227.

5. Assoun, *Freud and Nietzsche*, trans. R. Collier (London: Continuum, 2007), 3–4.

6. Freud, "Letter to Ludwig Binswanger"; *Correspondence, 1927–1939*; "Letter to Fleiss"; and *Minutes of the Vienna Psychoanalytic Society* – all cited in Assoun, *Freud and Nietzsche*, 21, xxiv, 20, 7–8. Freud, "On the History of the Psychoanalytic Movement (1914)," in SE14, 15–6.

7. Freud also discusses his distaste for world-views in his 1926 *Inhibitions, Symptoms and Anxiety*, SE20, 95–6, and in the last of his 1933 *New Introductory Lectures on Psychoanalysis*, SE22, 158–82. Assoun, *Freud and Nietzsche*, xxix–xxx, 10, 37.

8. Thomas Brobjer also documents how it was Nietzsche's training in historical studies and methods that was critical for his understanding of the Ancient Hellenes, whence emerged the impetus to launch his revaluation of our contemporary post-Christian values. Bass, *Interpretation and Difference*, 2. Brobjer, "Nietzsche's View of the Value of Historical Studies and Methods," *Journal of the History of Ideas* 65 (2004): 320–1. See also Brobjer, "The Origin and Early Context of the Revaluation Theme in Nietzsche's Thinking," *The Journal of Nietzsche Studies* 39 (2010): 12–29.

9. The harshness of the positivist ideological tradition on Freud's claim to scientific status is seen in the interviews collected by Todd Dufresne. Among them, Frank Sulloway suggests some of the 'self-analysis' made 'a causal agent of Freud's originality' actually came from his awareness of developments in sexology, which he *then read into* his own analysis and clinic. Perhaps a more balanced position would be that while Freud is not nearly as pseudo-scientific as the positivist wishes, he is also not yet as strictly scientific as he hopes. Dufresne, *Against Freud: Critics Talk Back* (Stanford: Stanford University Press, 2007), 55–6.

10. For analysis of denaturalizing's Platonic and Hebraic origins, along with its modern secular derivatives and unconscious formations, see also Nietzsche, *The Will to Power*, 299, 37, 292, 203, 298, 430; and *Anti-Christ*, 24–6.

11. Freud's discusses the 'internalization or turning inwards' of aggression by civilization in his 1937 'Analysis Terminable and Interminable' (SE23, 244). He links this process of 'turning it inwards' to the superego and formation of conscience particularly in his 1930 *Civilization and Its Discontents* (SE21, 130). Further, when Lacan in his *Ethics* puts 'at the heart of everything Freud taught' that 'the energy of the so-called superego derives from the aggression that the subject turns back on himself' (SVII,194), he inadvertently, without acknowledgment, puts Nietzsche at the heart of everything psychoanalysis discovers. For fuller treatment of the links between Lacan and Nietzsche via the super-ego acting as a nihilistic ascetic ideal, see Themi, *Lacan's Ethics and Nietzsche's Critique of Platonism*, 36–7, 53, 107, 140, 142, 178, 195, 216, 223. For an earlier analysis of the Freudo-Lacanian superego that neglects the debt to Nietzsche and the insights afforded, despite several references to him – including to the *Genealogy of Morals* where bad-conscience and the ascetic ideal are treated at great length – see Johnston, "The Vicious Circle of the Super-Ego:

The Pathological Trap of Guilt and the Beginning of Ethics," *Psychoanalytic Studies* 3.3/4 (2001): 411–2. Zupančič, *The Shortest Shadow*, 50, 53, 81.

12. Ons, "Nietzsche, Freud, Lacan," in *Lacan: The Silent Partners*, ed. Žižek (New York: Verso, 2006), 85.

13. Assoun, *Freud and Nietzsche*, 27–9, xxiv, xxvii, xxxix.

14. Assoun, *Freud and Nietzsche*, 9.

15. Assoun, *Freud and Nietzsche*, 6–11, 186.

16. Hume's treatment of the 'is-ought' or 'fact-value' dynamic is in *A Treatise of Human Nature* (London: Penguin, 1986), III, 1.1.

17. Zupančič, *The Shortest Shadow*, 43.

18. Brobjer also records how the Nietzsche of the late 1880s was generally critical of positivism's fantasy of 'pure facts', and along with Paul Franco observes that a greater 'unity' between art and science was implied from the start of Nietzsche's oeuvre and increasingly finds balance across time. For further explanation of both Nietzsche's 1886 defending of 'idealists against positivists' in *Beyond Good and Evil* and Book V of *The Gay Science*, and his 1888 defending of 'positivists against idealists' in *Twilight of the Idols*, see Themi, *Lacan's Ethics and Nietzsche's Critique of Platonism*, 117–23. Brobjer, "Nietzsche's Reading and Knowledge of Natural Science: An Overview," in *Nietzsche and Science*, eds. G. Moore, Brobjer (Aldershot: Ashgate, 2004), 35, 44, 46. Franco, "Nietzsche's Human, All Too Human and the Problem of Culture," *The Review of Politics* 69 (2007): 234, 242.

19. Alain Badiou also marks how Lacan's 'anti-philosopher' stance is from opposing Plato (and Parmenides) with concerns for difference, slippage, becoming, and change – making Lacan like Nietzsche closer to Heraclitus, who Nietzsche indeed had 'set apart with high reverence' for *not* having 'rejected the evidence of the senses because these showed plurality and change' (TI III, 2). For earlier and fuller discussion of Nietzsche's praise of realist-empiricist and naturalist pre-Platonic philosophy and culture, along with Lacan's criticism of the mystical ontological traditions of Plato and Aristotle vis-à-vis their unconsciously sexualized form-matter distinction, see also Themi, *Lacan's Ethics and Nietzsche's Critique of Platonism*, 8–9, 119–20, 125–6. Badiou, "Lacan and the Pre-Socratics," in *Lacan: The Silent Partners*, ed. Žižek, 12–3, 15.

20. For further discussion of Lacan's critique, evaluated also through an even stronger anti-Christocentric Nietzschean prism, see Themi, *Lacan's Ethics and Nietzsche's Critique of Platonism*, 97–105.

21. For Nietzsche's affirmation of Goethe as a Dionysian overman with his realist, Renaissance type naturalism and holism, who 'strove against the separation of reason, sensuality, feeling, will' that was 'preached in the most horrible scholasticism by Kant, the antipodes of Goethe', see *Twilight of the Idols*, IX, 49–51. Leiter, *Nietzsche on Morality* (New York: Routledge, 2002), 122.

22. Thucydides by contrast blames not the highly respected Pericles but the private greed, ambition, and corruption of those who took leadership after his death for the ultimate decimation of Golden Age Athens, in Book II of his *History of the Peloponnesian War, Volume I: Books 1–2*, trans. C. F. Smith, Loeb Classical Library 108 (Cambridge, MA: Harvard University Press, 1919), II, 65–6.

23. Assoun, *Freud and Nietzsche*, 34, 32, 202n.

24. Roudinesco notes that the young Lacan also read Nietzsche keenly when breaking from his family's religion, writing for his brother 'a brilliant eulogy of Nietzsche's thought' to deliver at their Catholic college, and earning its wrath in response. The brother nevertheless went on to become a monk, while Lacan gravitated more to Freud. Bataille, conversely, all but declares himself Nietzsche's sole heir in proclaiming: 'I am the only one who thinks of himself not as a commentator of Nietzsche but as being the same as he' (AS III, 367). Roudinesco, *Jacques Lacan*, 13–4.

25. Zupančič, *Shortest Shadow*, 5–6, 26.

26. Gooding-Williams, "Nietzsche's Pursuit of Modernism," *New German Critique* 41 (1987): 98–9, 96.

27. For Nietzsche's praise of Renaissance at the expense of Reformation, where he took Judea to have triumphed once more over Greece and Rome by the 'plebeian (German and English) *ressentiment* movement called the Reformation', see also *Genealogy of Morals*, I, 16. For how German philosophy continued this as 'a *cunning* theology', and in particular Kant's 'crafty-sly scepticism' which 'made of reality an "appearance"' so that the fantasy of a moral *essence* of the cosmos is 'if not demonstratable yet no longer *refutable*', since 'the *right* of reason does not extend so far' and we can never know the thing-in-itself, see *Anti-Christ*, 10–12. The latter pronouncement should be used to qualify Zupančič's overstated or misleading claim that, because Nietzsche recognizes the misuses and abuses of empiricism, 'Nietzsche is and remains a Kantian' who believes 'empirical reality is already a construction'. Nietzsche's *empiricist* critique of poor uses of empiricism, where we mistake ourselves to have 'discovered in things only *that which we had put into them!*', can be found in *Twilight of the Idols*, VI, 3, a full discussion of which is in section 6.2 of Themi, *Lacan's Ethics and Nietzsche's Critique of Platonism*, 117–23. Zupančič, *Shortest Shadow*, 92.

28. Chloë Taylor cites 'three critiques of confession' in Foucault which could be 'critiques of psychoanalysis'. Lacan's critique of 'adaptation' in 'ego-psychology' is also well known. Taylor, *The Culture of Confession from Augustine to Foucault: A Genealogy of the "Confessing Animal"* (New York: Routledge, 2009), 119. Dylan Evans, *Introductory Dictionary of Lacanian Psychoanalysis*, 4–5.

29. Roudinesco, *Jacques Lacan*, 136.

30. Lacan is also applying Freud's 1915 article 'Repression', which notes how beyond 'conscious influence' repressed material 'proliferates in the dark' into 'extreme forms of expression', which are 'deceptive' due to excessive 'damming-up' (SE14, 149).

31. Caillois, *Man and the Sacred*, 15.

32. Noys conversely suggests Richardson 'overstates the case for a rapprochement between Bataille and surrealism'. But in trying to avoid a Platonic essentialism of human nature, Noys's rejection of Richardson's Bataillean social theory seems to flirt with constructionism, as if nature itself contained no durations. The abandoning of natural-kinds as stable referents, as if 'reality is merely textual', is the postmodernist 'neo-Kantian' appropriation of Bataille that Richardson rebukes for 'abstracting'

transgression from taboo – that is, from the animal, bodily, natural elements that are taboo's objects, and thus from what is 'concrete' and 'empirical' in Bataille's more detailed Freudo-Nietzschean anthropological notion of nature. Nietzsche and Freud, moreover, defer precisely to material-empirical nature to reject the failed Platonic type inflationary idealism, rather than use such failure as grounds to continue to reject nature itself, which would be to remain bound up in an altered expression of Christian-Platonism, and its ascetic ideal of denial, even further still. In this, postmodernism for Richardson 'tends to merely reverse the frame of reference so that it becomes the lack of historical structure that is just as dogmatically asserted'. But Nietzsche had already rejected such a binary between the desire for permanence (*being*) and the desire for change (*becoming*) in Book V of the *Gay Science*, replacing it with his aesthetic distinction between abundance and lack to discern how both the desire for being *and* for becoming are on the surface 'ambiguous' (GS, 370) and, depending on the context, can both be wrong as symptoms of *ressentiment* towards actuality. Richardson, *Georges Bataille*, 4, 6–8, 135n; and "Introduction," in Bataille, WS, 1. Noys, *George Bataille*, 22, 143n.

33. Richardson, "Introduction," in Bataille, WS, 4.

34. Hollier, *Against Architecture*, 108. Stoekl, "Introduction," in Bataille, VE, xi. Bataille, "Surrealism from Day to Day," WS, 41.

35. See Bataille, "Formless"; "Base Materialism and Gnosticism"; "The Use Value of D.A.F. de Sade"; and "Materialism"; in VE, 31, 45, 94–9, 15–6. But for that on Sade, the articles first appeared in *Documents* among others tackling the similar themes of 'low' versus 'high', as discussed here in section 3.1.

36. Spiteri, "Georges Bataille and the Limits of Modernism," *Emaj: Online Journal of Art* 4 (2009): 1, 11, 21–2. Bataille, *Story of the Eye*, 76; *Madame Edwarda*, 150.

37. In rejecting, then, the postmodernist *reduction* of transgression to 'subversion', Richardson risks the opposite prejudice of reducing transgression to 'impotence' towards taboo, as if it never alters but only ever 'completes and reinforces it'. But this depends on the context, on *which* taboo, in relation to *which* element of nature – and on the *type* of taboo–transgression structure at play – which in the Christian context *can* be restructured because of its forced narrowness. I showed in chapter 1 here how this is argued for by Bataille in such texts as *Eroticism*, and in chapter 2 how in *Story of the Eye* this argument is metaphorized by the final enucleation of the priest. Richardson, *George Bataille*, 6, 9.

38. Deleuze saw Nietzschean return connected here to 'diversity and its reproduction, of difference and its repetition', as a principal of 'the will to power'. Russell also connects this clinically to the perspectival flows of interpretation that occurs, so as 'to neutralize *ressentiment*'. Deleuze, *Nietzsche and Philosophy*, trans. H. Tomlinson (New York: Columbia University Press, 1983), 49. Russell, *Nietzsche and the Clinic*, 9–11, 22–3.

39. Deleuze calls Schopenhauerian pessimism a stage two '*reactive* nihilism', where the inflated ideals initially produced through the *negation* of life (stage one nihilism) are removed, but not the negativity that first caused them. A third stage is '*passive nihilism*', where new ideals are secreted instead of genuinely created only to preserve this negative life in a state 'close to zero' – with this whole trajectory taking

us 'From God to God's murderer, from God's murder to the last man'. Zupančič in part misses the three-staged nuance of Nietzsche's diagnosis of European nihilism in referring to only active and passive nihilism corresponding to only 'two types of the ascetic ideal', where active nihilism rejects *all* fictions from a 'passion for the real' – as if all fictional creations are equivalent and equally affirm or negate the real – and where passive nihilism simply refuses to create or will at all. The *active* will to reject the denaturing Christian-Platonic semblances, illusions, myths, and ideals, by use of philosophy, science, and psychoanalysis, is also an important *anti*-nihilist step for clearing the slate for future creations of better ideals which affirm nature and life as per *pre*-Christian-Platonic cultures, without necessarily having to again conflict with science by creating *anti*-nature myths to believe in literally. This again comes down to the problem of stipulating all desire, fantasy, fiction, etc., as equally a defence against the real drive of enjoyment – which is solved by clarifying a distinction between the mytho-poetic products of weak sublimations (which elide and hide from the real) and those of strong sublimations (which rather face and affirm the real), as discussed at the end of chapter 1 here and sections 2.2 and 2.3 of Themi, *Lacan's Ethics and Nietzsche's Critique of Platonism*, 30–40. Deleuze, *Nietzsche and Philosophy*, 148–51. Zupančič, *Shortest Shadow*, 63–5.

40. Spiteri notes Bataille's complaint in response was where 'surrealism merely pacified revolt, channelling discontent into the artistic and poetic practices that the bourgeoisie tolerated, despite the occasional scandal'. Stoekl, "Introduction," xviii. Spiteri, "Surrealism and its Discontents: Georges Bataille, Georges Ribemont-Dessaignes, and the 1929 Crisis of Surrealism," *French History and Civilization* 4 (2011): 154.

41. Bataille, "The Sacred Conspiracy (1936)," "Nietzschean Chronicle (1937)," and "Propositions (1937)," in VE, 179, 206, 200. These articles initially appeared in Bataille's Nietzschean journal *Acéphale*.

42. Richardson, "Introduction," in Bataille, WS, 11. Kendall, *Georges Bataille*, 170.

43. Kendall concurs with Noys in seeing Richardson's rapprochement of Bataille and surrealism as overstated but to the point of being 'doubly disingenuous', which is to go too far in the opposite direction, as Bataille's professions of being opposed but '*from within*', and beyond but still 'with and alongside' surrealism suggest. That is, Breton and Sartre were not 'a privileged *other* for Bataille' in the same way or to the same extent as Kendall nigh implies. Bataille's friend Leiris, for one, had also noted how it was 'a mutual esteem' that would bring Bataille and Breton back together again on literary projects such as 'the review *Minotaure*', or on political projects such as 'Contra-Attaque', despite Bataille preserving his status as 'outsider'. Kendall, *Georges Bataille*, 179, 170, 82, 219n. Leiris, "From Bataille the Impossible to the Impossible *Documents*," in Georges Bataille, Michel Leiris, *Correspondence*, trans. L. Heron (London: Seagull, 2008), 13.

44. Boothby, *Freud as Philosopher*, 144, 150–1. Lacan, "Some Reflections on the Ego," *International Journal of Psycho-Analysis* 34 (1953): 15.

45. For the Nietzsche-and-Lacan praise of tragic art and critique of the notion of catharsis of Aristotle, the former pupil of Plato – himself the pupil of Socrates – see Themi, *Lacan's Ethics and Nietzsche's Critique of Platonism*, 41–63.

46. I discussed in section 1.4 here how Bataille's use of Weber details why capitalist transgressions have 'more in common with the *disturbed* transgressions of the Christian age than they do with those sacred of the Hellenic'. The earlier version of this discussion quoted here is in Themi, "Bataille and the Erotics of the Real," *Parrhesia: Journal of Critical Philosophy* 24 (2015): 323–28.

47. This is where Kennedy suggests politics and art are equally important to Bataille, linked respectively to 'the necessity to fight oppression and exploitation' *and* to 'the necessity to leave all necessity behind'. However, in a more recent article, in trying to point out that transgression is not 'inherently progressive', he risks the mistake of asserting that transgression thus is inherently un-progressive, which could be read as too conservative – where really it is neither progressive nor regressive inherently but depends on the context of taboo, and the level of psychoanalytic and philosophical know-how imbued in the transgressor. A key example I have stressed throughout my published work of the last six years is how the transgression of artificially narrowed Christian taboos on sexuality in particular *have* had a progressive function, and continue to, which *has* allowed for restructure, and is something highly implicit and often argued for in Bataille's work: from the enucleation of the priest in the 1928 *Story of the Eye*, to the heavy criticism of Christianity in the 1957 *Eroticism* and 1961 *Tears of Eros*. Kennedy, *Towards an Aesthetics of Sovereignty*, 275; and "Between Law and Transgression: Literature as a (Non-) Civilizing Strategy in the Early 20th Century," *Open Library of Humanities* 6/1.17 (2020): 15.

48. A full and detailed discussion of how the onto-theology of Christian-Platonism, with its inflationary idea of the Good, substitutes an imaginary for the real and thereby distorts the symbolic is in chapter 1 of Themi, *Lacan's Ethics and Nietzsche's Critique of Platonism*, 7–22.

49. Sass, "Lacan: The Mind of the Modernist," *Continental Philosophy Review* (2015) 48: 409–11. Greenberg, "Modernist Painting," in *The New Art: A Critical Anthology*, ed. G. Battcock (New York: Dutton, 1973).

50. Freud's full quote reads, 'And finally we must not forget that the analytic relationship is based on a love of truth – that is, on a recognition of reality – and that it precludes any kind of sham or deceit'. See the 1937 article, "Analysis Terminable and Interminable," in SE23, 248.

Chapter 5

From Dionysos to Devil
Bataille's Evil Happiness of Literature

We are in the 1949 article, 'Happiness, Eroticism, and Literature', where Bataille begins his discussion by reducing literature to a 'quest for happiness', but reduced Freudianly to 'sexual pleasure'. What was meant as a piece for the *Critique* journal he founded after the war, in this case reviewing the sensualist surrealist writings of Malcom de Chazal, soon produces some of the finest thinking Bataille has had to offer on the deepest processes of creative writing – where happiness can often seem like the very thing farthest removed (WS, 186–7).[1] The previous chapter saw how the positive influence of Nietzsche on psychoanalysis itself reaches through to Bataille's challenge to the surrealist branches of modernism, shedding more light on the aesthetic criteria that through Bataille we have here been developing. Now, we shall examine further Bataille's philosophy of art apropos of his express writings on *literature* – to see what this can offer for an aesthetics in terms of future writings of creative works, such as 'the novel', which Bataille famously also wrote himself.

First, I discuss how his 'Happiness, Eroticism, and Literature' posits literature as a paradoxical quest for happiness, and ground this with Nietzsche's critique of Kant's ostensibly contrary notion of 'disinterest' as characterizing the aesthetic sphere. Bataille's 1957 *Literature and Evil* work will also be considered in this context, positing as it does, rather, a quest for a kind of 'Evil' in literature, which I will argue is the mark of an under-analysed relation between law and desire that fails to make space for periodically affirming the return of certain repressed or tabooed desires, and thereby consigns Dionysus to the Devil. Next, I discuss Bataille's writings on poetry, which invoke it as a way to smash through the rut that can befall prose literature, so as to offer us potentially a more *immediate* experience. This will be observed in the work of Jacques Prévert and René Char, despite the *absence* of poetry's ability to any longer form the unifying social myths for community.

Finally, I turn to the paradoxical need for separation Bataille posits between the poetic and the rational that must also be a path between the two, which I suggest are equivalent, in Lacanian terms, to the intimately related yet still distinct imaginary and symbolic modes of registering the often heterogeneous *real*. I argue that a clarity of consciousness and affirmation of these distinct yet connected realms constitute Bataille's aim for future writings and novels – to foster our ability to *think-within* the raw, tumultuous experience of that which remains forever *real* in them.

5.1 LITERATURE'S QUEST FOR HAPPINESS OF THE EROTIC

This section considers the paradoxical 'quest for happiness' Bataille discerns of literature in his 1949 *Critique* article so as to evaluate it relative to the 'quest for evil' he later posits instead in his 1957 collection of essays *Literature and Evil*, the earlier versions of which also first appeared in *Critique*. Nietzsche's criticism of Kant's seemingly contrary notion of 'disinterest', as constituting the authentic *aesthetic* experience, will also be brought to bear here – not least because Nietzsche is the major philosophical reference of Bataille and also at one point equates aesthetics with happiness, while subjecting Kant's to a famous critique.

Nietzsche's critique of Kant's aesthetics is found in Essay III of his 1887 *Genealogy of Morals*, which sets out to deconstruct the *ascetic* ideal of self-denial inherited of our various Christian-Platonic traditions of the West. Here Nietzsche can be found dismissing the Kantian idea as such that 'one can even view undraped female statues "without interest"' as bearing all the 'naivety of a country Vicar', despite any pretentions to objectivity as a 'spectator' in emphasizing only those particular 'predicates of beauty' which 'establish the honour of knowledge', namely 'impersonality and universality' (GM III, 6). For this emphasis conceals an ascetic denial, which Nietzsche will contrast not only with the story of Pygmalion, the sculptor who literally fell in love with his own sculpture – so *besotted* with it was he – but also with the novelist Stendhal, who makes for Nietzsche the far more accurate 'sensual' and 'happily constituted' appeal to aesthetic beauty as rather 'the promise of happiness' (GM III, 6). And it is just this promise, affirmed by Nietzsche as the *real* of aesthetics 'in the realm of the beautiful' from a 'refined first-hand experience' of it – as a 'great *personal* fact' and 'abundance of vivid authentic experiences, desires, surprises, and delights' (GM III, 6) – that Bataille likely had in mind when beginning his own analysis of literature with a perceived quest for happiness. Although soon enough he comes across a paradox involved extending our analysis *beyond* personal interest in what I suggest is actually a *hyper*-interested Nietzschean way – involving as it does the 'eroticism' that Bataille will define in *Literature and Evil* as 'the approval of life up until death' (LE, 10).

This *paradox* in happiness, which Bataille follows Nietzsche in seeing literature as a kind of promise of or quest for, occurs because it can refer to the happiness of 'both acquisition and expenditure', which are different in kind for Bataille and why, when it comes to happiness, our 'representations vary in accordance with our frame of mind' (WS, 189). For the first sense of happiness is where 'happiness is *always* confounded with the resources which make it possible' (WS, 189), because 'before we can be happy we must find the means to be so', which, Bataille notes, means 'the thought of happiness thereby urges us to work to attain it' (WS, 188). This is what gives the happiness of security in the steady accumulation of means, wealth, and comfort, which is depending on the rational pursuit of determinate goals and interests in the sphere of work.

It is the results of this work that give what Bataille will note is the specifically longer 'duration' of happiness (WS, 190), in the safe-space governed and secured by the taboos we place on certain parts of our animal desires and instincts pertaining mainly to sex, violence, and death. But by doing so for Bataille, 'to recall its material data' (WS, 188), there is also a sense where 'we introduce a distance between ourselves and happiness' (WS, 188), which means our happiness is not complete unless there is also a contrary movement for transgressing such taboos. This is Bataille's second sense of happiness, which is that of the *expenditure* of our accumulated resources, from the *discharge* of power, wealth, and pent-up animal drive. It is the most intense happiness of the most transient 'instant' (WS, 190), and, Bataille notes, although it yields a most *personal* of satisfactions, it can also risk going too far, *beyond* self-interest in the most 'interested' of ways. Such are the two movements of happiness that Bataille posits as the essentially violent conflict of literature, reflecting 'these violent contrary movements within us' (WS, 187).

When it comes to living life, Bataille had already discerned before turning to discuss literature that this conflict of happiness is because 'for man the sexual act is animality', where 'man in a normal state' often 'condemns it' – for potentially it 'consumes our reserves' to such an extent that it 'frightens us because it enraptures us and it enraptures us all the more profoundly because it frightens us' (WS, 186–7). Lacan's *Seminar VII* articulation of the '*jouissance* of transgression' (SVII, 194–5) as the 'original state', and *least* 'indirect or even sublimated' (SVII, 200) form of drive satisfaction – going *beyond* our usual pleasure principles by transgressing the morals usually constraining us – speaks to this frightful enrapturing as well (SVII, 194–5, 200). But so too does Lacan's later *Seminar XVII* depiction of *jouissance* as that which always 'begins with a tickle and ends in a blaze of petrol' (SXVII, 72).

It is with such insights in mind that Bataille can then express that while 'sexual pleasure is by its very nature happiness', 'one of resolution and gushing forth', it 'nevertheless has the sense of unhappiness' (WS, 186), since *direct* sexual happiness is what we must shed in order to *work* to gain the means to acquire it – consign it thus to the absence of night. This is such for Bataille that 'either we betray our truth of the night during the day', where we are under taboo's sway and fixated nigh neurotically on the happiness of security and accumulation, 'or we hypocritically aspire simply to denounce the conventions of the day' (WS, 187) – where instead we enter the perverse space of transgression and the deepest form of drive satisfaction, so powerful in its sovereignty that we may wish never to return, and believe this is all too possible.

Here Bataille will complain of how the conflicting happinesses of accumulation and expenditure both seem to confine us 'within the conditions of falsehood', but are also especially 'found in literature, to which they give the disguised face of truth' (WS, 187). And by noting this truth as disguised, Bataille is pointing to our varying degrees of unconsciousness about these two forms of happiness, a lack of clarity playing itself out in different forms of literature, negatively and in various ways. This is where we find literature simulating, stimulating, staging, intensifying happiness's conflict even while masking it – such that Bataille will here remark that the 'quest for happiness that causes us to write or read seems in truth to have the contrary meaning of unhappiness' (WS, 187). He points to how tragedy, for instance, often 'brings terror rather than pleasure', and how even the 'joy of comedy' is 'equivocal' in involving laughing at someone's 'misfortune', while the novel also 'requires vicissitudes which produce anguish' – because actually, 'the depiction of happiness', pure and simple, 'is boring' (WS, 187). This is such for Bataille now that literature even portrays a 'vocation for unhappiness', which means 'if the writer evokes pleasure he does so with dark overtones suggesting something distressing' (WS, 187).

We get a sense for what Bataille's *directive* for literature would henceforth be when he sets his critical gaze to it through this happiness-unhappiness dynamic he has been offering. He laments, for example, the 'recent literature' that also 'covets happiness too much', to the point of 'poetic insipidity' – with a recent anthology of it even giving him 'the feeling of defeat' (WS, 187). Here he can strike a contrast with *classical* tragedy, where, actually, 'the unhappiness serves as a stimulant, a failure which reveals the power to confront it' (WS, 188). For we can see this in plays like Sophocles' *Antigone*, where Lacan can mark Antigone's 'beauty effect' (SVII, 281) as the blinding *lure* for us to face and affirm our tragic and transgressive, incestuous truths, when the chorus invokes the name of Oedipus, her Father – which also speaks to Nietzsche's notion of how *pleasure* here 'characterizes *strong* ages and natures' (WP, 852), as a 'display of fearlessness in the face of the fearsome and questionable' (TI IX, 24).[2]

But now instead we often get what Bataille will bemoan as the 'feeble display of failure or shameful pleasures', such that at any point 'if the body triumphs', the language expressing it 'has the power only to acknowledge a movement of retreat' (WS, 187). This retreat is where 'recent literature' for Bataille, insofar 'as it portrays sexual pleasure, tends more strangely to betray happiness and to misunderstand the poetic sense of unhappiness' – leading it neurotically to 'deny joy without having affirmed it' (WS, 188). The end result of this is thus an unsatisfying 'tribute to unhappiness – which balances a desire for the happiness it really is' (WS, 188), resulting overall in 'the rhetoric of unhappiness', where, Bataille concludes, 'literature becomes weary and cannot really discover its initial pure blaze' (WS, 192).

So much for the initial quest for happiness that literature had promised, at least from the initial vantage point Bataille seemed to share with Nietzsche and Stendhal at the price of Kant. But what Bataille is diagnosing here, with this loss of literature's *initial pure blaze*, is our loss of ability to properly experience, understand, and depict what he calls the 'felicitous animality' (WS, 191) of the second type of happiness that comes *from* transgression. This is because we remain fixated instead at the petrified level of an *all-too* human taboo, zealously governing the space of work and acquisition by morality and reason, by means-ends calculations concerning further growth in acquisitions in the future. And we can see the fixation to this realm playing out in literature as what Bataille calls the 'absence of incisive movements of anguish', or the 'reduction of "privileged moments"' (WS, 188) – where one can no longer experience the sovereignty of what Lacan directly calls '*jouissance* of transgression' (SVII, 195), or later in his *Seminar XXIII*, in the context of discussing the writings of James Joyce, the '*jouissance* of the real' (SXXIII, 63).

This loss of *incisive moments* is due to what we can mark vis-à-vis Lacan's *Seminar X* as the anxiety which 'operates as a signal' (SX, 160) of the oncoming real – at the 'fault-line where anxiety is produced' (SX, 182) – causing us to retreat due to the potential harm involved in going *beyond* the pleasure principle, in what is now opening up as precisely 'the gap between desire and *jouissance*' (SX, 175). For this gap is where 'masochism' is what Lacan later observed in *Seminar XXIII* can be 'the main share of the *jouissance* endued by the real' (SXXIII, 63). But it is also where Dominique Hecq discerns that the enigmatic Joyce writings Lacan examines in this seminar are less the traditional symptom and more a way of letting the anxiety *organize* the writing so that it 'harmonizes with castration', where castration can refer to the great distance or separation from the material real created by certain austere forms of moral law, reason and taboo – but also when such great distance, and the *under-analysed* imaginary that cocoons it in an alleged feeling of safety or superiority, is suddenly torn away.³

So what we mostly get now instead, then, due to the express retreat before our *deepest* desire which would reach the real in transgressive *jouissance*, is what Bataille notes is the 'predominance of everyday life' (WS, 188), which again hearkens back to Nietzsche's critique of Socrates' Euripides for causing the condescension of Greek Tragedy from its 'grand and bold traits' to the 'civic mediocrity' of the herd (BT, 11) – where everyday taboos of moral-rationalism lord it over desire, uproot and cocoon it, and reign supreme across all times, even in our best artistic spaces meant for due release. This is why Bataille will lament that 'happiness is confounded with the resources which make it possible' (WS, 189), in a humanity now utterly 'devoted to the world of things and reason' in a way so 'stubborn' it very much recalls our lost or latent 'animality' (WS, 190) – playing itself out in some *unconscious* form – which eventually, when the repressed drive returns condensed in a symptom, or displaced externally in a blind acting-out, 'consigns our most intimate moments to something monstrous, something shameful' (WS, 190).

5.2 LITERATURE AS CONDESCENSION OF DESIRE TO EVIL

In the previous section we arrived at the loss of the primordial, animal sense of happiness important to humankind in life and literature, a loss which figurately consigns – the Greek god of sexual ecstasy, intoxication, and transgression – to the Judaeo-Christian Devil. Now we turn to Bataille's 1957 *Literature and Evil* to examine further this process, where the happiness initially promised of literature seems to condescend to a demand for Evil, which is a demand that needs to be explained.

The very final work Bataille published in his oeuvre, the 1961 *Tears of Eros*, actually gives the key to this literary demand for Evil – documenting as it does eroticism's loss and distortion across the history of painting, particularly in the Christian era. For here Bataille notes the annulment of any adequate positive space for the erotic return of prohibited libidinal impulses, meaning they could only reappear 'distorted', 'piously cursed' with a 'sense of guilt', as 'repulsive images of sin', sadistic crime, the Devil, and the fires 'of hell' (TE, 79, 82–3). Freud had even made a similar observation on the history of religious culture in his 1910 *Leonardo* essay, noting how 'so much of the divine and sacred was ultimately extracted from sexuality that the exhausted remnant fell into contempt' – whereas originally 'genital-worship' was a sign of 'pride and hope' and the very 'connection between official religions and sexual activity', striking a contrast with our today where so many feel the act required to propagate humankind is an offence to 'dignity' that renders one 'degraded by the process' (SE11, 97).

This historical *debasement* of the genitals, and attempted un-sexing of religion and aesthetics marked by Bataille's 1961 *Tear of Eros*, is precisely what to keep in mind when approaching his slightly earlier 1957 *Literature and Evil* collection, which focuses on novels such as Emily Brontë's *Wuthering Heights* and William Blake's poem *Heaven and Hell*. For the latter are at the birth of the modern world and romantic reactions to its excess where, as Nietzsche saw, the abnegations of Christianity are preserved in the same old ascetic ideal but in a purer, more rationalized form – streamlined now only of its religious 'exteriors, its guise and masquerade' (GM III, 25).

The hyper-rational modern world thereby consigns the erotic to the irrational, the origins of which are in the Christian reduction of eroticism to Evil. But in between is Brontë's *Wuthering Heights*, which Bataille perhaps surprisingly calls 'surely the most beautiful and most profoundly violent love story' and 'one of the greatest books ever written' (LE, 9). Bataille in fact felt that 'there is no character in romantic literature who comes across more convincingly or more simply than Heathcliff' – in the 'basic state' of a 'child in revolt against the world of Good' and the 'adult world', and 'committed, in his revolt, to the side of Evil' (LE, 13). But this commitment is such that 'there is no law which Heathcliff does not enjoy breaking' (LE, 13), and Bataille will cite the 1955 study of Jacques Blondel to compare Heathcliff's speech to the executioners in Sade's *Justine* – where the act of 'destruction' is valorized to yield a 'divine', 'sensual' 'ecstasy' like no other, and at the very least, Heathcliff would add, to 'treat' oneself to 'an evening's amusement' (LE, 13–4).[4]

Despite these monstrous emissions, or perhaps even because of their elemental excess, Bataille finds that '*Wuthering Heights* has a certain affinity with Greek tragedy' (LE, 14). This is because 'the subject of the novel is the tragic violation of law', where the author 'agreed with the law', but the 'emotional impact' of the play is actually 'communicating the sympathy' that was felt 'for the transgressor' (LE, 14). Bataille explains this sympathy in terms of the *lure* one feels for 'forbidden' fruits – where, he notes, 'the ban beautifies that to which it prevents access', which serves to 'magnify it', and is 'no less an invitation at the same time as it is an obstacle' (LE, 15).

We can also find Lacan two years later in his *Ethics* seminar similarly noting the eternal 'attraction of transgression', which, among 'religious circles', only a 'comic optimism' could ever hope to fully suppress (SVII, 2). In any case, it is the *excessive* violence of the transgressor – whether it be incest, parricide, or self-enuclation in the case of tragedy, or the necrophilia and more sadistic, vengeful torture of *Wuthering Heights* – which might suggest a corresponding excess of taboo that thereby both requires, and causes, an equal opposite force to allow for the drive's sublimated release. And this explains why in his 1958 Television interview on *Literature and Evil*, Bataille perhaps cryptically refers to both the force of taboo *and* the violence of transgression as 'two opposite kinds of Evil'.[5]

These two forms of evil are in actual fact related to the two forms of happiness we earlier discussed, where the happiness of social security coming from taboo, moral law, and accumulation sees the happiness of transgression and expenditure as Evil – *but also vice versa* – where the happiness of transgression may look upon the violent imposition of taboo back to stop it as the real and actual Evil. Both sides of this equation are, of course, coequal in value for Bataille: transgression for release, and taboo to gives us something in reserve to later release – and part of the essential conflict of life parading itself across the page with various levels of clarity, or lack thereof, in our various kinds of literature.

By adding *more* consciousness or clarity about this conflictual interrelation, moreover, Bataille would like to lessen the 'evil' wretchedness that each side of the relation, and thus our whole contradictory totality itself, may otherwise take. And we can see this in his turn to the poetry of Blake, who much like ourselves to this day, Bataille concedes, could not quite 'solve this contradiction' where 'by affirming Evil Blake was affirming liberty' – even though 'the liberty of Evil is also the negation of liberty' (LE, 78) – but who nevertheless somehow managed, quite stunningly in fact, 'to restore life to original energy' (LE, 80).

Bataille thus begins his Blake chapter in *Literature and Evil* with the pronouncement: 'If I had to name those English writers who moved me most, they would be John Ford, Emily Brontë, and William Blake' – for there 'in the excessive violence of their work', Bataille suggests, 'Evil attains a form of purity' (LE, 65). In Blake's case, this was to 'reduce humanity to poetry and poetry to Evil' (LE, 65), but it is no longer the evil of slow, sadomasochistic torture and murder that we find in other traditions founded on the suppression of the fullness of libido; rather, Bataille affirms, 'He wrote an apology for sexual freedom and, rumour had it, wanted to force his wife to live with his mistress' (LE, 67).

Moreover for Bataille, although 'Blake was in no way a philosopher', he 'pronounced the essential with a vigour and a precision that might make a philosopher envious' (LE, 75) – with 'visionary writings' that also offered 'no opposition to the clarity which psychoanalysis would like to introduce', despite their often 'dreamlike incoherence' (LE, 73). Bataille cites, for example, the 1793 *Marriage of Heaven and Hell* where, Blake writes, nigh anticipating with exactitude Bataille's own position: 'Good is the passive that obeys reason. Evil is the active springing from Energy'; but 'Energy is the only life, and is from the Body; and Reason is the bound or outward circumference of Energy' (LE, 75). And the message for Bataille of Blake's conclusion, here, that 'Energy is eternal delight', is that 'instead of turning away from Evil, man should look it boldly in the face' (LE, 75).

Blake's refusal to look away from what Judaeo/Christian-Platonic metaphysics often crudely mislabelled 'evil' in the moralistic sense was because, Bataille notes, 'in Blake's life the joy of the senses was a touchstone', such that 'sensuality set him against the primacy of reason', and he 'condemned the moral law in the name of sensuality' (LE, 75). This condemnation is evident in a line of Blake's, which could have fitted perfectly in Nietzsche's 1888 *The Anti-Christ* a century later, which reads: 'As the caterpillar chooses the fairest leaves to lay her eggs on, so the priest lays his curse on the fairest joys' – which Bataille reads *resolutely* as calling for 'sensual happiness, for the exuberance of the body' (LE, 75). Nietzsche, of course, had also similarly ascertained, in his sustained genealogical critique of Judaeo-Christianity, that wherever the priest appears to formalize life's affairs it is always 'to denaturalize them', but precisely in a way that *accurses* their natural, animal, and biological instinctual endowment that is *of* the body and the earth, while pretending instead to 'sanctify them' (AC, 26).

The theological term 'Evil' for Bataille, however, still does valuable work in the world of Blake, for it serves to affirm a difference from what Bataille calls 'that subterfuge which denies true sensuality by seeing it solely as health' – and is rather 'on the side of Energy, which is Evil, which restores it to its deepest significance' (LE, 75). Such a significance Bataille can especially evince in Blake's re-grounding, *re*-naturalizing, or *de*-transcendentalizing of marriage and love, when he writes: 'In a wife I would desire/What in whores is always found – The lineaments of Gratified desire' (LE, 76).

The findings since of psychoanalysis, and especially Lacan's rejection of any 'moralizing intention' residual in it via 'an oblative' or 'idyllic advent of the genital relationship'[6] – along with his debunking of 'Woman with a capital *W*, indicating the universal' of eternal purity, of which 'there's no such thing' because 'she is not-whole' (SXX, 72–3, 57) – should also demonstrate that one should not at all assume that Blake has only professed a masculine or 'active' desire here. Rather, along with Bataille's own work, Blake is giving expression to what Lacan calls 'the truth revealed in the ancient mysteries that "Eros is a black God"'[7] – whose other formulation is that there is 'no sexual relation' (SXVII, 116) – pointing to the *absence* of any pre-given idealized *rapport* between the sexes, linked 'in copulation' to a moralistic Good as if it were 'nature's intentions that this form a whole, a sphere' (SXVII, 33). For our animal impulses of sex will always subsist but appear shockingly perverse from the lofty vantage of the denaturing Good, which demonizes *real* difference through an inflationary structure, that is ever little more than illusion or dream.[8]

Bataille, nevertheless, concludes his treatment of Blake problematizing his comments on the Terror of the French Revolution, referring to the 'fearful symmetry' (LE, 77) of Blake's *The Tyger* as imbued of what in the poem *Europe*, as the 'furious terrors flew around' in the 'vineyards of red France', would 'couch upon the prey and suck the ruddy tide' (LE, 79). Bataille finds that Blake here has 'exalted the blind release of brute force' as a 'divine form of excess', and as 'portions of eternity too great for the eye of man' (LE, 78) – which in revolutions is too opposed for Bataille to the 'dictates of Reason', and thus 'does not lead to any coherent attitude' but only 'poetic disorder' (LE, 79). Hence, although he portrayed almost similar views himself in the 1930s, Bataille now, in 1957, is without finding *total* resolution in Blake, as inspirational as he was to him, of the question of violence contained in Evil – adding much complexity to the 'insoluble contradiction' (LE, 78) between the happiness (or 'evil') of taboo and the happiness (or 'evil') of transgression, that by thinking literature we have been discussing. Perhaps, then, a resolution might best be sought or found in Bataille's turn to the poetic works of his dissident surrealist colleagues of postwar Paris.[9]

5.3 POETRY'S FORCE OF SOVEREIGNTY FROM THE RUT OF LITERATURE

This section considers how for Bataille the more recent poetry of his contemporaries might restore a *positive* sense of immediacy with the real of our drives, while leading not to chaos but to their more lucid co-relation with the rational world of discourse which, Bataille contends, prose literature can leave us alienated within. More specifically, we shall examine Bataille's discussions of Jacques Prévert and René Char – so as to look further into this ostensibly irreducible conflict of law and transgression.

By going further into poetic immediacy, we are also in a sense following the stated premise of Lacan's *Ethics* of going 'more deeply' *into* 'the real' instead of 'the ideal' or 'unreal' as per the manner of 'superficial opinion' (SVII, 11). For by better understanding the real first, the ideals we construct are likely to be better informed, secured and rooted, and thereby eschew the unconscious 'guilt' and 'catastrophes' of 'neurosis and its consequences' where, Lacan notes, 'desire keeps coming back' and 'demands insistently that the debt be paid' (SVII, 319). To this end, Lacan's *Ethics* also provides a focused reading of *Antigone*, the work of Sophocles the *poet*, to grant a truer picture of the *real* of desire – just as Bataille's own examination of poetic immediacy is now to further illuminate desire therein.[10] Bataille's ultimate aim in this will be to find a more clarified delineation between the times for taboo and moral-rational law, and the spaces for transgression with the return of repressed desire – to better enable a knowing conduit, clear path, and lucid relation between the two, which more *thoughtful* literature can both benefit from and contribute to.

Beginning then with the 1946 *Critique* article, 'From the Stone Age to Jacques Prévert', we can see that by invoking the stone age Bataille's suggestion is that 'the poetic effect brought about by Prévert's texts take us back from our time', all the way to the early 'stammerings of humanity' (WS, 147). This is key for Bataille's attempt to recover the archaic know-how of *pre*-Christian-Platonic cultures in regulating separate times for the sacred and the profane: where the sacred moment was that of the transgression of prohibitions, and profane time marked return to taboos.

This sacred and profane dynamic, established by Durkheim's 1912 *The Elementary Forms of Religious Life*, is what corresponds to transgression and taboo when viewed through early religion's lens – an understanding of which Bataille sharpened and honed with his College of Sociology cofounder Caillois in the 1930s, whom Bataille credits with the written formulation of Mauss's largely orally transmitted discovery of the taboo–transgression correlation in 'the history of religion' (E, 65, 257). It shows how the sacred once involved transgression that both deified and went *deeper into* our repressed, bodily animality – as opposed to the later Christian-Platonic dualism, with its roots in the denaturing Judaic and Orphic-Pythagorean traditions respectively, which instead has the sacred trying to further purify, transcend, escape further away, as if for Good.

While Christianity's roots in late Judaism is well known from the Old Testament Bible, it should also be noted how the *ascetic* afterlife fantasy, of *metempsychosis*, in Plato's texts such as *Phaedo* (114b–d) and *Republic* (X, 614a, 619e, 621d), came from the minor Orphic current of Greek religion, which influenced Pythagoras and later Plato. E. R. Dodds even suggests Plato may have been influenced to adopt his 'transcendental psychology' through 'his personal contact with the Pythagoreans of West Greece when he visited them in about 390 BC': that is, *after* the decline of the classical period – distorting thence the common 'beliefs about the soul', entailed in such myths as those around Persephone in the Eleusinian mysteries, into a 'Puritan psychology'. For as Rohde was to put it, sounding at his most Nietzschean, while there was the promise of a blessed afterlife as part of the panhellenic Eleusinian mysteries, it was *not* in the manner of the Orphism which influenced Pythagoras and later Plato, for it contained 'no strange revaluation of values, contradicting the general opinions of the time', and no view of 'the beyond' that made 'this earth seem dark and mean' and 'death superior to life'.[11]

With Plato and Paul, the latter was done by making a life spent renouncing the body, its senses, and *sensuality*, a pre-condition of entry into heaven – where the reward, as stated in *Phaedo*, was the fundamental fantasy finally realized to 'live henceforth altogether without bodies' (114b–c). Maudemarie Clark accordingly dubs *Phaedo* a 'great panegyric to the ascetic ideal'.[12] But it is expressly the *role of poetry*, in the other, *non*-ascetic religions, that is here Bataille's focus in discussing Prévert – 'who is not part of the literary scene', 'writes for the cinema', and 'prefers films to books because he is attracted by what is immediate' (WS, 140) – to discern how this might re-enable a grateful return of the *real* of pent-up animality instead.

Bataille invokes how 'powerful emotion has always been expressed poetically', how it could never be 'expressed absolutely', or 'translated into words', except if it were 'by means of poetry' where 'every emotion was sung out' – even calling *purely* literary poetry, which Greek tragedy never was, 'a sort of mutilated song' (WS, 137). This again speaks to Nietzsche's thesis of the 'birth of tragedy out of the spirit of music', the full title of his 1872 first-born work (BT, 7, 16–7), which is not at all an extraordinary claim for those familiar with classical scholarship, where it is already suggested in 335 BC in Aristotle's *Poetics*. For Aristotle records how tragedy in fact 'came from the prelude to the dithyramb', while even comedy came 'from the prelude to the phallic songs', where 'tragedy then gradually evolved' until 'it was Aeschylus who first raised the number of the actors from one to two', then 'curtailed the chorus and gave the dialogue the leading part' – while later still 'three actors and scene-painting Sophocles introduced'.[13]

Hence it is through an awareness of origins that Bataille can suggest that 'what cannot be sung is outside the domain of poetry', while referring also to its 'antipodes' of such things as 'business affairs' (WS, 138) – where along with consistent, predictable behaviours a soberly clear, deterministic language is required. And it is in this linguistic sense that poetry, with its endlessly potent metaphors, is, for Bataille, 'literature which is no longer literary' – insofar as it cuts through and 'escapes from the rut in which literature is genuinely entrapped', and 'undercuts the desire in us to reduce things to the dimensions of reason' (WS, 138). But this is only if we are 'touched by a sovereign emotion', Bataille must add, which takes 'the actuality of men outside the self' – where outside our usual perimeters, standing out *in ecstasy*, the 'overwhelming power of poetry' is to 'communicate the condition of the poet' (WS, 138). It is thus for Bataille that 'poetry gives expression to what exceeds the possibilities of common language', and 'uses words to overturn the order of words' – as the 'cry of what, within us, cannot be reduced; what, within us, is stronger than us' (WS, 138). And with this irreducibility Bataille can also be seen portending what Lacan later calls the 'intimate exteriority or "extimacy" that is the Thing' – which is the drive *in the real* made visible, and signifying, as Lacan by no coincidence also notes that was discovered originally on the 'cave walls' of 'prehistoric art' (SVII, 139).[14]

Bataille will speak further to this primal poetic state of immediacy in his later 1951 *Critique* article, 'René Char and the Force of Poetry' (WS, 129–34). But in speaking now of *force*, Bataille can begin with a contrast between 'confined existence' and 'sovereign existence' (WS, 129) – with the *force* of poetry belonging to the latter. This is what he defines as 'not in the service of any enterprise, not even of its own egoistic interest' (WS, 129). But the difference between this dis-interest and, say, Kant's notion of 'aesthetic disinterest', is that there is nothing transcendental about Bataille's sovereignty. It goes deeper *into* the subject's drives, rather than cathect itself metonymically to the cognitive functions of understanding, inflating even as they do in Kant's aesthetics to try and grasp the imagination that somehow 'takes the lead' in a creative 'free-play'.[15]

Kant's itself remains an imaginary aesthetics while still under the altruistic sway of 'denaturalizing' immortal souls in a possible Christian heaven, categorically centred on the Good, which is sheer escapism from the optic of the much more Nietzschean and Dionysian Bataille.[16] For Bataille's aesthetic sovereignty corresponds to the earlier *Pre*-Christian-Platonic force of the sacred, involving religiously sanctioned transgression both aesthetic *and* erotic in kind, in returning our repressed bodilyness as 'poetic and divine though animal' (E, 153). And we can see the difference also in the fable Lacan's *Ethics* seminar finds in Kant, where Kant believes 'the gallows' set up outside the chambers of a woman of erotic appeal would be 'sufficient deterrent' (SVII, 108). For 'our philosopher from Konigsberg was a nice person', Lacan must note, his 'stature' and 'passions' aside (SVII, 108), and unaware of what Freud would later call 'object sublimation' or the 'overvaluation of the object', provoking 'transgression beyond the limits normally assigned' towards 'the level of *das Ding* [the Thing]' and 'what is commonly known as perversion' – that which occurs, and forever *reoccurs,* within the libidinally infused realm of the senses (SVII, 109).

Lacan in fact returns to Kant's moral fable in his 1963 'Kant with Sade' article of *Écrits* (Éc, 659), remarking how it neglects that 'defiance of or even contempt for the gallows' can be the very motivation for one's goal – *like fuel to the fire* – because 'the Law is something else', much more connected to desire and its incestuous origins, 'as we have known since Antigone' (Éc, 660). This was the article that was actually first published 'in the journal *Critique*' (Éc, 645) a year after Bataille ceased editing it upon his death. And in this Nobus also notes that earlier Bataille, who Lacan had known 'intellectual convergences' and an 'existing "family relationship"' with, himself gave a lecture to the *Collège Philosophique* in 1947 which 'alluded to Kant's conception of fine art in the *Critique of Judgement* as "intrinsically purposive", and thus emblematic of moral action'.[17]

It is the alienation of humanity, in an 'anti-natural' moral purpose by Kant and the whole of Christendom, that what would drive Nietzsche to despair of the 'whole labour of the ancient world *in vain*' (AC, 25, 59) – with Paul Bishop for one calling this section 59 of *Anti-Christ* here cited 'one of the clearest statements of Nietzsche's assertions of classical ideals', and noting that it includes what in *Will to Power* is called 'the joyous, benevolent, Goethean attitude towards sensuality' (WP, 118), which Christianity lost.[18] But 'Solitary tears are not wasted', the cry from Char will here ring out, whom Bataille now cites in referring to how 'the task of poetry, through its eye and on the tongue of its palate, is to cause this alienation to vanish by revealing how ridiculous it is' (WS, 130).

Bataille, then, is most pleased to note where Char writes of how 'we still manage to rise up up up', 'exploding with our execrations as much as with our loins' – the 'instant when beauty', made to wait by the necessities of *confined* existence, 'rises from common things', 'connects everything' and 'inflames all' (WS, 130). 'Nothing tempers this plenitude', Bataille remarks (WS, 131). And in invoking this beauty in the plenitude of its sovereignty, we have reference not only to Blake's utterance of 'exuberance is beauty' from the *Proverbs of Hell*, which Bataille quotes as the dedications page of Vol. I of *Accursed Share*, but also to the 'abundance' of natural instinct Nietzsche held to constitute the genuinely strong aesthetic state – over-against the weak depersonalized 'lack' of Kant's – *bestowing* to things from a libidinalized fullness (GS, 370).

This fullness speaks to the aesthetic process of *sublimation* Lacan articulates in Freud, which involves a satisfaction of the drive without so much repression or neurosis, through a higher valuation of an earthly object in a *closer* signifying proximity to the Freudian Thing (SVII, 216–17). Even Zupančič can observe here that in Lacanian theory 'sublimation gets closer to the real', rather than turn away again 'in the name of some idea'.[19] And as such, Lacan will playfully define sublimation as 'raising an object', 'to the dignity of the Thing' (SVII, 112), preserving thus a knowing *conduit* between the dignified high and the low Thing that is its source, which the high does not seek to wholly deny by becoming evasive – *or indignant*. But the difference between Lacan's Freudian Thing, which he often calls *das Ding*, and Kant's thing-in-itself (*das Ding an sich*), which it is a play on too, is, as Grigg notes, that the Thing is 'the real' that is normally 'excluded from the symbolic field' of ordinary but defensive representations, that can still return to interrupt them, 'intruding into the subject's experience in a way that finds him or her devoid of any means of protection' – *forcing* here through the speaking body that ineluctably we all are.[20]

Grigg will cite the clinic of 'hallucination' regarding this forcing, and Lacan's 'Response to Jean Hyppolite's Commentary on Freud's "Verneinung"' which states: 'That which has not seen the light of day in the symbolic appears in the real' (Éc, 324) – along with Freud's formulation from his famous 1911 *Schreber Case* of 'what was abolished internally returns from without' (SE12, 71). A knowing sublimation, moreover, based both on psychoanalytic knowledge and a Nietzschean affirmation of what was otherwise abolished, brought together and enhanced here through Bataille's re-eroticizing aesthetics, is precisely what can forge a *way out* of such pathogenic vicissitudes of the drive's ever polymorphous striving for satisfaction – at least in general, or reasonably favourable cases. Alas for Kant, most conversely, as Nietzsche deemed his onto-epistemic thing-in-itself to be a fraudulent construct deliberately placed outside the reach of reason, simply to preserve the fantasy of Christian dogma actually being 'true'.[21]

Here Bataille can turn his treatment of Char's force of poetry into what could be considered a proto-Lacanian ontology, invoking the poetic as an opening to the *impossible*, which is one of the terms Lacan uses to describe the *real* himself – as both impossible to integrate and 'the pre-historic Other that is impossible to forget' (SVII, 71). Bataille's emphasis, however, is expressly on the feeling of 'insipidity' attending 'the possible' our existence depends on, wanting to remind us of an existence beyond its confined normal limits. For if we always 'limited ourselves to what is possible', Bataille explains, we 'remain enclosed, moribund', in 'banishment from the totality of being' where we would instead be 'exceeding the limits of the possible and going to the point of death' (WS, 131). This invokes Bataille's formulation of the erotic as 'assenting to life up to the point of death', which he not only makes in his 1957 *Eroticism* (E, 11) but also in the *Literature and Evil* chapter on Brontë of the same year, expressed now as 'the approval of life, up until death' (LE, 10). And for Bataille, whether it is as literature or life, it is very much 'our whims, and this taste for the impossible', that 'alone signify that we can never concede the separation of the individual fixed in the feeble limits of the possible' (WS, 131).

Bataille, then, perhaps surprisingly at first, will affirm Char's reference to the 'fear, irony, and anguish' elicited by the 'presence of the poet who bears the poem' as 'not mistaken' – for it is only here the 'pure happiness' at risk, corresponding to Bataille's first happiness of confined taboo-governed self-interest, which on its own, as Char will put it, is merely a 'happiness screened from the eyes and its own nature' (WS, 131–2). This is where Bataille can again in proto-Lacanian terms refer to 'the impossible' as 'what we lack', but also, moreover, as that 'by which we restore', by transgressing the limits invoking 'death', 'obscenity', and a 'totality' that 'causes us to tremble', is 'completely other', and 'gives us a sacred shiver' (WS, 132). Bataille's own distinct emphasis on *not* retreating before this sacred shiver, as vehiculated by the poetic through the space of literature, stems from his conviction that 'today humanity sees its right to exceed the possible in a sovereign way denied' – but through his poetry he finds here that 'Char's morality' is precisely the 'calm exuberance' that 'reminds sovereign man that nothing can prevail against him' (WS, 132).

Bataille had earlier finished his Prévert article in much the same way, with similar sentiments, having sojourned through early religion's use of poetry to invoke the sacred and the logic of sacrifice – sacrificing as it does words and things alike from their normal use-value which as such 'could not communicate with desire' (WS, 148), committing them thus to desire's flame. As opposed to our today, however, Bataille must lament, where 'present day society is vulgar and constructed from man's flight from himself', and where one mainly 'hides behind a set design' – which is such that 'poetry that evokes this society' most necessarily now 'is also the negation of it' (WS, 153).

Society is obviously not something we want to *completely* negate, but without separate yet coordinated times for workaday taboos and sublimated spaces for restorative transgression, we will never escape this difference between the two forms of happiness involved emerging as a devastating conflict. To further allay this conflict, then, we can seek to augment Bataille's preferred aesthetics of literature – which puts it on the side of transgression in relation to the taboos it violates – with Lacan's *tripartite* episteme of the real, symbolic, and imaginary, read as constituting in their entirety what Bataille himself invokes as the 'totality of being' (WS, 130).

5.4 ART AND POLITICS: SEPARATE CONNECTION OF THE IMAGINARY AND SYMBOLIC IN THE REAL

When Lacan in his later 1975–76 *Seminar XXIII* on Joyce, *The Sinthome*, examines the way that 'art – the artisanal – can foil, as it were, what imposes itself as a symptom', he does so by invoking what is 'namely, truth' (SXXIII, 14). For here Lacan is pointing to the creative *reopening* of the symptom to its lost source, that now, through the artist, as 'the fourth term known as the sinthome', perhaps more knowingly and optimally 'completes the knot of the imaginary, the symbolic, and the real' (SXXIII, 27). In Joyce's case, Lacan suggests this was by creatively refashioning, re-making or 'wanting a name for himself' *as* an artist, as 'compensation for the paternal failing' (SXXIII, 77) and parental deficiencies generally inherited through the symbolic function of 'Name-of-the-Father' – which, Lacan adds, 'is certainly God' – and where with '*the sinthome*', à la Joyce, 'one can just as well bypass it, on the condition that one make use of it' (SXXIII, 116, 147).

It is the known foreclosure effects of the Judaeo/Christian-Platonic God-Father that leads to our incapacity to appropriately regulate or make sense of desire, sourced as He was in what Lacan earlier called the 'ferocious ignorance' of 'Yahweh himself' on 'sexual knowledge' (SXVII, 136), along with the 'profound incompetence' of the Platonic Socrates on the 'topic of tragedy' (SVIII, 81–2) – all of whom Nietzsche includes as among the great 'despisers of the body' (Z I, 4). This despising is what in Bataillean terms results in the warped interrelation between taboo and transgression – where the former, as too blind, negative and hyper-strict, can only foreclose the truth of the latter, which thus requires *real* creativity as one of the potential ways out.

In discussing such ways out of what psychoanalysts discern as an 'instability in the signifiers of sexual difference', Michael Newman analyses the artwork of Hans Bellmer by linking his sinthomic *recreation* of the symbolic, via the real, to Joyce's – which in Bellmer's case is what sees 'the artist takes the place of the failed father who is at once the overbearing Nazi and a pathetic invalid, obscene and inadequate'. Newman also cites Colette Soler for how the sinthome's broaching of the real here 'can contribute actively to the formation of the – or a – Symbolic', where, depending on its calibre, it can eschew the psychotic withdrawal into madness to instead 'involve an intervention into the Symbolic, such as Joyce's creation of polyvalent or equivocal words from lalangue'. For Bellmer, Newman adds, this is where 'the "active" relation to the creation of a symbolic involves the anagram and the trait', evinced in his drawings, sculptures, and dolls – which he identifies with both to mock and seduce the Father he also emulates in *engineering* such constructions. But this is also the very Bellmer, of course, who provides the stunning *base*-surrealist illustrations for Bataille's erotic novellas, namely *Story of the Eye* and *Madame Edwarda*.[22]

There are a number of postwar articles in *Critique*, and elsewhere, where Bataille gives us further perceptive formulations of an *actively restructured* dual necessity between *taboo* (the symbolic relation of critical distance towards the real) and *transgression* (the return of the prohibited real *in* the erotic imaginary) – equating roughly to our separate times for work and play, politics and art, or reason and the unconscious, respectively. Bataille writes, for instance, of 'Marx's doctrine' as 'the only effective application of intelligence to practical facts as a whole', insofar as it brings 'the sort of clear-cut decision that a science brings into a particular domain' (WS, 156). But elsewhere, in sensing the danger of overreach, he quotes also the surrealist Jean Maquet declaring that 'after the experience of the past twenty years, it would today be a radical-socialist stupidity to refuse to save a place for a Pascal or a Rimbaud', a 'Baudelaire, Nietzsche, Dostoyevsky or Chestov' (WS, 128).[23] This is because again, for Bataille, 'no one can neglect this problem', concerning our two very different but equiprimordial modes of being: For 'it is a question of mankind's harmony with itself, of poetry's harmony with what is useful, and the harmony of the passions with material needs' (WS, 157).

In thinking this harmony, we have found Bataille concerned with 'the necessities of the path, the bridge, between the two domains' – where, as he puts it, we take 'account of material needs', but also give 'the passions, which only poetry generally welcomes, a place and necessity in the ordering of the industrial world' (WS, 157). This is for Bataille so as to formulate 'a project of productive organization in which poetry would not be immediately expelled, as it usually is' (WS, 157), which calls to mind Nietzsche's critique of Plato's *barring* of the poets from an ideal *Republic*, as the metaphysical origins of our failure to get the balance right in the various traditions ensuing in the West – where Nietzsche in his *Genealogy of Morals* will thence call 'Plato versus Homer' the 'complete, the genuine antagonism' (GM III, 25).[24]

I suggest that to get the balance right here between the poetic and the rational is a matter of the right amount of distance-*and*-nearness between the two domains, appended to how the different 'forms of sublimation' underpinning these two key aspects of civilization amount to a different optimum of distance-nearness to 'the Thing' (SVII, 129). Such a differential of amounts and distance is what is especially propitious through Lacan's focus on the Thing or Id's unconscious signifying aspect, by distinguishing 'the *Trieb* [drive]', at the level of the psyche, from 'the *Instinkt* [instinct]' (SVII, 90), at the level of the soma – pointing to how different types of ideations around what Freud in his *Three Essay* calls 'the frontier between the mental and the physical' (SE7, 168), which elsewhere he also calls 'the frontier between the spheres of psychology and biology', imply different amounts of openness and distance.[25]

Science and rationality, for example, as Lacan suggests, could almost 'foreclose' the Thing with its extra critical symbolic distance (SVII, 131) – while art in the imaginary, in the throes of its passion, would usually bear the remit of a risk and reward of 'encircling' closer (SVII, 141). But we sense the delicate balances involved when Bataille is critical not just of Sartre's attempt to make literature serve a predefined political commitment – which takes it *too far* from the Thing and can mean a neurotic's renunciation – but also of an 'art for art's sake' movement that now zeros in *too close*, which in the case of surrealism could lead to what Bataille saw as only an 'empty liberty', 'monotonous' as well as 'powerless' (WS, 180).[26]

What Bataille wants instead, here, is a kind of affirmation of this empty liberty by the intelligence that experiences it, which gets us close as possible to the Thing with enough knowledge of it not to get lost, withdrawn from the world, or too close and burnt. And we can see this very nuance at play when Bataille commends the painter André Masson who, like 'Rimbaud or Blake' before him, 'did not dissociate poetic vision from intelligence', which made his work 'distanced from pure surrealism' – as 'the thought it expresses is no longer, as in automatic writing, disengaged with the world', but is rather 'integrated with it and invades it' (WS, 181). Masson's work, then, for Bataille, has 'a quality of totality' that is 'limited neither by discursive thought nor by the automatism of the dream' – which is why Bataille condemns the critic who once said of it, 'We do not want thought painting' (WS, 178). I have shown in this chapter that Bataille would have similar rebukes for those critics who would say the same thing about 'thought literature', or properly wholistic attempts to *think* the novel, while experiencing it also as *real jouissance*.

Getting this distance-nearness relation right is, of course, never easy, or predetermined in advance, and Bataille laments how forever 'the antagonism between poetry and consciousness (the latter connected to reason) is at the heart of our lives' (WS, 125). And this can be such for Bataille that 'consciousness experiences what really slips away' – such as with 'sexual pleasure', which is 'given to man only in the night', and 'in our intimate returns to the pink depths of life' (WS, 125). But consciousness can still be more connected than not to this by the intelligent author, as we might see in Bataille's description of the dazzling copulations of his eponymous heroine of *Madame Edwarda*, with Bataille himself actually seeing 'Chazal as the first writer to achieve the equivalence of sexual pleasure and language' (WS, 126), to whom we began this chapter with reference.

Returning then to the 1949 *Critique* article, 'Happiness, Eroticism, and Literature', where our analysis began, and Bataille will quote Chazal writing of sexual pleasure as 'the grey hound race of desire', or as 'time assassinated for a moment and rendered invisible with touch', and even as that which 'enables us to taste through the other's palate' (WS, 195). But meanwhile, in his own more darkly toned *Madame Edwarda*, Bataille will write of her *jouissance* with a driver in the back of his taxi, during which Bataille supported her quivering body from 'the nape' – as 'that stream of luxury', that 'glorified her being unceasingly', made her 'unceasingly more naked', and 'her lewdness ever more intimate' (M, 157–8). One could also mention the provocative scenes of Bataille's *L'Abbé C*, where the priest catches sight of the heroine's 'naked bottom' while on his knees, with 'arms out-stretched' and mouth 'hanging open', giving an impromptu mass (Ab, 45) – although it is likely a step too far to include how later after witnessing her copulation with Charles his libertine brother, this priest evinces his silent presence by her window with 'a piece of stinking filth' (Ab, 98).

The latter calls to mind not so much an erotics but rather the neurotics of the symptoms of Freud's *Wolf Man* case, perhaps surfacing a repressed and thus distorted passive desire to anally take the woman's place (SE17, 78–81). And, lo and behold, and Bataille's priest character can even be found confessing later in the book: 'Who am I? Could I be Eponine in bed with Charles?' – to which he adds: 'Halfway to a diverting joke; that helps me because I am ashamed of it' (Ab, 136).[27] In light of this, Freud would also consider if the faeces signifier produced here is a distorted gift of recompense for the act of voyeurism, while simultaneously a sign of derision and contempt, as something offered both 'contumely, and as a regressive expression of making amends' (SE17, 81). This would indeed match the priest's ambivalent, obsessional, ascetic structure in the novella, which earnt him the ironic nickname of '"the abbé", "the cure"' (Ab, 13). But in Lacanian terms, what matters only is that we ourselves fasten the real, symbolic, and imaginary in a more conscientious way, with our own singularly enhanced levels of *psychoanalytic* knowledge and experience of *jouissance* – such that symptoms dissolve, opening out like a conduit to their source *in* the real – with different emphases in place during the times for work, reason, and taboo (*the symbolic*), and the times for artistic, erotic play, release, and transgression (*the imaginary*).

Having come, then, to literature and the novel as a place for the transgressive but actively sublimated or *sinthomic* release and expression of normally prohibited drives, acts, thoughts and behaviours connected to our most intimate, or *extimate*, animality – we should commend Bataille for having shed his light on this process which will hopefully, on the basis of this work, shine ever more radiantly in future works and in our appraisals of them and of those gone past. The next chapter will consider how a novel by Bataille himself, on *politics* itself, might meet still the aesthetic criteria we have been extracting from his work – calling as it does for a separation of art and politics – so as to deepen their understanding. For an enhanced clarity concerning the distance and nearness of the poetic-literary with the rational-prosaic, and the two different but equally necessary forms of sublimated happiness involved, is what we have seen here is more than possible – which relieves the burden of deeming impossible more of the *real* than we otherwise could, while relegating it to 'evil'.

So, if there is to be something of a politics of the novel, perhaps it shall be as a meta-politics, or even a 'hyper-morality' – that is, as an ethics which is also an erotics enhancing the consciousness and enjoyment demonstrated in the depths of the *real*-oriented thinking here.

> But this concept does not exclude morality: on the contrary, it demands a 'hypermorality'.
>
> —Bataille, 'Preface', *Literature and Evil* (1957)

NOTES

1. Richardson notes that the editorial rationale of *Critique* was to solicit scholarly reviews of books that produced a distinct argument extending on them. Richardson, *Georges Bataille*, 60.

2. For Lacan's analysis of this lure brought together with Nietzsche's in many ways similar Dionysian affirmation of Attic tragedy, see Themi, *Lacan's Ethics and Nietzsche's Critique of Platonism*, 51, 53–4, 57, 61–2. Sophocles, *Antigone*, line 856, 'you are paying for some crime of your fathers [πατρῷον δ' ἐκτίνεις τιν' ἆθλον]', in *Sophocles II*, trans. H. Lloyd-Jones, Loeb Classical Library (Cambridge, MA: Harvard University Press, 1998), 82–3.

3. The latter un-analysed imaginary is implied in the definition of castration Hecq gives in a 'minimalist glossary' at the end of her article, pointing to the imaginary *phallus* as the object a child must at some point renounce trying to be for the mother's desire in the final phase of the Oedipus Complex – suggesting that 'castration may also refer to a state of lack existing in the mother prior to the infant's birth', which is 'evident in the mother's desire' as 'her own incompleteness, which the subject perceives as a desire for the imaginary phallus'. Hecq, "Uncanny Encounters: On Writing, Anxiety and jouissance," *Anatomy & Poetics* 6 (2005) http://www.doubledialogues.com/article/uncanny-encounters-on-writing-anxiety-and-jouissance/ (accessed June 22, 2020).

4. Blondel, *Emily Brontë: Expérience Spirituelle et Création Poétique* (Paris: PUF, 1955).

5. In his definitive 1957 *Eroticism*, Bataille notes the cases where the 'compression' force of taboo 'is not subservient to the explosion' of transgression that follows as its 'complement', but rather what 'gives it increased force' – like fuel to the fire (E, 65). Pierre Dumayet, interviewer, "Georges Bataille: Literature and Evil" https://www.youtube.com/watch?v=5XCnGuK8CVc (accessed June 23, 2020).

6. Lacan, *Triumph of Religion, preceded by Discourse to Catholics*, 44.

7. Lacan, *Triumph of Religion, preceded by Discourse to Catholics*, 44.

8. Horbury stresses where certain feminist literatures falling prey to the universal ~~Woman~~ of the Good can become an escapist fantasy against the real of sexual drives *within* as well as without – noting even where psychoanalysis is used, it is by focusing 'only on those aspects of Freud that serve the pre-established wishes and (unconscious) fantasies of feminist discourses'. Among a number of insightful papers on this, see also Estela V. Welldon, "No Longer a Taboo: Understanding Female Perversion in Motherhood," in *Perversion Now!*, eds. D. Caine, C. Wright (London: Palgrave-MacMillan, 2017), 147–54. Lacan, *Triumph of Religion, preceded by Discourse to Catholics*, 44. Horbury, "What Does Feminism Want?" 582; and "A Psychoanalytic Ethics of the Pornographic Aesthetic," *Porn Studies* (2019): 11–12.

9. Kendall marks how Bataille differed with Simone Weil's position in the 1930s which saw revolution as moral and rational rather than as the 'liberation of the instincts' considered 'pathological' – while also noting Weil as the basis of 'Lazare, the ugly 'Christian' revolutionary', in Bataille's political novel *Blue of Noon* (1935). I

will discuss in chapter 6 here how the Bataille of this *Blue of Noon* period is still quite close to Blake's position, which he later surpasses without necessarily going back to take up Weil's. Kendall, *Georges Bataille*, 103, 119.

10. Lacan's analysis shows Antigone's *desire*, in opposition to Creon's edict of the common good, is a critique of the Sovereign Good to come with Socrates, Plato, Aristotle, and Judaeo-Christianity, the central problematic of 'Western moralism' to which, right from *Seminar I*, Lacan attributes our unconscious 'race towards destruction' (SI, 277). For a detailed demonstration of this see chapter 3 of Themi, *Lacan's Ethics and Nietzsche's Critique of Platonism*, 41–63.

11. Dodds, *The Greeks and the Irrational* (Berkeley: University of California Press, 1951), 137, 149, 209. Rohde, *Psyche: Vol. 1*, 219–23, 228–9.

12. Plato, *Phaedo*, trans. H. N. Fowler, in *Plato I*, Loeb Classical Library, ed. J. Henderson (Cambridge, MA: Harvard University Press, 2005), 391. Clark, *Nietzsche on Truth and Philosophy* (Cambridge: Cambridge University Press, 1990), 169.

13. Aristotle, *Poetics*, 1449a10–19, trans. W. H. Fyfe, in *Aristotle in 23 Volumes* Vol. 23 (Cambridge, MA: Harvard University Press, 1932); available with the Greek at *Perseus Digital Library*, ed. Gregory R. Crane, http://www.perseus.tufts.edu/hopper/text?doc=Perseus:abo:tlg,0086,034:1449a (accessed Jan 30, 2020).

14. As discussed here in section 3.2, Bataille's extensive treatment of prehistoric art's depictions of *divine animality* is in the posthumous collection of his many lectures and articles on the topic *The Cradle of Humanity* (CH).

15. Kant's depiction of the aesthetic 'free-play of imagination and understanding', and the 'delight in the object' that is 'independent of interest', is in his *Third Critique*. See Kant, *Critique of Judgement* (1790), trans. J. C. Meredith (Oxford: Clarendon, 1952), I 9, 6.

16. For Nietzsche's critique of Western moralism's excessive and inflationary 'denaturalizing of natural values' (AC, 25), enjoined with Lacan's analysis of Socrates in Plato's *Symposium* and Freud's handling of Hebraic tradition, see chapters 4 and 5 respectively of Themi, *Lacan's Ethics and Nietzsche's Critique of Platonism*, 65–8, 70–1, 74, 78–9, 82–3, 85, 87–8, 91, 97–105.

17. Nobus, *The Law of Desire: On Lacan's "Kant with Sade,"* xvii, xxix, xxx, 141.

18. Bishop, "Nietzsche's Anti-Christianity as a Return to (German) Classicism," in *Nietzsche and Antiquity*, ed. Bishop, 448–52.

19. For detailed analysis of Nietzsche's major aesthetic distinction of abundance and lack in terms of Lacano-Freudian sublimation, which overcomes the false reduction of all desire to absolute lack by noting instead the gradations of distance and amounts in the relation of signifier to Thing in Lacan, see section 2.3 of Themi, *Lacan's Ethics and Nietzsche's*, 36–40. Zupančič, *Shortest Shadow*, 77.

20. Grigg, *Lacan, Language, and Philosophy*, 8.

21. Cf., Nietzsche, *Anti-Christ*, 10, and the chapter, "How the 'Real World' at last Became a Myth," in *Twilight of the Idols*. A fuller analysis of the latter key chapter, which exposes the mythical real world of metaphysics as a weak creativity stemming from lack and *ressentiment* 'ascetically repressive in its moral effects and anti-empiricist in its epistemic effects', can be found in sections 2.3 and 6.2 of Themi, *Lacan's Ethics and Nietzsche's Critique of Platonism*, 36–7, 119–20. It was this very chapter

of *Twilight of the Idols* that Heidegger called Nietzsche's 'magnificent moment of vision' in volume I of his Nietzsche lectures. Heidegger, "Nietzsche's Overturning of Platonism," in *Nietzsche: Volumes One and Two*, 202.

22. Newman, "The Ball-Joint and the Anagram: Perversion and Jouissance in Hans Bellmer," in *Perversion Now!* eds. Caine, Wright, 158–9, 163–5. Soler, *Lacan – the Unconscious Reinvented*, trans. E. Faye, S. Schwartz (London: Karnac, 2014).

23. Ffrench notes that Bataille's central question of the 1930s, played out in his political novel *Blue of Noon*, was, 'How is it possible to counter the threat of fascism when the latter thrives on an exploitation of the *jouissance* that is foreclosed in the Marxist schema?' In other words, ffrench suggests, 'if Marxist politics fails because of its neglect of the erotic, is this "part maudite [accursed share]" always going to be taken up by the spectacle of fascism?' I will take up this precise problem in the following and final chapter 6. Ffrench, "Dirty Life," in *The Beast at Heaven's Gate: Georges Bataille and the Art of Transgression*, ed. A. Hussey (Amsterdam: Rodopi, 2006), 63.

24. Plato had invoked a quarrel between philosophy and poetry as an ancient antagonism in *Republic*, Book X, 607b.

25. For the reference to biology see Freud's 1913 article "The Claims of Psycho-Analysis to Scientific Interest," in SE13, 182. For full discussion of how the drive-instinct distinction, along with that between object and Thing, informs Lacan's proposed solution to the problem of sublimation in Freud as a four-fold, see also section 2.2 of Themi, *Lacan's Ethics and Nietzsche's Critique of Platonism*.

26. Kennedy, too, notes Bataille's critique of Aestheticism for creating only 'dilettantes detached from society', but also, moreover, that Bataille's 1950 'Letter to René Char on the Incompatibilities of the Writer' is directed against Sartre's opposite aesthetic 'discourse on commitment, or literary engagement'. Kennedy, *Towards an Aesthetics of Sovereignty*, 173, 258. Bataille, "Letter to René Char on the Incompatibilities of the Writer," trans. C. Carsten, *Yale French Studies* (1990): 34, 37–9.

27. For a recent Lacanian analysis of hallucination in Wolf Man, who hallucinates his severed finger as what is foreclosed from the symbolic (genital difference, 'castration') returns in the real in a signifying-symbolic form which is *imaginary in content*, see Grigg, "Signifiers in the Real: from Schreber to Wolf Man," *Psychoanalysis Lacan* 4 (2020): 1–4. For a Lacanian approach to trans phenomena which suggests the originary bisexuality uncovered by Freud is itself an original trans aspect *not* necessarily reducible to a psychotic structure, see Patricia Gherovici, *Transgender Psychoanalysis: A Lacanian Perspective on Sexual Difference* (London: Routledge, 2017), 89–95, 146. For how Lacan's notion of sinthome is useful for avoiding the hyper-pathologizing of trans phenomena, see also Sheila L. Cavanagh, "Transsexuality as Sinthome: Bracha L. Ettinger and the Other (Feminine) Sexual Difference," *Studies in Gender and Sexuality* 17.1 (2016): 27–44.

Chapter 6

Eternal Returns

Erotic Politics in Bataille's Blue of Noon

The previous chapter saw the increasing importance Bataille attached to the necessity of a separation of art and politics, while also maintaining a clear consciousness of the residual path or distant relation between the two. This leads to the question of how one might even broach the topic of politics in art at all, which Bataille famously did in his 1935 novel *Blue of Noon*. But it was only much later in 1957, again nearing the end of his oeuvre, that Bataille at the prompting of others decided to publish it. Feeling vastly distanced from 'the anguish' which had earlier *driven* him to write it, and unsure whether this 'ground was a guarantee of quality', Bataille finally 'deferred to the judgement' of friends and the book was launched – despite feeling that already by 1936 'the Spanish Civil War and the World War had rendered insignificant the historical events connected with the plot of the novel' (BN, 154-5). For 'confronted with tragedy itself', Bataille remarks in the Foreword, 'why pay any attention to its portents?' (BN, 154–5). Since then, of course, we have also witnessed both the collapse of European communism and several crises of confidence in liberal capitalism – leading, inexplicably, to the resurgence of fascist sympathies throughout the coveted traditions of the West.

This chapter will read *Blue of Noon* as a key analytic locus for prescient concerns about the return of fascism and seeming insufficiency of genuine attempts to oppose it. It will also deploy the genealogy of Bataille's postwar economics treatise, *The Accursed Share*, to ground such of his activist works of the 1930s which ranged from the scholarly and literary to the 'ferociously religious' (VE, 179) – as with his secret Nietzschean society of *Acéphale*. I suggest his analysis of how the twin rivals of capitalism and communism both arose from the decline of the Monarchic, reveals us trapped in the same split-subject of politics as before. This is especially with our twenty-first century return of fascism, which I shall contend only more consciousness of erotic truth – as manifested by the protagonists Troppmann and Dirty of *Blue of Noon* in their final confrontation with death – could ever help us mitigate in favour of reason.[1]

6.1 SUPERFICIAL SOCIALISMS – THE CASE OF LAZARE

This section examines the narrator Troppmann's strained relationship with the socialist character we find in Lazare. It considers how the critique of Lazare implied is part of how *Blue of Noon* portends the resurgence of fascism so well as to make it not only explicable in its *hidden erotic sense*, but also grounds for a more genuine opposition – positioning *Blue of Noon* as a fundamental text that has stood the test of time more than Bataille would have known.

The book opens 'in London, in a cellar, in a neighbourhood dive', where Troppmann and his consort Dirty are once again 'drunk' (BN, 11). The debauched scenes to follow will bear on much significance, not least because Troppmann's relation with Dirty is in part a fictional projection of Bataille's to Laure (Colette Peignot). Kendall, for instance, notes that 'Laure certainly suggests some of the characteristics of the anti-heroine Dorothea, or Dirty, as she is called' – while ffrench also records how later 'a version of the italicized "Part One" of *Blue of Noon* appears as a "chapter" of *Inner Experience* [1943]', based on 'an experience of "atrocious" enlightenment Bataille underwent in Italy in 1934, with his lover Collette Peignot (Laure)'.[2]

The introductory scene in London, moreover, culminating in a room at the Savoy with Dirty soiling her 'sumptuous evening gown' (BN, 11) – where 'in terror the servants saw that water was trickling across the chair and down the legs of their beautiful guest', as 'a noise of slackening bowels made itself ponderously evident' (BN, 17) – is also thought to be the sole surviving fragment of the novella *W.C.* Bataille wrote and destroyed in 1926. This was the one that so offended the surrealism of Breton, during the period where Bataille's worrying obsessions led his own friends to encourage him to seek treatment with the psychoanalyst Dr Borel.[3]

Even in Bataille's estimation, in his later 1958 'Autobiographical Note', *W.C.* was 'of violent opposition to all dignity' (AN, 108) – with Stoekl marking 'one of the book's few readers' to be Bataille's surrealist friend Leiris, who recalls its account of Dirty and narrator 'indulging in an orgy with the female stallholders in a fish market', with later chapters further juxtaposing 'the extremes of aristocratic luxury' with low 'vulgarity'.[4] Leiris himself was to be treated by Borel in 1929, as was Laure during the 1930s writing of *Blue of Noon*, with Kendall suggesting that just as Bataille's analysis in 1927 precipitated the novella *Story of the Eye*, his lover's analysis in 1934 'spurred him to return to the form' with *Blue of Noon* – as he was *driven* again to be 'remembering, repeating, and working-through', as Freud would say, the mnesic signifiers of the drive towards the nether regions of the mind, wherein lie the 'repressed instinctual impulses which are feeding the resistance'.[5]

Some of the initial malaise of *W.C.* has, then, by some of the same stimulus of *Story of the Eye*, transferred itself across to open *Blue of Noon* eight years later, with Bataille himself noting cryptically, in a later 1943 preface to *Story of the Eye*, that in the past he 'gave the author of *W.C.* the pseudonym Troppmann'[6] – before adding, disturbingly, somewhere *in* the first-person: 'I masturbated naked, at night, by my mother's corpse'.[7] This atrocity is something Troppmann as protagonist will confess to his three main feminine interests of *Blue of Noon*, including Lazare, who, French notes, 'bears undoubted similarity to Simon Weil', the socialist revolutionary Bataille had activist relations with in the 1930s – with Kendall also suggesting that 'Simone Weil provided the basis of Lazare, the ugly "Christian revolutionary"', while citing 'Simone Petrémont, Weil's friend and biographer' who worked with Bataille at the Bibliothèque National, as one who 'swears to the resemblance'.[8]

Weil had become associated with Bataille around the activist group, *The Democratic Communist Circle*, of the early 1930s, which produced the journal *La Critique Sociale*. The aim, there, was to expand Marxism by further incorporating influences from philosophy, psychoanalysis, and French Sociology, in a project which Kendall notes 'was forbidden by Stalinist orthodoxy'.[9] It is where between 1932 and 1934 Bataille published his first important articles, 'The Notion of Expenditure', 'The Critique of the Foundations of the Hegelian Dialectic', and 'The Psychological Structure of Fascism' (VE). But it is also where he first met Laure, who at the time was with Boris Souvarine, the founder of the *Circle*, just as Bataille at the time was still married to the Sylvia who would go on later to marry Lacan, and whom the estranged wife of Troppmann, Edith, of *Blue of Noon*, is partly modelled on.[10]

Troppmann's confessional scene with Lazare, moreover, in Part Two of the book following the debauched openings with Dirty, is the first invocation of the directly political concerns of *Blue of Noon* – but also with what I suggest is the perennially disruptive *non*-relation of the erotic sphere to the political, which Bataille's distinctive contribution as a writer and scholar has done so much to throw light on. Here Troppmann is feeling 'most unhappy' (BN, 27), because Dirty has abandoned him, which he confesses to Lazare among a host of other sordid details. His connection to Lazare is that he had been financing the printing of a 'tiny monthly review to which she attached great importance', within which 'she defended Communist principles that were a far cry from the official Communism of Moscow' (BN, 30). But it is expressly how her 'macabre appearance', 'ugly and conspicuously filthy' (BN, 29), combines with her obsession to champion 'the cause of the downtrodden' (BN, 31), that somehow seems to make her the only person who could rescue Troppmann 'from dejection' (BN, 30) – following the loss of his exceptionally 'beautiful' but erotically wild and profligate Dirty (BN, 34).

As the story ensues, Troppmann gradually comes to learn that this saviour effect Lazare has on him is because she has 'the mind of a priest' (BN, 94, 38), is basically 'a Christian' (BN, 63), with an excess for negating desire only to match Troppmann and Dirty's opposite drive – through *direct* satisfaction – to 'eliminate every possible urge' (BN, 20). And it is in this context of her priestly role, of the ascetic ideal, of being 'calm as a priest hearing confession' (BN, 38), that Troppmann finds himself confessing to her his double life with Dirty, which had already reached unimaginable 'levels of unnaturalness' (BN, 35). This includes how he eventually found that 'in bed with her' he 'was impotent', despite never having 'had any woman more beautiful or exciting as Dirty' (BN, 34), which he initially links to his 'necrophiliac' (BN, 37) moment by his mother's coffin – the incestuous aspect of which he conceals by mentioning to Lazare only that it was an 'elderly woman' (BN, 38).

Lazare is horribly exposed in her sexual naivety in response to this problem of impotence, with her constantly presumptuous interpositions of a selfless, altruistic notion of love (BN, 34, 39), which irritates Troppmann greatly, sensing also 'contempt' or envy in Lazare's tone – herself 'physically revolting' with 'her grimy nails and the almost cadaverous hue of her skin' – 'for another woman's good luck' (BN, 36). So Troppmann goes on himself to explain by connecting his impotence now not just to necrophilia, corpses, and the episode by his mother's, but also to how he seems to have no problem performing when he is with 'a prostitute, for instance', or any other woman that he himself admits 'contempt for' (BN, 35).

The thing with Dirty is that while she is just as debauched as prostitutes, even 'irredeemably debauched', she is not like those 'who earn their living by it' (BN, 36), she charges no fee, which gives her to him a sacredness that makes him want to 'grovel at her feet', respecting her now 'too much' (BN, 35). As Freud explains with impotence, then, in his 1912 article 'On the Universal Tendency to Debasement in the Sphere of Love', again it is a case of 'where they love they do not desire and where they desire they cannot love' (SE11, 183) – although here in a newly twisted way. For Troppmann's love for Dirty is not the usual desexualizing *agapic* love of Lazare and the Christian tradition, modelled on infantile myths of a virgin Mother with a pure and perfect victim as Son. Rather, it is much closer to what Bataille discloses in his genealogy of the sacred as the Eros of archaic pre-Platonic Greece, which exalted Dionysos, Aphrodite, Maenads, Nymphs, and thus the sacredness of *more* of the polymorphous *base* of desire – *in the real* – than the denaturalizing monotheisms of the Judaeo/Christian-Platonisms to follow.

As Bataille was to elaborate later in his 1957 *Eroticism*, and the 1952 volume II of *Accursed Share* which is its earlier draft, where 'Christian repression was not able to prevent the pagan festivals from continuing', in its attempt to cleave the sexual *animal* elements from sacred being, 'the worship of Satan replaced that of the old deities' (AS II, 131–2). For 'only the devil remained part beast', with horns being along 'with his tail the sign first of transgression and then of degradation' (E, 136), which 'is why it is not absurd to recognize a *Dionysos redivivus* in the Devil' (AS II, 132). And it is similar with Dirty's wild and bestial Maenadic Aphrodite *redivivus*, insofar as she transgresses those very taboos on animal sexuality 'without which we would not be human beings' (E, 134). But not in the same way as low prostitution, Bataille would contend, where a 'poverty-stricken' and 'unhappy plight absolved them from the need scrupulously to observe the taboos' (E, 134-5) – who do not, then, have the luxury of taboos but are forced to sexual animality by necessity of accumulation, rather than out of a sacred erotic expenditure. In this, Bataille concludes, shedding light on Troppmann's ability to perform with them but not his beloved Dirty – but also on the neurotic split of Freud's description of the tendency to '*debasement* of the sexual object' (SE11, 183) – low prostitution 'generally excited a disgust like the one most civilizations claim to feel for sows', meaning those with unconscious prejudice against libido, who separate it much from sacredness and affection, can finally perform, like filthy animals, with a prostitute who in their mind is already that low, where 'even if she is not ashamed of it', Bataille interpolates, 'she does know that she lives like a pig' (E, 134-5).

This neurotic split is also marked by Freud as 'the two directions personified in art as sacred and profane (or animal) love' (SE11, 183) – which is where under Christian-Platonism animality is cleansed from the sacred and relegated to the profane, while the sacred becomes inflationary transcendental, separated from body and earth. Troppmann's impotence only differs from the normal neurotic structure in being a case of fearing loss of love of a *sensual* object of 'overvaluation' (SE11, 183). But it can also be from the extreme nature of the acts they perform: when she is 'staring' at him 'with eyes like an animal's' (BN, 15), in a 'place crowded with men' while their 'eyes were getting ominous' (BN, 11) – as this for Troppmann 'always left this taste of corpses' (BN, 35), sensing the danger, fearing the loss of death itself no longer in any merely external metaphorized form, as per his diagnosis of 'necrophiliac' (BN, 37-8). 'I was afraid of her', Troppmann had earlier thought to himself at the Savoy, 'while she was gasping for breath, panting like an animal' (BN, 14) – with Dirty also admitting, 'I'm scared myself', and, moreover, 'Scared to death' (BN, 18).

As Bataille was to again so aptly put it later in *Eroticism*, 'we are not always strong enough to will this', when it comes to this transgressive life, for eventually 'we come to an end of our resources and sometimes desire is impotent' – where, 'if the danger is too great, if death is inevitable, then the desire is generally inhibited' (E, 86). But Lazare's insistent naivety in response to all this, becoming 'indifferent' (BN, 37), with a 'hint of contempt' – refusing to see how Dirty's prostitutional acts with a waived fee was 'how that women could be uplifted by it' (BN, 36) – leaves her looking at Troppmann as if he 'were a presumptuous brat' (BN, 38). But this leaves Troppmann himself looking at her 'with loathing' (BN, 40), while thinking to himself, as she returned to the topic of politics to assume moral grief at the goings on: 'this foolish, ugly girl horrified me by the consistency of her preoccupations' (BN, 42). And so, in order 'to embarrass her', Troppmann rejects her presumption he must have been 'upset' to be in Vienna where recently an 'assassination took place' – where actually he was just distraught at being abandoned by Dirty without goodbye, retorting thus to Lazare: 'even if there'd been a war, it would have mirrored what was going on in my head' (BN, 42).

It leaves Lazare stunned that such an otherwise serious intelligent being could be in a state of mind where war might reflect it and make him happy – and not at all because it may lead to a progressive 'revolution', which she then reflexively sought to contend, only to be shut down again with: 'I'm talking about war, not about what it could lead to' (BN, 43). 'Nothing could have shocked her more cruelly than what I had just said' (BN, 43), Troppmann concludes, in the privacy of a tortured 'philosopher's head in which since then' a 'shriek of horror' would attend – of which Bataille remarks, in the *W.C.* preface to *Story of the Eye*, whenever struck with such 'lugubrious' urges (SE, 75), giving 'dreamy vision a disastrous sadness' (SE, 67).

6.2 SUPERFICIAL SURREALISMS – THE CASE OF XENIE

Troppmann begins 'seeing less of Lazare' (BN, 44). But in his constant stumblings from table to table of various clubs with copious drink he neglects himself and grows violently ill. He also meets his third major feminine interest of the novel in Xenie. This section examines Troppmann's sometimes tender but often cruel treatment of Xenie, a transitional object following his growing rejection of Lazare which followed his own rejection *by* Dirty. It suggests Xenie metaphorizes both the foreignness of leftist politics *and* avant-garde aesthetics to the erotic real that Troppmann seeks to uncover in his obsessions with death, which fascism seems to be able to utilize at will – albeit it as connected with what Bataille later, in the 1953 volume III of *Accursed Share*, calls 'the backward, nationalistic forms of violence' (AS III, 368).

Regarding this backwards nationalism, Bataille here is specifically referring to how the sovereign subjectivity of Nietzsche's thought tends to be co-opted politically, wherever its importance is not instead left 'suspended, as it were' (AS III, 368). In his 1933 article 'The Psychological Structure of Fascism', moreover, Bataille notes fascism's ability in general to exploit the sovereign '*heterogeneous* elements' that 'censorship excluded from the conscious ego' – which, 'given what we know about repression', are 'described by psychoanalysis as *unconscious*' (VE, 141-3). Here fascism is marked as that which 'taps', 'from the bottom up' (VE, 153), so to speak, the *base* behaviours of 'impoverished classes' (VE, 142, 154), of 'the various unconscious processes such as dreams or neuroses' (VE, 142), and the sovereign destructive passions and other 'such apparently anachronistic phantoms' (VE, 153), to create a mystical 'concentration' or 'condensation of power' that can be frighteningly 'both military and religious' (VE, 153-4).

This is where Andrew Hussey's analysis of the political context of 1930s France invokes 'what Walter Benjamin called the "aestheticizing of politics"', which creates an 'aesthetic sympathy with fascism' through what for Bataille is discernible as 'an element of sensuality'.[11] By drawing on Freud's seminal 1921 essay on *Group Psychology and the Analysis of the 'Ego'*, moreover, as the 'essential introduction of the understanding of fascism' (VE, 160), Bataille will mark fascism's success in this being by 'the affective flow' of 'moral identification' with 'a leader', whose '*force*' is thus 'analogous to that exerted in hypnosis' (VE, 143). Insofar as there is an 'internal domination', like that 'uniting a chief to his soldiers', Bataille even notes the leader's 'presence' as 'a negation of the fundamental revolutionary effervescence that he taps' (VE, 153) – forming, thus, 'the analogy with hypnosis', when 'the affective relations of the followers to the leader' project the latter as a 'transcendent object of collective affectivity' (VE, 154), who in Freudian terms is then internalized and set up as an '*Ego Ideal* or the *superego*' (VE, 160).

Freud indeed had observed of such groups, in his *Group Psychology*, the 'number of individuals who have put one and the same object in place of their ego ideal' and have thus 'identified themselves with another in their ego' – which in the case of 'artificial groups', such as 'the Church and the Army', puts the leader in the locus of something like a 'kind elder brother' or 'substitute father' (SE18, 116, 93-4). Such is the libidinal affectivity that Bataille observes is then bundled together with 'the mystical idea of race', which indeed 'lacks an objective base', but 'is nonetheless subjectively grounded' (VE, 155) – as with 'the State', or the 'glorious existence of a nation raised to the value of a divine force' (VE, 154). And all this is what seems to render reason itself now impotent, Bataille laments, such that leftist 'revolutionary movements that develop in a democracy are hopeless' (VE, 159).

Later in the 1953 *Sovereignty* volume III of *Accursed Share*, Bataille will again stress, 'against both classical and present-day Marxism, the connection of all the great modern revolutions, from the English and the French onward, with a feudal order that is breaking down' (AS III, 279). This is because Bataille is all too aware that on the left 'there have never been any great revolutions that have struck down an established bourgeois domination', that 'all those that overthrew a regime started with a revolt motivated by the sovereignty that is implied in feudal society' (AS III, 279). This feudal form of sovereignty for Bataille, which is 'a distorted, even detestable' externalization of subjective drives for 'a *sovereign* use, for an unproductive use, of wealth' – such as 'the splendour' and 'yearly maintenance budget' of 'the construction of Versailles' (AS III, 280) – is one which thus could not adequately industrialize, and is completely *other* to the bourgeois society forever investing in the accumulative 'production of the means of production' (AS III, 282). Only fascism has overthrown the latter, which while it is again, as Richardson puts it, a 'perverted and nostalgic form' that is parodic of 'mankind's drives', it nevertheless, like initial feudalism, 'responds to a deep yearning for a meaningful experience of the sacred' that the economic reductionism of the establishment and the left mostly fails to match.[12]

Richardson, then, marks the 'acute perception' of Bataille's observing in *Accursed Share* of how communism or socialism, unlike fascism, has only ever overthrown 'industrially backward countries' (AS III, 273), namely those with 'an agrarian or feudal social structure', but never the capitalist ones that Marx foresaw and hoped (AS III, 265). And it is only by shedding our ignorance of the *libidinal* base of such historical 'divergence' (AS III, 265), or 'aberration', and continuing 'to seek its meaning' (AS III, 280), that we might hope to address the fascist weddings of *It* with death – as I suggest the encounters of Troppmann in *Blue of Noon* can help serve to demonstrate.

The key moment between Troppmann and Xenie, for instance, is when he tells her too of masturbating by his mother's corpse (BN, 75–6). 'But this time things were stranger' (BN, 75), Troppmann concedes, for indeed he specifies this time that the 'elderly woman' *was* his 'mother', and it was not as a confession but in order to express his 'contempt for her' (BN, 77) – for *Xenie*, that is – where he 'was smiling' as the thought of it sent her into 'a spasm' as 'she gave in, let herself go, and her body slumped limply down' (BN, 77). This effectively for Troppmann reduces her to the level of a corpse, but also to that of a prostitute 'in a whorehouse' (BN, 77), as gets her undressed and drinking to the point where he can 'tell her "Lie down" and she'll lie down, or "Lick the table" and she'll lick the table' (BN, 80).

What Troppmann is arguably trying to do here is break the hold of the normal taboos and prohibitions constituting what he takes to be the superficiality of Xenie. This is such that through enactment of a kind of symbolic death she can be *back in the real* where her 'natural' and 'pretty', animal 'nakedness' can stand out (BN, 51, 67, 69, 74), and he can perform the act with her – as she goes on to assume, through his rituals of humiliation, 'the appearance of a dead woman' with 'the pale breasts of a prostitute' (BN, 85). Ffrench also suggests that when 'Troppmann is driven to stab Xenie's naked thigh, beneath the table', when they first meet at a club, it is from 'a drunken wish to break through the veneer of her social face', expressing in general how 'Bataille seeks to reach that place where a being is undone', such as 'an animal at its throat', or 'a woman under her dress'.[13] This thwarts the intent of 'poor little Xenie' (BN, 74) to 'take care of' him (BN, 67), ease his pain through a 'love' (BN, 74) that is 'motherly' (BN, 76), and restore him back to normal taboos – having earlier said to him: 'Everybody knows you lead an abnormal sex life'; 'I'm very stupid and I laugh a lot. There's nothing but dumb ideas inside my head', but 'people who have loathsome habits, like you – it's probably because they're in pain' (BN, 67).

All of this sees to it that 'tears were streaming' from Troppmann's eyes, 'in spite of' himself (BN, 67). But with this drawing out of involuntary tenderness, Troppmann soon feels Xenie's 'presence disagreeable' (BN, 68), which leads to another key moment where he suddenly goes shouting mad at what the *superficial* surrealists and aesthetic dilletante's did – presumably like Xenie herself in all her involvements 'in literary goings-on' – in heaping praise and admiration on the works of 'De Sade' (BN, 68). Troppmann calls them 'con artists' who, unless they are dead, in 'jail or underground', are really 'bootlicking' of masters, 'bursting with conceit', and far too scared themselves to 'eat shit' (BN, 68). Kendall also notes in this that Troppmann 'undoubtedly has the Surrealists in mind' in his outburst towards the flatterers of the ultimately 'heterogeneous object – Sade', directed in this instance towards the 'literary dilettante, Xenie', who, 'with her uninformed openness and good intentions', and 'foolish overreaching', Kendall concludes, is a character that 'surely stands in for a member of the literary avant-garde'.[14]

In and around such outbursts, however, there are still the moments when Troppmann imagines that he can be happy with the relatively facile but also quite natural and pretty Xenie, whose very name in Greek even connotes her status as 'an intruder, an alien' (BN, 124).[15] For Xenie is foreign to the erotic excess in the real like Dirty and Sade, but also to the excess in ascetically renouncing it like Lazare – even though Troppmann 'belatedly recalled how Xenie used to proclaim her Communist views whenever she had the chance' (BN, 122). And it is only later when *out of the blue*, like a plane descending from 'the blue of the noon sky' (BN, 107), that Dirty announces she will be coming back to Barcelona to meet him, that Troppmann is finally able to surmount both Xenie *and* Lazare in his libidinal economy – including any activist investment he maintained in the worker's revolution enacted by what he had earlier referred to as 'communists, or socialists, or whatever' (BN, 63).

This last indifferent phrase occurs in Troppmann as a question of 'why are you' (BN, 63) when he meets Lazare's stepfather, a communist who 'taught philosophy in a country *lycee*' (BN, 58). Lazare's response of 'we must not abandon the downtrodden', and 'one can always save one's own soul', is what finally exposes her as fundamentally 'Christian', which leaves Troppmann asking: 'Why "must?" What's the point of it?' (BN, 63); to go with his earlier: 'Why should I give a damn?' (BN, 61) – feeling now 'outraged with shame' (BN, 63) at having gotten caught up in her schemes, as if 'caught in a trap' (BN, 58). But it is not until later that he is able to work through the priestly, super-egoic hold Lazare has on him, a hold indicated by his apparently only 'silly idea', when meeting her stepfather, that he 'might have to ward off the evil eye' (BN, 58).

Three more scenes are worth revealing on this super-egoic hold and its eventual overcoming. First is when he hears that Lazare has been spotted in a Barcelona dive-bar, where known perverse performances take place 'of a boy in girl's clothing' (BN, 86-7) – and where she is found, moreover, requesting that one of her comrades 'stick pins into her skin', allegedly in preparation 'for withstanding torture' (BN, 89). The *phallicness* of the act here is quite extant, from active to passive, suggesting that as a kind of 'saint' (BN, 90), of a sexually repressed and puritan virginal state, she can only accede to libidinal desire and what Lacan's later . . . *Or Worse* seminar calls 'the phallic function' or 'business of castration' (SXIX, 25, 92), through sado-masochistic symbolic displacements – essentially her own way of *dressing like a girl* for one brief moment, like the transvestite performers on the stage.

Second is where the phallic symbolism again re-emerges, when she flirts with the idea of death with another comrade – getting him to 'hold the barrel' of a revolver 'against her chest', where 'it was no joke', and daring him to pull the trigger (BN, 91). This leaves Troppmann feeling 'obsessed with the revolver, by the need to shoot, to empty the chamber – into her belly, into her' (BN, 93). It is almost as if to force her to the function of receptivity to the phallus, which in Lacan is not a function she can wholly exist without even as 'a *pas-toute*, a *not-all*, a duality' (SXIX, 92), would be to free him of the strange hold she has on him. But this disturbing hold was also visible on the other Barcelona workers and activists who equally 'were appalled' by her presence at this bar and 'couldn't understand her being there' (BN, 89) – as if Jesus himself, or even his Mary, were spotted consorting in the Red-Light district, living it up at the lowliest brothels.

Ffrench notes in this that here 'Lazare does not represent a "clean" Marxism', at least not anymore, but rather her own bizarre version of 'a "dirty" flirtation with death and base, perverse sexuality' – which ultimately, however, ffrench must add, can only project a Christian salvation 'beyond the grave' or horizon of the 'revolutionary project'.[16] This is indicated in a third moment of much significance, in addition to these dive-bar libidinal displacements into irrational excess by this otherwise sober, stoic, and hyper-moral subject, where Lazare insists that the workers raid the prison instead of the armoury. This is despite the fact that the act is merely symbolic, and in terms of revolutionary aims, where what is required is that the movement puts 'weapons into the hands of workers', unproductive, and, Troppmann concedes, of absolutely 'no use to anyone' (BN, 110).

By this time, however, Troppmann is buoyed at the news of Dirty's return, and seems even to *enjoy* the further evidence of his inkling of Lazare's Christian neurosis coming to the fore, with the perverse drive behind it becoming more manifest. He no longer feels, then, 'like a trapped animal' (BN, 106), expendable to the Other's cause, or understands how he ever really 'could have been afraid of Lazare' (BN, 108). In the end she was at the same time the 'most humane being' he had ever seen while 'also a monstrous rat' (BN, 115) – 'a bird of ill omen; a dirty, trivial bird' (BN, 107) – suggesting again the perverse core behind the most repressively inflated moral ideals, *accursing* our libidinal drives unconsciously with violence and death. But Dirty's foreshadowed return has enabled Troppmann to feel that he 'might even be coming to life', and he 'smiled now' whenever he 'thought of corpses, or of Lazare' (BN, 121). It enables him to see Lazare as a priestly introjection, connected not just to the hypnotic superego of Freud's *Group Psychology,* which by no means belongs to fascism alone, but also to the lascivious renouncing of libidinal life in favour of death. Hence, 'not running away' becomes 'easy' when he sees her in Barcelona, trying still to facilitate the worker's revolution, for he already 'was, in fact, far away' (BN, 115) – that is, *distanced* from any guilt-bondage to her latently perverse Christian commitments, with their deferred irrational post-mortem salvations, to the meek or downtrodden working class.

It remains to be seen, however, in what state Dirty will herself arrive, and how Troppmann will co-respond in the moment – not just emotionally, but also intellectually and physically apropos of his previously confessed impotence with her, that seemed at the time somehow connected to death, debauchery, *a strange sacred respect*, and corpses.

6.3 LIBIDINAL DEMANDS FOR DEATH – THE RETURN OF DIRTY *DORO-THEA*

Dirty, whose name is 'merely an abbreviation – a provocative abbreviation – of Dorothea' (BN, 101), in fact arrives in a state near death, strangely announcing that if she were not sick she 'wouldn't have come', but now that she was, 'sick at last', they were 'going to be happy' (BN, 131). Stranger still, the letter she sent had opened with 'I grovel at your feet', but was even apologizing for not having actually died, 'for not having had the courage to kill herself' (BN, 101) – that is, for being left instead, much like Troppmann from a debauched neglect, hovering precariously at the threshold. This section analyses Troppmann's final encounter with Dirty, which is also a final confrontation with death. It suggests the libidinal demands for death inherent in Dirty are most *directly* connected to the deepest elements of erotic life, as opposed to the superficiality of Xenie or the ascetics of Lazare's moralistic obsessions. This will allow us to see most fully just what is involved in the easy exploitation of *jouissance* by fascism.

Doro-thea literally means 'gift of the goddess' in the Greek.[17] And it is very much a *pre*-Christian-Platonic kind of gift that the goddess here has for offering, where the erotic is yet to be so cleansed from the sacred religious – where it is only through 'the Christian position with regard to sacred eroticism', as Bataille later notes, that 'eroticism has become sin' (E, 129), and where 'eroticism, having lost its sacred character, became unclean' (TE, 74). Dorothea's gift is rather closer to that of the erotic drive in all its polymorphous libidinal fullness, which, of course, as one pursues it, can risk too much – 'to the point of death' (E, 11; LE, 10), as Bataille will put it – so powerful it is in its sovereignty unleashed. This is why Dirty and Troppmann feel so connected to death in their erotic attempts to restore and attain to libidinal fullness, where it 'always left this taste of corpses', as Troppmann recalled, 'especially in London' with the unimaginable 'levels of unnaturalness one can reach' (BN, 35), that opened *Blue of Noon* in 'a room at the Savoy' (BN, 12).

But this connection of eroticism with death is also a reaction to the 'well-behaved' 'way of life' (BN, 18) that others would culturally try to re-impose – who are 'scared', as Dirty remarks at the Savoy, while trembling herself, without succumbing, which is 'why they never dare let anything show' (BN, 18). The savagery with which culture can try to reimpose repression on the erotic can leave death-wish as the only way back to the animal, libidinal, bodily real – given that one is already guilted and shamed, discredited socially, for trying to be who they really are, and residually unconscious about the displacements of libido that can only now return as monstrous and disavowed, and acted-out, projected *as* the repressed in the form of some deathly symptom.

This paradoxical linking of the erotic to death is what is wonderfully metaphorized in the graveyard scene between Dirty and Troppmann near the end of their final encounter. It was 'the first time in a long while that she had let herself go' (BN, 144), but for Troppmann too, as 'Dorothea opened wide' and he 'bared her to the loins', feeling that 'her naked cleft lay open' to him 'like a freshly dug grave' – surrounded as they were below, as they slid onto a precipice, by candle lit graves which were mirrored above by stars in the night, giving the topsy-turvy feeling of 'falling into the void of the sky' (BN, 145).

Bataille will later enumerate further psycho-physiological and ontological 'parallels' between 'death and sexuality' throughout his 1957 *Eroticism*: in terms of both the bodily organs of 'reproduction' (E, 61-2), and the disruptive 'violence' (E, 42) of the drive's 'excessive' (E, 83) aspect, when 'the danger is too great' (E, 86); and in terms of nature's own 'cycle of change' (E, 55), in its eternal becoming of 'generation' with 'squandering', 'annihilation' (E, 61), 'decomposition', and 'corruption' (E, 55), in the 'continuity of being' (E, 13). But it should also be noted that one of the key strategies of ascetic hyper-repression is to then artificially conflate or reduce the libido to risk of death so as to dissuade us of its access – in what amounts to a skewed consequentialist analysis that merely bespeaks the empty threat: *touch and you shall die or burn in hell for eternity*.[18]

The falling down in order to go high, moreover, of Troppmann and Dirty's erotic graveyard scene, can also signify the pre-Christian sense of the sacred erotic so important to Bataille's genealogy: where as we return to base sexuality, after traversing our usual taboos, we find its 'low' *real* sublimated in the imaginary to become 'poetic and divine though animal' (E, 153) – and where Bataille's aim is to 'lift the curse' on the drive and make its ineluctable *share* of being less *accursed* again (AS I, 9). But it also speaks to his dissident surrealism of the late 1920s, which sought to reclaim for consciousness the base-material elided beneath the heights of hyper-sublimation, inflated as they often were towards neurotic substitution through repression both of satisfaction *and* knowledge. Only now we find Bataille transferring the erotic intervention to a new domain with his dissident or base Marxism of the 1930s, to expose why democratic and revolutionary leftism fails and fascism succeeds when the bourgeois centre collapses. In keeping with this is also Kendall's observation that the *La Critique Sociale* journal of the Democratic Communist Circle 'would replace *Documents* as Bataille's primary venue of publication for the next three years', after this base surrealist journal that caused his dispute with Breton 'lost its funding in January 1931' – where just as '*Documents* brought ethnography and aesthetics into encounters with one another and with psychoanalysis, *La Critique Sociale* set about revitalizing Marxism through very similar encounters'.[19]

If Marxism needed this revitalizing, or else was doomed to falter, it is because even at the price of morality and rationality, people will unconsciously seek a return to a sacred that somehow signifies, and even gives them access to, their distortedly repressed libidinal desire. This again is wonderfully encapsulated not just by Troppmann's frequently obsessed revulsion with Lazare (BN, 36, 93), but also by the absurdly underhanded and perverse libidinal manner of the Nazi boy-band he finds playing at the end of *Blue of Noon*. For though 'some of them were blonde, with doll-like faces', Troppmann senses the 'long drum major's stick', keeping the time, to be held 'obscenely erect, with the knob at his crotch', which 'looked like a monstrous monkey's penis' – such that 'like a dirty little brute, he would then jerk the stick level with his mouth; from crotch to mouth, from mouth to crotch, each rise and fall jerking to a grinding salvo from the drums' (BN, 151).

Here ffrench suggests that while Troppmann is 'not a Marxist hero', his attraction to Dirty embroils him in fascinations with such abjection and death that the 'infinite loss of a fall upwards into the starry sky', of the graveyard copulation scene, is the 'only possible counter to the Nazi parade' that 'elevates death into a phallic obscenity' – with the 'erection of power and the upright posture of the military regime' opposed now by 'the fall, the collapse, the fading of desire into abjection and impotence'. In this ffrench also notes others of Bataille's fictive works to operate this strategy of 'desublimation' – that is, of 'putting into play the fundamental human need for elevation and the corresponding physical reality' which 'brings it down low' – so as to restore a more grounded cyclical balance to our inflated ideals, as if now, 'like Troppmann and Dirty', one were only 'to fall upwards into the void in the sky'.[20]

Stein on this also interprets that Bataille has 'juxtaposed Dorothea's and Troppmann's own abandonment', which illuminates the 'comic-tragic character of all authority', to the 'tragically abandoned way that the Nazi youth who clung to a false Icarian pose lost themselves in a sadistic ideal of "purity and perfection"'.[21] So, when it comes to the final sight of this Nazi band, Troppmann finds the 'hateful automatons' obscene, but also 'terrifying', where 'each pearl of music in the night was an incantatory summons to war and murder' (BN, 151). But it is interesting to wonder whether Dirty, who before having briefly left was openly fantasizing of war and death again, would have had the same shriek back in horror at the signifier of the brutal reality set to unfold. For what is evidenced in Dirty's still expressed 'wish there would be war', that Troppmann would 'like it, too', and 'be killed' – and that she would tell 'a really nice man' each time one of his children were killed while 'dressed in black' in 'a puddle of blood' (BN, 148) – is the externalizing of the repressed well-springs of desire in distorted form, reduced to death, which the restoration of libidinal eroticism seems initially to entail: metaphorizing as it also does the smashing of the strictly repressive, domesticating taboos of docile bodies, and *denatured* enculturation.

In short, a fuller restoration of the erotic sphere renders both the leftist ascetic negation of it and the far-right's parodic exploitation of it equally absurd, as if it were Lazare now leading the band of perverted blonde-beasts, with Xenie handing out the flyers. But until that time of consciousness is reached, the far right has ever its chance to prevail, as a distorted mirroring of what is really going on in people's heads. Such is the way that Troppmann is left with Bataille's horrendous portent of 1935 that 'against this rising tide of murder', it will be impossible to set anything but 'trivialities', or the 'comic entreaties of old ladies' – like ugly Lazares, or superficial Xenies – with all things 'surely doomed to conflagration' (BN, 151).

6.4 SPLIT-SUBJECTS OF POLITICAL ECONOMY – LEFT, RIGHT, LEFT . . .

This doomed portent in the political brings us lastly to the problem of the bourgeois centre, whose constant corruption cycles of boom and bust create the great discontent and power vacuum to exploit in the first place: both in the 1930s of Bataille's Troppmann and, unfortunately, in our today. For as Bataille traces out in his postwar *Accursed Share*, particularly in its volumes I and III on *Consumption* and *Sovereignty*, the problem is in capitalism's overreliance on special '*isolated* interests' in determining the production and use of resources – which, though it enables some space for individuality, ambition, desire and innovation, also allows for greed, superficiality, corruption and externalized destruction by failing to connect up, in enough substantial ways, 'with any *general* interest whatever' (AS I, 176–7). Communism for Bataille is then an attempt to mitigate this individual greed and corruption, what he calls the 'deceptive appearances' (AS III, 368) or 'caricatural aspect' of the 'bourgeois debasement of sovereignty' – with its 'comedy of sovereignty' *reduced* to mass accumulation 'in the world of things' (AS III, 360) – but does so at the expense of having 'renounced sovereignty' (AS III, 313), 'personal sovereignty' (AS III, 324), or 'subjective life' (AS III, 360) all together, and is thereby 'eliminating the difference between men' (AS III, 350) in an *ascetic* way, 'in order to produce better' (AS III, 313).

Hence 'they place their sovereignty in renunciation' (AS III, 325), as Bataille laments of communism, forming a version of that 'ascetic ideal' as a means to power that Nietzsche bemoans of the whole of malaise of Christianity and its ideological descendants. This is where Nietzsche observes how 'the chief trick the ascetic priest permits' is the very 'exploitation of the sense of guilt' that they themselves have caused by shaming animality and the *natural* differences entailed – causing the 'bad conscience' that leaves Nietzsche bewailing that 'for two millennia now we have been condemned to the sight of this new type of invalid, "the sinner"' (GM III, 20).[22]

In the case of communism for Bataille, this renewed asceticism specifically imbues 'a resolute contempt for individual interest, for thought, for personal conventions and rights' – that culminates 'in that complete negation, pushed to its extreme consequences, of individual reality' (AS I, 150). Bataille will deplore, for instance, 'the rift it brings about' between what people *really* love, and what in fact they are prepared to acknowledge or 'openly say' – where now 'a kind of timidity, of bad conscience, of shame' takes hold when they compare 'the concerns of communist politics' with their erotic life, desire, or philosophical thought and questioning, with 'what engages them personally' (AS III, 329).

At the level of political economy, there is even something uniquely identical for Bataille to the twin rivals of capitalism and communism in both favouring a 'primitive accumulation' (AS III, 274, 360) of the means of production – that which only 'gives primacy to accumulation' (AS III, 315, 310), rather than to the not so obviously utilitarian or immediately productive expenditure that is otherwise more connected to desire, beauty, contemplation, the aesthetic and the erotic which really is what is free, 'what is sovereign' (AS III, 315). For Bataille also notes that communism historically is just the *belated* '"industrial revolution" which the rich countries accomplished long ago' (AS III, 274), of 'poor countries' trying to catch up to 'the richest countries' (AS III, 309), which 'calls for changes that Marx couldn't have foreseen' – *or even approved* – as he knew too well that its horrors would only mimic those initially suffered 'in England' (AS III, 274-5, 265).

To Bataille, of course, 'all accumulation is cruel', as 'all renunciation of the present for the sake of the future is cruel', but particularly then when done so reductively, rapidly – referring also to the work of Isaac Deutscher on how 'Stalin inevitably calls to mind that period of intense "primitive" accumulation in England whose excesses and cruelties Karl Marx described in the last chapter of volume one of *Capital*' (AS III, 274–5).[23] This is done regardless by the 'agrarian, industrially backward countries with a juridical structure that is more or less feudal' (AS III, 273); that is, Bataille notes, the 'industrially underdeveloped countries' which had 'kept the forms of feudal society' and thus, for Marx, 'were ripe for bourgeois revolution, not for socialist revolution' (AS III, 265). But as Bataille interpolates it, writing around 1953, here 'the Russian bourgeoise not having accumulated' meant they were too weak and that 'the Russian proletariat had to do it. And the Chinese proletariat will have to do likewise' (AS III, 275).

Against this primitive logic, one must stress how Marx himself even notes with Engels, in their famous *Communist Manifesto*, how 'the first direct attempts of the proletariat to attain its own ends', when 'feudal society was being overthrown', had 'necessarily failed' – due to the 'then undeveloped state of the proletariat', and the 'absence of the economic conditions for its emancipation', which 'could be produced by the impending bourgeois epoch alone'. In keeping, moreover, with the later concerns of Nietzsche and Bataille on ascetic renunciation, Marx and Engels also mark how 'the revolutionary literature that accompanied these first movements of the proletariat had necessarily a reactionary character', which indeed 'inculcated universal asceticism and social levelling in its crudest form'.[24]

Alas for 'Lenin and Trotsky', Bataille recounts, who while aware on Marxist principles that socialist revolution in their country had little chance of success, with such principles in mind were also fortified with the mistaken belief that 'revolution was near in all Western Europe', such that 'the victorious proletariat of the advanced countries' would soon be able to help (AS III, 269). As the vanguard of a poorer country, moreover, they still wanted to develop faster for themselves and immediately break any external hegemony – even though 'with a view to industry' and 'accumulation' they knew too well that their own bourgeois were weak, corrupt, and as Bataille puts it, simply 'not able to do anything' (AS III, 275).

Hence the revolution went ahead anyway, 'carried out by the militants who quoted Marx as their authority', succeeding 'in countries with an agrarian or feudal social structure' where, Bataille notes, even 'peasants had a decisive part in them' (AS III, 265). And all the while they were imbued with the hope or fantasy that once they won they would suddenly remember the implacable nature of the lost erotic sphere on which their decades of ascetic toil had functioned precisely on the exclusion of, or even remember this as a problem. We should recall the *banning* of psychoanalysis in the Sino-Soviet forms of communism[25] – but also the ceaseless, sometimes hostile resistances to psychoanalysis and the *truth* of the erotic it bears even in our much more liberal academies and cultural forms of the West right up to this day.

With respect to the latter, Horbury refers to Lacan's *Seminar XVII* four-discourses to mark how in particular, 'as a protest discourse, feminist discourse has been equated with the productive discourse of the hysteric', but once institutionalized 'takes on the structure of the university discourse', and does so through 'bypassing the critical phase of the analyst'. In a process now sadly not exclusive to the various forms of feminism or the Academy alone, Horbury stresses in this that 'no genuine revolution in their discourse can occur', only the perpetuation of a 'politics of the symptom *as* a solution'. And this is where as with any of the artificial group structures outlined by Freud – such as army and church (SE18, 93–4, 116) – in internalizing or 'adopting an ideal-ego built upon another's affective discourse', rather than seeking analytic knowledge of an egoic symptom's source, 'the subject remains split-off from what motivates them, their desire, and their enjoyment'.[26]

Freud discusses the '*cultural hypocrisy*' involved in his 1925 article, 'The Resistances to Psychoanalysis', in terms of the 'bad conscience' society has accrued in setting up such 'a high ideal of morality' that can really 'bear heavily on the individual' (SE19, 219). For this has led to sexual instincts in particular being 'tamed insufficiently', in a way 'psychological wrong' as devoid of understanding – leaving them 'readier than the rest to break loose' and resulting in 'insecurity' in the guarding of a 'precarious situation by forbidding criticism and discussion', with psychoanalysis included (SE19, 219). This self-censoring should come as little surprise, however, when it comes to the modern West. For as Bataille notes of capitalism's origins in Calvinism and the Protestant reformation, its focus on expending accumulated resources only on the *further* growth of the productive apparatus, functioned to a substantial extent on the same ascetic exclusion of eroticism of earlier Christian-Platonism and the later communist East – devalued still as useless, non-productive expenditure or *waste* so as to channel ever more time into the furnaces of the industrial revolution, and its alleged eternal growth rate of production.

Even though in capitalism this was later viewed as being done by 'free choice', as opposed to the Marxists' authoritarian 'blanket decision' (AS III, 310), Bataille saw how it ultimately comes to express the reductive austerity of Benjamin Franklin's formulation of 'time is money' (AS I, 126) – with any cruelties, greed, or ill-gotten gains involved dressed-up morally 'as diligence and industry' (AS I, 122), by the ostensibly 'humble, saving, hardworking' (AS I, 123). This is what becomes cloaked in the veneer of what Lacan observed as the Calvinist doctrine of *God rewards the rich*: that 'God rewards the people he loves with plentiful goods' (SVIII, 57) – which is here seen as a proof of one's morality to such an extent that it is even, as Bataille notes in citing Tawney, as reward for all one's ascetic self-denial, diligence and toil, 'a proof salvation has been attained' (AS I, 123).[27]

Gone in the post-Christian West is the overturning of money tables, or the other biblical ascetic idea of more chance a camel passing through the eye of a needle than a rich man through the gates of heaven.[28] But again it is merely a case of what Nietzsche calls *not* the opposite but the 'latest expression of the ascetic ideal' (GM III, 23), where, when it comes to the 'denial of sensuality', it is again only 'a particular mode of this denial' (GM III, 24) – where as allied now with modern science it 'became stronger', 'more elusive', and 'more captious' (GM III, 25), as 'one of the latest phases of its evolution' (GM III, 27). But given this new asceticism of how even our (neo)liberal, apparently hedonistic 'capitalist society reduces what is human to the condition of a *thing*' in the form 'of a commodity' (AS, I, 129), Bataille suggests that unless we 'discover an outlet founded on reason' for the drive and consumption for which, nevertheless, 'erotic pleasure – the instant consumption of energy – is the model' – then devoid of a fuller consciousness of *jouissance*, 'the only possible outcome is war' (TE, 149).

Bataille was astute to note that capitalism was only 'avoiding paralysis' after World War II because the 'extreme tension' of the Cold War was *forcing* them to spend with the *gift* structure of 'the Marshall Plan' (AS I, 184). For this was 'favourable to a less unequal distribution of resources, to a circulation of wealth that the increasing unevenness of levels paralysed', causing the very 'working-class agitation' that the Plan now 'tries to remedy with a rise in the Western standard of living' (AS I, 184). But on this Bataille will also differ with the economist François Perroux, in sensing that while 'the plan may be an "investment in the world's interest"', it may very easily be 'warped in the direction of the American interest' when its 'integration into the real political game becomes the question', which is something that Bataille found was really 'not treated in Perroux's work' (AS I, 183).[29]

This warping of the Plan is because for Bataille, 'in short, it has to be financed', where the way it was set up 'demands' a nation like the United States with 'a national income out of proportion with that of other nations' (AS I, 179). But this only points to the original 'failure' of the 'Bretton Woods agreements' (AS I, 175), Bataille regrets, and the 'inadequacy of the International Bank and the Monetary Fund' (AS I, 177) – which, in their residual deference to special interests, to 'the rule of *isolated* profit' (AS I, 176), could only have 'presented a negative version of the Marshall Plan's positive initiative' (AS I, 177). Bataille in fact saw how this was such that 'without the salutary fear of the Soviets (or some analogous threat), there would be no Marshall Plan' (AS I, 183) – a Plan which ultimately amounts, then, to 'the struggle of two economic methods', in 'an organization of surplus against the accumulation of the Stalin plans' (AS I, 173), when *coldly* integrated into 'the political game that opposes America and the USSR throughout the world' (AS I, 175).

What emerges here for Bataille is precisely our political '"schism", a complete rift' – *from left-to-right* – that 'divides not just minds, but the mind in general' (AS I, 169). And this is such that some, Bataille notes, will insist on seeing only 'an inhuman will embodied in the USSR', or 'the work of evil in the politics of the Kremlin'; that is, as merely the cruel 'continuation of a regime relying on a secret police, the muzzling of thought and numerous concentration camps', as if these dreadful horrors had not also 'responded to a pressing need' (AS I, 188). Bataille himself foresaw that 'calm would be completely unwarranted' if the Iron Curtain and Wall were to come down, as indeed occurred nigh three decades after his death, as three decades on from this, further still, we find ourselves as Bataille anticipated with 'more reason than ever to be afraid' (AS I, 188). For capitalism again has tightened its austere grip, squeezing fascism out the sides – as we find ourselves thrown back, in a seemingly bewildering time-warp, to a kind of 'post-modern 1930s'.[30]

Not enough was done to develop the aesthetic spaces for erotic consciousness, expenditure, expression and enjoyment – but it is in going back to such works as *Blue of Noon*, and the genealogies of *Consumption*, *Eroticism* and *Sovereignty* that Bataille as philosopher subsequently wrought in his three-volumed *Accursed Share*, that we are able to secure and continue the slow intellectual advances that have nevertheless been made: so as to finally oppose what Troppmann, at the close of *Blue of Noon*, would aptly portend as *the rising tide of murder*.

> As I found myself confronting this catastrophe, I was filled with the black irony that accompanies the moments of seizure when no one can help screaming. The music ended; the rain had stopped. I slowly returned to the station. The train was assembled. For a while I walked up and down the platform before entering a compartment. The train lost no time in departing.
>
> —Georges Bataille / Henri Troppmann, *Blue of Noon*, May, 1935

NOTES

1. See where Bataille states, 'consciousness of erotic truth anticipates the end of history' (AS II, 190). While consciousness and reason may seem anathema to readings of Bataille focused on his a-theology works of the occupation, as Stein points out, 'this stress on mysticism and inner-experience represents only one period of Bataille's total output' and addresses 'just one element of Bataille's more complex notion of heterology and excess' – where Bataille's interest in such states, on the boundary of where science reaches its ever-shifting limits, does not at all make him 'a simple irrationalist opposed to the use of reason in any form'. Stein, "The Use and Abuse of History: Habermas's Misreading of Bataille," 53–5.

2. Kendall, *Georges Bataille*, 120. Ffrench, "Bataille's Literary Writings," in *Georges Bataille*, eds., Hewson, Coelen, 192. For the reprinting of Part One of *Blue of Noon*, see part 3 of Bataille, *Inner Experience*, 82–3. For the work of Laure (Colette) Peignot see *Laure: The Collected Writings*, trans. J. Herman (San Francisco: City Lights, 2001).

3. Kendall and Stoekl note that it was Dr Camille Dausse who specifically made the referral to Borel, given his known affinity for working with artists. Kendall, *Georges Bataille*, 47, 49, 121. Stoekl, "Introduction," in Bataille, VE, x.

4. Leiris mentions this in his contribution to the *Hommage à Georges Bataille* of *Critique* (1963), where he also notes that 'one episode of this novel [W.C.] survived as the story of Dirty' which was 'first published on its own' for the magazine *Fontaine* (1928), then 'used again as the introduction to *Blue of Noon*'. Stoekl, "Introduction," in Bataille, VE, x. Leiris, "From Bataille the Impossible to the Impossible *Documents*," in Bataille, Leiris, *Correspondence*, 10; first published in *Critique* 195–196 (1963): 685–93.

5. Kendall, *Georges Bataille*, 119. Freud, "Remembering, Repeating, and Working-Through (1914)," SE12, 147, 155.

6. Leiris records how Bataille once spoke to him 'about a novel in which he fictionalized himself in the guise of the famous murderer Georges Troppmann (his partial namesake) but which later took the form of a first-person narrative', which could 'have been W.C.' Kendall notes the actual murderer was 'Jean-Baptiste Troppmann, who murdered a family of eight in 1869 and was guillotined for his trouble', known because 'Rimbaud includes the names of the murderer and his victims' in his '"Paris" poem contributed to the *Album Zutique*'. Kendall also suggests that the 'Henri' of *Blue of Noon* might reference one of his victims, Henri Kinch, while 'in a French-English pun, Troppmann can be read as meaning "too much man"'. Leiris, "From Bataille the Impossible to the Impossible *Documents*," in Bataille, Leiris, *Correspondence*, 9–10. Kendall, *Georges Bataille*, 48.

7. Kendall cites Bataille's 'La Cadavre Maternal' to record how two years before this 1930 episode with his mother's corpse he had 'held an orgy in her apartment, in her bed, on his birthday', the memory of which kindled his desire before the corpse but also froze it: so he had to go 'into the kitchen to finish' – while his wife Sylvia, pregnant with daughter Laurence, was 'asleep in the next room'. Diana Boczkowski analyses a similarly strange episode with Pierre Molinier who, after his sister's death, 'experienced an orgasm while caressing her legs during the wake' – becoming thence 'the inventor of surrealist photography' in his ensuing work, where 'legs proliferate'. Bataille, "W.C. Preface to *Story of the Eye from Le Petit: 1943*," in SE, 76. Kendall, *Georges Bataille*, 83–4, 219n. Bataille, "La Cadavre Maternal," in *Oeuvres Completes* 2 (Paris: Gallimard, 1970–88), 130. Boczkowski, "Neither Loss nor Mourning, but Perversion," in *Perversion Now!*, eds., Caine, Wright, 171.

8. Ffrench, "Dirty Life," in *The Beast at Heaven's Gate*, ed. Hussey, 69. Kendall, *Georges Bataille*, 119. Simone Petrémont, *La Vie de Simone Weil* (Paris: Fayard, 1973), 308.

9. Kendall, *Georges Bataille*, 88–9, 94.

10. Due to the mechanism of condensation, Kendall also gives examples of why it is impossible to fully 'equate' anyone in Bataille's life 'completely with a figure from his fiction'. Kendall, *Georges Bataille*, 93, 107, 119–20.

11. Hussey, "Fascism and the Politics of 1930s France," in *Georges Bataille*, eds. Hewson, Coelen, 56, 51.

12. Richardson, *Georges Bataille*, 92–3.

13. Ffrench, "Bataille's Literary Writings," in *Georges Bataille*, eds., Hewson, Coelen, 196.

14. Kendall, *Georges Bataille*, 79, 120.

15. The ambiguity of the term 'Xenie' in Greek in denoting hospitality while also connoting foreignness is that hospitality is usually what one shows to strangers or foreigners, to whom we may equally seem both strange or foreign. See entries ξενία and ξένιος in Liddell and Scott, *A Greek-English Lexicon*, 1188–9; also available at Crane, ed. *Perseus Digital Library*, http://www.perseus.tufts.edu/hopper/morph?l=ceni%2Fa&la=greek&can=ceni%2Fa0&prior=ce/nhqen#lexicon (accessed June 30, 2020).

16. For more on Simone Weil's known desexualized virginal presence and her mystical Christian conversion experience, see the discussion with Beatrice Han-Pile, Stephen Plant, and David Levy in BBC Radio 4, *In Our Time*, "Simone Weil," prod. Natalia Fernandez, https://www.bbc.co.uk/programmes/b01nthz3 (accessed June 30, 2020). Ffrench, "Dirty Life," in *The Beast at Heaven's Gate*, ed. Hussey, 70.

17. See entries δῶρον and θεά in Liddell and Scott, *A Greek-English Lexicon*, 465, 786.

18. This over-wrought threat is a version of the 'second death' (SVII, 251, 254, 260, 285) that Lacan discloses when discussing Antigone, who first dies to the socio-symbolic order when banished for defying Creon's law, whereupon she awaits her actual physical death as a second. In terms of the Christian-Platonic afterlife structure that was to dominate from the century after Sophocles, the second death is of the allegedly immortal soul's chances in an imagined heaven. For more discussion of the second death see Themi, *Lacan's Ethics and Nietzsche's Critique of Platonism*, 41–3, 47, 52–5, 60–1, 146n, 150n.

19. Kendall, *Georges Bataille*, 86–7, 89.

20. ffrench, "Bataille's Literary Writings," in *Georges Bataille*, eds. Hewson, Coelen, 194–5, 198, 200.

21. With appropriate rigour Stein also concludes that from a gross misreading 'Habermas misses all together the nuances of Bataille's anti-fascism and his subtle critique of the Enlightenment's tendency to totalize rational discourse'. In Lacanian terms, the latter is the fantasy of reducing the entirety of the imaginary register to the symbolic, as if for Good. Stein, "The Use and Abuse of History: Habermas's Misreading of Bataille," 53, 55.

22. See essay III, "What Is the Meaning of Ascetic Ideals?" in Nietzsche's *On the Genealogy of Morals*.

23. Deutscher, *Stalin: A Political Biography* (London: Oxford, 1949), 342.

24. Karl Marx, Friedrich Engels, *The Communist Manifesto*, in *Karl Marx: Selected Writings*, ed. L. H. Simon (Indianapolis: Hackett, 1994), 182–3.

25. For the entry of psychoanalysis into China before the Communist era, its banning from 1949 as a bourgeois superstition, and its 'accelerated reintroduction since the late 1980s', see David Scharff, "Psychoanalysis in China: An Essay on the Recent Literature in English," *The Psychoanalytic Quarterly* 85.4 (2016): 1037–67.

26. The difficulty that analysts themselves can encounter here is expressed in Frederick Hacker's observation that the same act of social protest can be interpreted by some as an 'uncontrolled acting out of unresolved Oedipal and other infantile conflicts', while by others as a 'heroic sublimation authentically expressing a truly humane vision'. A full discussion of Lacan's four-discourses of *Seminar XVII*, including the master's and analyst's discourses and the rotations between them and that of the university and the hysteric, can be found in section 6.1 of Themi, *Lacan's Ethics and Nietzsche's Critique of Platonism*. Horbury, "Digital Feminisms and the Split Subject: Short-circuits through Lacan's Four-Discourses," *CM: Communication and Media* XI.38 (2016): 135, 160. Hacker, "Sublimation Revisited," *International Journal of Psychoanalysis* 53 (1972): 218.

27. R. H. Tawney, *Religion and the Rise of Capitalism*, 112.

28. See *Matthew* 19:25, *Mark* 10:25, *Luke* 18:25 in *The Bible*; and Lacan, *Seminar VIII*, 49, 60.

29. Bataille is referring to Perroux's *Le Plan Marshall ou l'Europe Nécessaire au Monde* (Paris: Librairie de Médicis, 1948).

30. This evocative phrase belongs to Yanis Varoufakis, the economics professor with a well-articulated theory of how a surplus-recycling mechanism should amend the crises of capitalism and contemporary regressions to extremist political forms. A Bataillean *general* economic analysis of capitalism and the 'superstructures' of fascism would also, however, add much needed philosophical and psychoanalytic specificity and depth to the economic sophistication of his oeuvre – especially for tackling the motivational deficits encountered where the plea for rationality is read as a special consideration or demand for charity. While Bataille's own point of departure on 'the Bretton Woods agreements', 'their failure', and 'the inadequacy of the International Bank and the Monetary Fund', was Perroux (AS I, 175) – the atomic physicist Georges Ambrosino was also originally meant to co-author the *Consumption* volume I of *Accursed Share*, to assist with the studying of 'the movements of energy on the surface of the globe' (AS I, 191n). A Varoufakis work on the current Eurozone corruption has recently been made into a film by Costas-Gavras. Varoufakis, *And the Weak Suffer what they Must? Europe's Crisis and America's Economic Future* (New York: Nation Books, 2016), xvii, 238. Costas-Gavras, *Adults in the Room* (Athens-Paris: KG Productions, with Odeon, France 2 Cinéma, Wild Bunch and Canal+, 2019).

Conclusion

This book began as an exploration of how Bataille's erotics of the real, broaching the heterogeneous objects of taboo that *touch* the drive's *jouissance* in the real, might contribute to Lacan's ethics of psychoanalysis. This was where the latter was broadly construed as an ethics of desire, self-knowledge, and sublimation I situated from the space broke open by Nietzsche's debunking of Plato's Supreme Good for inflating *too far* from earthly, bodily nature to the point of moralistic ignorance, prejudice, and destruction – particularly in its later Christian form from the close of the Greco-Roman empire. A new ethics founds itself on the basis of Nietzsche's critique, of what he dubbed the 'anti-nature' turn in morality (TI V, 4; EH IV, 7), and Lacan's own ethics – able to draw also on *Freudian* experience – could throw much light on this at the level of the polymorphous libido and its partial drives, with its mnesic entanglements forever repeating, and working through, in the passes and the gorges of the signifier.

The aim, then, was to see how Bataille's genealogy of erotics, as a history of the shifting, mutating structures of taboo and *jouissance* of transgression across time, might further develop – and be itself developed by – this Nietzsche, Freud, Lacan *revolution*, or '*revaluation of all values*' (EH IV, 1), as Nietzsche coined it, in the field of ethics. But of particular importance soon became the role of *aesthetics* in this, emerging as the superlative space for a sublimated outlet of an erotics on the basis of an ethics. And here the task became to further articulate the connections between ethics, erotics, and aesthetics, and how Bataille, increasingly, began to theorize a distinction which is also a relation between art and politics approximating to that between transgression and taboo – so as to better stress their independent sovereignty in terms of *libidinal* as well as political economy.

On reaching the age of sixty, moreover, in 1957 as his recognition continued to grow with the publication of *Eroticism, Literature and Evil*, and *Blue of Noon* all in the same year, Bataille was commissioned by the original publisher of *Critique* to found another journal. It was to be illustrated like his earlier *Documents*, but this time focussed solely on eroticism, and subtitled 'Sexology, Psychoanalysis, Philosophy of Sexuality'.[1] By the close of 1958, however, with Bataille unwilling to cede his scholarly frame to the publisher's demand for ever more scandalous content, the project collapsed. And so, consequently, while again indicating the centrality of sexuality and aesthetics to his mature concerns, Bataille reconfigured the illustrations he had collected into what would make up his final text: that on the history of artistic erotic expression, of *eroticizing* aesthetics, *The Tears of Eros* of 1961.

It almost counted as a secret history of being. But featuring the photo of a torture oddly given to him by his analyst Borel more than thirty years prior, it was to be banned by the French Ministry of Culture, after Bataille's death in 1962. In this perhaps it even serves as a final reminder of the need for a more harmonious interrelation, which is *neither chasm nor conflation*, between the oft-excessive expressions of art and moralistic demands of politics: corresponding in Bataille to the dual and sometimes *duelling* necessities of transgression and taboo.

In considering, then, how the different discourses of Lacan and Bataille, as an ethics and erotics of the real respectively, might extend on each other, chapter 1 suggested focus on the heterogeneous real was necessitated by the distortions Nietzsche points to when Plato's ideal of the Good was *inflated* in the imaginary as if it were real, exacerbated by Christendom to ape cruelty itself, then artificially 'naturalized' or overturned, without overcoming, throughout our Modernity of today. Lacan's *Ethics* Seminar itself had called for an enquiry that goes 'more deeply into' the real instead of the ideal, that looks at what occurs 'between Aristotle and Freud' (SVII, 11) and introduces 'an erotics that is above morality' (SVII, 84) – a directive reissued in his *Anxiety* Seminar as 'any morality is to be sought out, in its principle and in its origin, on the side of the real' (SX, 148) – despite the initial unease this can cause.

Emerging from this was how only an *erotics* of the real can prevent an ethics from again taking-flight in what Lacan calls a 'moralizing hustle or a bluff, whose dangers cannot be exaggerated' (SVII, 312) – namely that which only ever *re-finds* its disavowed real by distorted projections onto an *Other* that is demonized in the process. The Christian Dark Ages, with its crusades and inquisitions, its neuroses and psychoses, is forever testament to that – as Nietzsche's strident rejection of the Christian-Platonic metaphysics central to Western morals first saw. I suggested through Bataille that restoring something more of a *living-openness* to the erotic means an ethics no longer has the need to disavow what it can now more fully *enjoy* – empowered here psychoanalytically within the restructured other limits that our pre-Platonic cultures can help exemplify.

Bataille's genealogy of the *sacred* from the optic of the taboo–transgression relation proved insightful here – as formulated through his engagement with the anthropology of Mauss – as did Nietzsche's analysis of the *Birth of Tragedy* in pre-Platonic Greece and of the myths they made use, helping us to re-conceive of a kind of aesthetic space that enabled this mutual supporting of ethics and erotics to take place. Traversing, however, from our initial Palaeolithic *animal-to-human* transition to the classical age and then to what Lacan called 'Socrates' profound incompetence' on tragedy (SVIII, 81) – that which protracted in the Platonism to follow, including in Aristotle's attempted materialist 'conversion' of it (SVIII, 5) – what was evident was the *loss* of the religious aspect of erotic transgression, leaving us with lack of access to our latent animality, which was thereby abandoned, discredited, and relegated *to* the unconscious.

After Plato, transgression was a spitting on the dignity of the Good, rather than its expected complement through a periodic need to return to the real – a repression worsened when Christianity reduced transgression to *sin*, which left it condemned, and hearkened back to what Lacan saw as 'Yahweh's ferocious ignorance' of sacred practices based specifically on nature and *sexual* knowledge (SXVIII, 116, 136). Modern science's attempts to later reclaim a positivity for taboo-objects then fell short, because the relation of taboo-and-transgression remained insufficiently understood – functioning inconsistently, *in* the unconscious, to *externalize* a material reference interspersed still with unanalysed fragments of idealism. After two millennia of repression, blindness about desire still held sway, as *inner*-experience of its configuration of the partial drives and objects disclosed by Freud was relegated to a past of morose naiveties in confessional praxis, while sex-positivism went about in its *all-too* merry way.

As Richardson put it, this is because Judaeo-Christian ideology progressively 'served to tear our inner experience from itself' by installing 'work ethic to all areas of social life' – cutting 'adrift' the chances of any genuinely knowing erotic transgression with a 'puritan detachment', that now even permissiveness cannot restore.[2] Here is where, through Bataille's engagement with Weber on the rise of Calvinism from the Protestant reformation, we saw how a foreclosure of transgression on the ethical plane of libidinal-economy was transferred further into *political*-economy, as the aim of accumulation became only *more* accumulation and 'profit' constitutes the Good. Anything heterogeneous thus becomes waste, or reduced to a *pseudo*-symbolic service of goods through a *violent* commodification of the globe. For capitalist homogeneity overwhelms 'every aspect of life', Richardson concludes, so that 'sacred forms like festival, play, and sacrifice can no longer be integrated' – never adequately anyway, beyond the mean begrudging *eye* of the market – due to what Bataille calls the 'unreserved surrender to *things*, heedless of consequences and seeing nothing beyond them' (AS I, 136).[3]

Violence can indeed be so ubiquitous that Bataille at one point will simply equate *nature* with it (E, 40). But this is not to say that ideology, whether Christian, Platonist, or Calvinist, does not make it worse, where within each irruption one can still discern the *signifier* leaving its trace – pointing to a foreclosure playing itself out as a destining trying waywardly, vengefully, to unfold. Chapter 2 then saw how Bataille's 1928 erotic novella *Story of the Eye*, with its stunning 'linguis-tricks' that did not escape the attention of Barthes and Lacan – wrought around a narration of transgression akin to that at the level of words – might metaphorize a break from this infinite regress of excessive taboo that displaces into ever more destruction, which then paradoxically calls for, and hypocritically profits from, more and more rounds of precisely the kinds of repressive taboo that initially were the cause.

Combining here the linguistic approach of Barthes with the similarly formal approach to analysis of Lacan was found to shed more light on the eye metaphor's meaning, as its metonymic cross-cutting, between different relations of verbs and nouns, was shown to go beyond the bar of resistance normally characterizing a fetish series of objects – to reveal, rather, the whole of Bataille's *Freudian* Thing in all its mnesic, unconscious formations. This pertained to the primal scene of his blind, syphilitic father's upturned eye while urinating – while the child Bataille was secretly *watching* – a memory overlaid by that of his mother's dress *looking* like it was pissing the creek water, when later she went mad, tried to drown herself, and Bataille *saw* her *there*.

Such horror seems to predestine the young Bataille here, even later as analysand. But it is in *working-through* such material in a dissident surrealist way, under the auspices of the analyst Borel, that the violence of the *Story* inflicted on the metaphoric substitutes of the eye – in their cross-cutting copulations with liquids such as milk, yolk, and urine – is eventually shown to uncover the *gaze*, to mix in fluidity with seeing itself. This is what metaphorizes as an attack on the sources of repression that would fixate taboo and spurn the sacred play of transgression – culminating in the attack on the *Eye* of the Priest, standing in for 'the eye of bad conscience' in the final climatic scene. The gratuitous element of the violence, particularly on ostensibly innocent characters such as the pretty cyclist or the luscious streetwalker from Madrid, also indicated a transitional Sadean stage for working towards a more finely balanced relation of taboo and transgression: although the early Bataille was already more advanced than Sade in this, whose excesses by comparison lacked any decent meaning.

In sum, it was found that the meaning of the eye is the gaze apropos of the *split* between them articulated by Lacan, as per the substitution metaphor formulated in *Écrits* to cross the bar separating conscious from unconscious, or signifier from the signified of the sexed drive *in the real*. This further confronts the meaning of the text that the young Bataille intuited through his analysis, opening up the possibility of a better ethical response to the heterogeneous real of animality, forever raging beneath the bars of Western metaphysics and savagely vengeful in its returns. In this I recommend a healthier, more open relation to taboo, where the bar is not so fixed and disavowed but more suitably nuanced and porous, enables a world where violence can be attenuated through more properly sublimated outlets for erotic transgression, within an overall structure of a widened taboo. Lastly, I suggested the excessive violence of Bataille's *Story* metaphorizes a signpost along the road of a balance that remains to be gotten right, both in the genealogical development of Bataille's own oeuvre *and* in our own sociohistorical world at large.

Chapter 3 then uncovered what further kinds of aesthetic criteria can be extracted from such of Bataille's interventions in the artistic world, starting from the critique of aesthetics enacted by his early work with *Documents* – as a critique of the more idealist surrealists – which increasingly incorporated a passion for Palaeolithic art and Nietzsche. I suggested, moreover, that by reading Bataille's early and later work together along with Nietzsche's previous interventions into aesthetics – but also with the kindred psychoanalytic concepts discovered by Freud just after Nietzsche and articulated further by Bataille's contemporary in Lacan – we could further understand just what kinds of aesthetics, and roles for aesthetics, Bataille would recommend.

As Kennedy was to put it, in a thesis later commended by Richman for lifting scholarly recognition for 'sovereign aesthetics', politics and art become equally important to Bataille but linked to two very different necessities and freedoms: 'the necessity to fight oppression and exploitation, on the one hand, and the necessity to leave all necessity behind, on the other'.[4] This is why I argued that a sovereign aesthetics must be a structured but transgressive opening onto our normally quite rightly prohibited animal roots – as a *jouissance* of the real that is a *joy in the real* – affirming more the sovereignty of the present moment than subordinating it to concerns for future. It is the most direct enjoyment that is possible, namely one that is neither neurotically ignorant of its sexual and aggressive base material, nor its perverse and formless animal origins, but which can nonetheless be safely affirmed through the psychoanalytically disclosed mechanism of sublimation that governs artistic process. For this is what can be *raising* an object, an ordinary earthly, animal, bodily object, to what Lacan called the *dignity* of the Freudian Thing, that it affirms and also in a sense, at least in part, condescends to below.

With such a reopening, sublimated *conduit* of raising and descending, we overcome any mutually exclusive binaries of high or low, beauty or ugly, neurosis or perversion, or worse, and so on, stifling the history of aesthetics and culture analysis, through a more knowing, all-encompassing cycle of affirmation of the Nietzschean eternal return. For as Freud pointed out it in his *Three Essays*, there is always 'a mixture, in every proportion, of efficiency, perversion, and neurosis', depending on the 'completeness or incompleteness of the sublimation' (SE7, 238) – but even in the works of our greatest achievers such as *Leonardo da Vinci*, whose 'extraordinary capacity for sublimating the primitive instincts', in those sovereign moments of enhanced efficiency when he managed to surpass his neurotic vacillation, 'left his epoch far behind' (SE11, 133-4). It means that by encouraging the Nietzschean aesthetic state of physiological *abundance*, linked to the divine animality that Bataille beholds of Palaeolithic art to have bestrode across all the non-Christian-Platonic religions at the heart of the West, we ourselves can overcome the forced reduction of art to *lack*. For such a reduction remains caught in what Nietzsche's 1886 *Beyond Good and Evil* saw as 'the fundamental faith of the metaphysicians' in '*the faith in opposite values*' (BGE, 2) – with the 'awkwardness' of its 'talk of opposites where there are only degrees and many subtleties of gradations' (BGE, 24) – as if the difference between lack and abundance were a binary or zero-sum game with a falsely hollowed out, excluded middle that implies because we cannot have absolute abundance, we must somehow (dis)content ourselves with absolute lack.[5]

I showed, then, how the eternal return between high and low can be *not* like a return-of-the-repressed *as* repressed in the depressingly neurotic symptom sense, or in the perverse disavowal sense which leads to blind fetish, or in the psychotic foreclosure of the symbolic sense that goes madly devoid of any mediation at all – and returns now *too explosively* in the real. Rather, this return is more like the classically attuned Apollo-Dionysos dynamic in Nietzsche, the ameliorated taboo–transgression or human–animal correlation of Bataille, but also the now deepened symbolic-imaginary distinction in Lacan. For here the imaginary corresponds to the greater dominance of the aesthetic realm governed by animal erotic transgression, and the symbolic to the greater dominance of the political governed by human reason and taboo – two modes for Bataille that should be distinctly preserved in keeping with their respective sovereignties, and differing relations kept with the real.

The Nietzschean affirmation of the whole of this cycle of eternal return, refocused between an equally valued human *and* animal aspect with the directives Bataille extracts from the paintings of Lascaux, is what delivers a criterion of aesthetics to foster sublimation of the right abundance of distance-*and-nearness* to the usually unconscious Freudian Thing. This is especially where the latter is psychoanalytically reattuned by Lacan to the signifying aspect of the drive, at what Freud so aptly called the 'frontier between the mental and the somatic' (SE14, 122) in his 1915 'Instincts [*Trieb*] and Their Vicissitudes' – *there* where endosomatic instincts meet their ideational representation, which constitutes what Lacan calls *the drive's* innate mixture of 'plasticity and limits' (SVII, 31). Aesthetic criteria can hereby emerge to overcome the nihilism of privileging *inflated* Icarian heights cut-off from our inherited animal roots, or of privileging the overdetermined lows this causes when such escapist flights run aground – which, whether in phobic or fetish form, are a return-of-the-repressed in some kind of monstrous, under-analysed, and thus un-sublimated form.

The emergence of such criteria also demonstrates the great value in reading Bataille's early dissident surrealism not only with his later passion for Palaeolithic art and the sovereignty of Nietzsche's rejecting of Christian effort to *denature* our animal body, but also with related psychoanalytic concepts such as sublimation and the real. This is particularly insofar as the aim is to sublimate a healthy strength of animal vigour, or *blooming* physicality, as Nietzsche terms the empowering function of the aesthetic state: one to more effectively defeat the reductive lack promulgated by the denaturalizing nihilism that taints the world in forms both high and low – by better importing the *real* of transgression, and its *jouissance, to* the totality of being.

Chapter 4 then saw how at the initial interface of philosophy and psychoanalysis, occurring between Nietzsche and Freud in the Germanophone context of the late nineteenth century, stands Nietzsche's more affirming comportment towards the drives relative to Freud – who while himself is no hyper-negater, still seems by comparison sometimes closer to a Schopenhauerian pessimism about desiring will, which tends towards resignation. This is where our previous metaphysical idealist, religious world-views are reacted against for their veiled nihilism or make-believe structure, but not the negative devaluations of earthly, bodily sexual life which they enshrined and of which they were symptom – leaving us stranded upon a stripped back earth with nothing but their underlying pessimism towards the real. We saw, then, how this residue of difference between Nietzsche and Freud, amidst all the many anticipations in Nietzsche of the findings of psychoanalysis, which Freud acknowledged, translated also into the more *erotic* kind of aesthetics that Bataille later took up in his more positive reinvestment of surrealism after the war – at the price of Sartre and the rise of existentialism – which Lacan's more modernist Freudian insights could be used to further support as well.

What emerged was how the modernist sensibility to dare to create the new, which surrealism partook in with its use of Freudian techniques of free-association, could become the grounds through which Bataille's work could radically restructure the relation of taboo and transgression, and thereby society, with a definitive role reserved for the arts. Nietzsche, here, supplies the force of Dionysos, Freud the detailed mechanisms of libido, and Lacan the deflationary ontology of the real, symbolic, and imaginary – all of which to help stabilize this transformative aesthetic practice within a psychoanalytic ethics of self-knowledge and sublimation, but also of erotic *experience*. Greek tragedy from our classical pre-Platonic past, and surrealist modernism closer to the present – along with the Renaissance project in between – provided examples of how we can strategically re-access what of enduring value was unjustly lost of our archaic past, by the torturous vicissitudes of Christian-Platonism, so as to *renew* ourselves for the present in future.

In short, what these findings serve to demonstrate is how *re*-reading Nietzsche and psychoanalysis back together, where they began in the late nineteenth-century Germanophone context, is beneficial both for psychoanalysis and philosophy *and* for culture in general. For by tracing this combined heritage from its source in Nietzsche and Freud forward to the twentieth-century Francophone context of surrealist modernism, where we find together the more Nietzschean Bataille and Freudian Lacan – across a span of time and place traditionally thought to be that of modernism itself – we find exemplified by what Bataille-and-Lacan were ensconced in, as combined Freudo-Nietzschean practitioners of the symbolic-and-imaginary modes of the real, an initial movement rearward that eventually enables us to leap radically forward, with a new *eroticizing aesthetics*, ethics, and ontology, suitable for our world's progressive amelioration.

Chapter 5 then discovered how Bataille's treatment of the literary arts specifically – including the novel of which he was, of course, a great exponent himself – soon comes upon his fundamental position in aesthetics as a whole. This was in discerning the key tendencies in literature to be a *conflict* between the happiness of taboo (as in accumulation and security) and the happiness of transgression (as in expenditure and risk), while also offering what could be extracted as a distinct programme to clarify and improve the situation – to make such a conflict less deadly. What began, then, with a discernible quest for 'happiness' in literature, channelling Nietzsche at the expense of Kant's more sterile notion of aesthetic disinterest, soon took on a dual structure embroiling us in what ostensibly looked like 'evil' – that is, in the periodic *transgression* of our fundamental taboos as necessary to 'happiness' as the taboos themselves – of which poetic literature in particular could afford us much insight.

In Lacanian terms, Bataille's articulation of this taboo–transgression conflict in literature, which becomes more like a *correlation* through a greater clarity of consciousness about the two forms of happiness Bataille enables, is itself the work of the register of the *symbolic*. This is what was defined from chapter 1 as the clear, conceptual use of words and concepts which are rational, knowledge and science based, logical and empirical, and where the later

Bataille as philosopher, scholar, reviewer of scholarly works, and editor of a journal normally exists – as do we presumably ourselves – in the space governed by the everyday, workaday, moral taboos, governing our reserves. But when immediately Bataille comes across a contrary need for transgression of these taboos, it is because such taboos create distance from the *real* of our animal-bodily drives pertaining explicitly to sex and death that are registered in terms of enjoyment (*jouissance*) – and the demand for the latter, as what Lacan calls the most 'direct satisfaction' (SVII, 92, 200) of the drive, is a debt that also, periodically, needs to be repaid. 'Sublimate as much as you like', as Lacan at the end of his *Ethics* even puts it, for still 'you have to pay for it with something. And this something is called jouissance' (SVII, 322). What this chapter demonstrated, then, is how this debt to the real can be repaid in a more psychoanalytically attuned *imaginary* register, through creativity and transgressive works of art such as poetic literature – which we saw through Prévert and Char does not reduce itself to the ostensive utility or pre-given use-value of words, and can thereby open up subjective possibilities in the *real* usually excluded for being evil or *impossible*.

I suggested that to get the balance right here between the poetic and the rational, always at loggerheads and approximating to the duelling happinesses of transgression and taboo – which to each other can look like opposite forms of evil – is a matter of the right amount of distance-*and*-nearness between the two domains of art and science. But this is appended to how in Lacan's *Ethics* the different 'forms of sublimation' underpinning these two key aspects of civilization themselves amount to a different optimum of distance-nearness to the real or 'the Thing' (SVII, 129). Here, then – as per 'the slope of that difference' opened up by Lacan's focus on the Thing's signifying outer by distinguishing 'the *Trieb* [drive]' from 'the *Instinkt* [instinct]' (SVII, 90)[6] – we saw how in art we want to be *closer*, but not to the point of an annihilating irrationality that leaves no route back, and also how in science we wanted more *distance*, but no so much that creativity is coldly foreclosed and our works resemble a successful paranoia.

Knowledge of this difference of degrees between art and science is what can also constitute the path between the two realms Bataille sought, to stop them interfering with each other. For such an interference we saw in Blake's exaltation of the tiger-like violence of the French Revolution, in a poem that affirms a politics that for the mature Bataille thus flies too far from reason. But such an interference we also saw in the art for art's sake sentiment that led one critic to condemn Masson for producing 'thought-painting', as if complete absence from intelligence was what in any way for Bataille art required, too.

I showed in this that Bataille would have similar rebukes for critics who would make the same condemnation about 'thought literature', or attempts to properly *think* the novel while still experiencing, as much as each instant allows, its transgressive force as a real *jouissance*. In Lacanian terms, what matters only is that we fasten the real, symbolic, and imaginary in a more analytically attuned and conscientious way, within the singularities of our own levels of knowledge and experience of *jouissance*. And this is such that symptoms dissolve, worked through the drive's signifying memorializations to open out to their source – with different emphases in place during the times for work, reason, politics and taboo, and during the spaces for artistic, erotic play, expenditure, release and transgression.

This stress on the distinction between art and politics, which is also crucially still a relation, raised then the question of just how to broach the topic of politics in art, if at all, and whether Bataille in fact himself had provided a superlative example of it. To this end chapter 6 then saw how the deathly expressions of eroticism in Bataille's 1935 political novel *Blue of Noon*, cast against the 1930s rise of fascism, can also help us understand how today fascism has again arisen amidst mute attempts to oppose. But for this it became important to understand how fascism's twin rivals of communism and capitalism both arose in rejection of the distorted sovereignty in the Monarchic feudal structure, which was ultimately for Bataille a medieval form of 'moralizing (enslaving) sovereignty mired in Christianity' (AS III, 368), which failed to produce. It was also important to recall how *before* that, at the roots of the Western traditions, was the in many key ways more optimal archaic paradigm discussed by Bataille, especially significant through Nietzsche's emphasis on *pre*-Christian-Platonic Greece.

In the course of analysing the figures of Lazare, Xenie, Dirty, and Troppmann, evinced was how latent therein, and struggling to re-emerge, is something of this archaic paradigm of the drive as erotic gift, rather than as accursed share, that could be better incorporated in our advanced symbolic structures today. This is so as to deepen while securing them for further advances – lest we regress to some barbarism on the right or puritanism on the left, which, of course, like Lazare's, is a moralizing-enslaving barbarism still. I argued thus that *Blue of Noon* is central to this task for our today, of mitigating the return of fascism and inadequacy of communism, spurred by the repeating crises of capitalism in the West. For it shows how a confrontation with libidinalized obsessions of death, worked towards greater consciousness through Bataille's genealogy of the sacred but accursed share, can help us resist the nationalist regressions of our most recent past – where, instead, like Dirty and Troppmann but with greater lucidity and analysis, we can only now *fall* into the void of the sky, as part of a cycle affirmed eternally as such: so as to better balance the human with the animal aspects of desire, and thus defuse the ticking bomb of the occluded, archaic instinctual world.

Previously the latter was relegated in its sovereignty, but Bataille as analyst saw how this is only 'insofar as consciousness deceives us', to think it something that *merely* 'seems to belong to the past', which in actual fact is 'leaving our most deeply rooted desires in the penumbra of the unconscious' (AS III, 225). Hence, the problem is still as Freud disclosed in his *Three Essays*, where the perverse component drives of the libido have only here undergone a 'repression', which, he adds, 'it must be insisted, is not equivalent to their being abolished' (SE7, 237). Moreover for Freud, as stressed in his 1914 *On Narcissism: An Introduction*, was how sublimation was meant to be the 'way out' of such repression (SE14, 95) – in that it enabled libidinal excitations to find 'an outlet and use in other fields' while boosting their efficiency, as 'one of the origins of artistic activity' (SE7, 238). This points to the importance of Bataille's articulation of a coordinated separation between art and politics for re-broaching such repressed contents of the sovereign unconscious – insofar as we are lured to the later by the artistic expression of it erotically as *jouissance*, even in some kind of symbolic death, but with a newly developed consciousness of it so.

In this *Blue of Noon* becomes the superlative example for how a work of art can masterfully broach the political without letting it also elide the importance of the erotic, for which the aesthetic should be the privileged place. This again is because art invokes the creative imaginary, fuelled by the drives and the return of ordinarily repressed animality, through a seemingly ruinous, non-productive expenditure – granting here the sublimated outlets the drives require by transgressing the taboos that govern accumulation, which should rather belong to the socio-symbolic register of science, reason, and the times to return to concerns of work, belonging more in the political. *Blue of Noon* demonstrates the need for this separation, and, by way of the moralism of Lazare, the superficiality of Xenie, and the raw erotics of Dirty-Dorothea, the consequences of its absence as a distorted political – while still excelling in its main aesthetic task, through Troppmann's many dream-like travails, of being an outlet for the singularly enhanced levels of expression of our erotic *jouissance*.

Such a coordinated separation of art and politics is what later emerged most fully from Bataille's abandoned attempts with *Acéphale* – that secret Nietzschean society forged in the fires of the late 1930s to reconnect art with religion, as if to weaponize it with the extra affective force required to *immediately* transform the political. But it is also what emerged from his creative atheological mysticism during the despondent days of NAZI occupation, which Bataille even invokes in the conclusion to the opening volume of *Accursed Share*, written as it was between 1946 and 1949. This is where in refusing to find completion in the political project of an 'improvement in the global standard of living', which he considers rather a 'starting point' (AS I,

189), Bataille insists that part of 'this book on economy' is situated 'in the line of mystics of all times', while being 'nonetheless far removed from all the presuppositions of the various mysticisms' (AS I, 197n), with their *literal* beliefs in 'divinities and myths' (AS I, 189) – to which Bataille feels he need oppose here 'only the lucidity of self-consciousness' (AS I, 197n).

And so, finally, after the war, mature and scholarly like a phoenix from the ashes, Bataille concludes with the emphasis that politics must remain *exclusively rational* by preserving and affirming the required separate time-space for the effusiveness of the animal drives in art, while both art and politics remain devoid of religion – such that there is much less under-employed libido lying about to be reappropriated in disingenuous ways: in secretly aestheticized, mystified and backwards tribalistic, and underhandedly re-sexualized ways.

No more significant achievement in a work of art, or philosophy, is possible, or more urgently needed for our today – where such things are again afoot, and to an extent forever will be. Such is the eternal incompleteness of the human condition, as always appended in some residual way to its initial Palaeolithic animal transition, by the establishment of taboo.

> More open, the mind discerns, instead of an antiquated teleology, the truth that silence alone does not betray.
>
> —Georges Bataille, *The Accursed Share: An Essay on General Economy Volume I, Consumption* (1946–1949, 190)

NOTES

1. For an account of Bataille's work on the 1957 Sexology journal, see Kendall, *Georges Bataille*, 206–7, 7.

2. Richardson, *Georges Bataille*, 104.

3. See also where Nietzsche writes, 'The most industrious of ages – ours – does not know how to make anything of all its industriousness and money, except always still more money and still more industriousness; for it requires more genius to spend than to acquire' (GS, 21). Further, in what equally applies to the left's obsessions with moralistic correctness, he notes, 'Our time, with its aspiration to remedy and prevent accidental distresses and to wage preventive war against disagreeable possibilities, is a time of the poor. Our "rich" – are poorest of all. The true purpose of all riches is forgotten' (WP, 61). The Christian-modern tendency to ban sex-work, for example, which worsens its problems, or to reduce it to a degraded commercialism, illustrates the absent sacred heterogeneity that could instead return, as perhaps with Napoleon's reaffirming-regulation of the bordellos, leading to their *Belle Époque* of

which Bataille saw the tail-end, or as with Solon's instating of them as Aphrodite *Pandemos* (for the people), with taxes generated for reciprocal gifts granted back to the polis. It is in this sense that Bataille hoped to deepen his *experience* of brothels as true churches again – namely as sacred temples of reciprocal erotic gift-giving beyond the narrowed mores of profits, 'sins', and production. I returned in section 2.3 here to Bataille's later exegesis of the logic of prostitution in *Eroticism* (132–7). A more recent defence of sex-work on consequentialist grounds is in Raja Halwani, *Philosophy of Love, Sex, and Marriage* (New York: Routledge, 2010), 170–7, 210–24. Richardson, *Georges Bataille*, 91.

4. Richman also notes that 'sovereignty is the recurrent keyword when Bataille writes about art' as it removes an object from 'the realm of things'. It is a shame, however, that Kennedy's thesis was published as a book in such an unedited, amateur form. Richman, "Art," in *Georges Bataille*, eds. Hewson, Coelen, 148, 158. Kennedy, *Towards an Aesthetic Sovereignty*, 275.

5. Nietzsche's deconstruction of faith in opposites is central to Deleuze's 1962 anti-Hegelian deployment of Nietzsche against belief in dialectics. Bataille himself discusses 'the mystical ancestors of the Hegelian dialectic' in his 1932 'The Critique of the Foundations of the Hegelian Dialectic', first published in *La Critique Sociale*, while noting where on Marxist issues, 'idealist prejudices' against nature aside, this otherwise 'religious form of thought' could still be useful to proletarian concerns 'as the class condemned by the bourgeoisie to a negative existence' (VE, 105, 107, 109, 114). Deleuze, *Nietzsche and Philosophy*, 157–8, 162.

6. Discussion of how the drive-instinct and object-Thing distinctions inform Lacan's solution to the problem of sublimation inherited from Freud should be sought in section 2.2 of Themi, *Lacan's Ethics and Nietzsche's Critique of Platonism*.

Bibliography

Agostini, Giulia. "Nietzsche." In *Georges Bataille: Key Concepts*, edited by M. Hewson and M. Coelen. London: Routledge, 2015.
Allison, David B. "Transgression and the Community of the Sacred." In *The Obsessions of Georges Bataille*, edited by A. Mitchell and J. Winfree. Albany: State University of New York Press, 2009.
Aristophanes. *The Clouds*. Translated by W. Arrowsmith. New York: New American Library, 1962.
Aristotle. *Poetics*. In *Aristotle in 23 Volumes, Volume 23*. Translated by W. H. Fyfe. Cambridge, MA: Harvard University Press, 1932.
Arppe, Tina. "Evil." In *Georges Bataille: Key Concepts*, edited by M. Hewson and M. Coelen. London: Routledge, 2015.
Assoun, Paul-Laurent. *Freud and Nietzsche*. Translated by R. L. Collier Jnr. London: Continuum, 2007.
Athanassakis, Apostolos N. and Benjamin M. Wolkow, eds. *The Orphic Hymns*. Translated by A. N. Athanassakis and B. M. Wolkow. Baltimore: The John Hopkins University Press, 2013.
Badiou, Alain. "Lacan and the Pre-Socratics." In *Lacan: The Silent Partners*, edited by S. Žižek. New York: Verso, 2006.
Barthes, Roland. "The Death of the Author." In *Image, Music, Text*. Translated by S. Heath. London: Fontana, 1977.
———. "The Metaphor of the Eye." Translated by J. A. Underwood. In Bataille, *Story of the Eye*. Translated by J. Neugroschal. London: Penguin, 2001.
Bass, Alan. *Interpretation and Difference: The Strangeness of Care*. Stanford: Stanford University Press, 2006.
Bataille, Georges. *L'Abbé C*. Translated by P. A. Facey. London: Marion Boyars, 2001.
———. *The Absence of Myth: Writings on Surrealism*. Translated by M. Richardson. London: Verso, 2006.

———. "The Absence of Myth." In *The Absence of Myth: Writings on Surrealism*. Translated by M. Richardson. London: Verso, 2006.

———. *The Accursed Share: An Essay on General Economy. Volume I: Consumption. Volume II: The History of Eroticism. Volume III: Sovereignty*. Translated by R. Hurley. New York: Zone Books, 1991, 1993.

———. *Acéphale 1936-1939*. Paris: Jean-Michel Place, 1995.

———. "The Age of Revolt." In *The Absence of Myth: Writings on Surrealism*. Translated by M. Richardson. London: Verso, 2006.

———. "André Masson." In *The Absence of Myth: Writings on Surrealism*. Translated by M. Richardson. London: Verso, 2006.

———. *L'Apprenti Sorcier: texts, letteres, documents, 1932-1939*, edited by M. Galletti. Paris: Editions de la Différence, 1999.

———. "Autobiographical Note [1958]." Translated by A. Michelson. *October* 36 (1986): 106–10.

———. "Base Materialism and Gnosticism." In *Visions of Excess: Selected Writings, 1927-1939*. Translated by A. Stoekl. Minneapolis: University of Minnesota Press, 1985.

———. "The Big Toe." In *Visions of Excess: Selected Writings, 1927-1939*. Translated by A. Stoekl. Minneapolis: University of Minnesota Press, 1985.

———. *Blue of Noon*. Translated by H. Mathews. London: Paladin Books, 1988.

———. "La Cadavre Maternal." In *Oeuvres Completes* 2. Paris: Gallimard, 1970–1988.

———. "The Castrated Lion." In *The Absence of Myth: Writings on Surrealism*. Translated by M. Richardson. London: Verso, 2006.

———. *The Cradle of Humanity: Pre-historic Art and Culture*. Translated by S. Kendall. New York: Zone Books, 2009.

———. "The Critique of the Foundations of the Hegelian Dialectic." In *Visions of Excess: Selected Writings, 1927-1939*. Translated by A. Stoekl. Minneapolis: University of Minnesota Press, 1985.

———. ed. *Critique (Journal)*. Paris: Les Éditions de Minuit, 1946–1962.

———. *Documents: Doctrines, Archéologie, Beaux-Arts, Ethnographie*. Paris: Jean-Michel Place, 1991.

———. *Eroticism*. Translated by M. Dalwood. London: Penguin Books, 2001.

———. "Formless." In *Visions of Excess: Selected Writings, 1927-1939*. Translated by A. Stoekl. Minneapolis: University of Minnesota Press, 1985.

———. *Guilty*. Translated by B. Boone. Venice, CA: Lapis, 1988.

———. "Happiness, Eroticism, and Literature." In *The Absence of Myth: Writings on Surrealism*. Translated by M. Richardson. London: Verso, 2006.

———. *Inner Experience*. Translated by S. Kendall. Albany: State University of New York Press, 2014.

———. "The Language of Flowers." In *Visions of Excess: Selected Writings, 1927-1939*. Translated by A. Stoekl. Minneapolis: University of Minnesota Press, 1985.

———. *Lascaux; or, the Birth of Art: Pre-Historic Painting*. Translated by A. Wainhouse. New York: Skira, 1955.

———. "Letter to René Char on the Incompatibilities of the Writer." Translated by C. Carsten. *Yale French Studies* (1990): 31–43.

———. *Literature and Evil*. Translated by A. Hamilton. New York: Marion Boyars, 1997.

———. "The Little One [Le Petit] by Louis Trente." In *Louis XXX: The Little One and The Tomb of Louis XXX*. Translated by S. Kendall. London: Equus Press, 2013.

———. *Madame Edwarda*. In *My Mother, Madame Edwarda, The Dead Man*. Translated by A. Wainhouse. London: Marion Boyars, 2003.

———. "Materialism." In *Visions of Excess: Selected Writings, 1927-1939*. Translated by A. Stoekl. Minneapolis: University of Minnesota Press, 1985.

———. "Method of Meditation." In *The Unfinished System of Non-Knowledge*. Translated by M. Kendall and S. Kendall. Minneapolis: University of Minnesota Press, 2001.

———. *On Nietzsche*. Translated by B. Boone. London: Continuum, 2004.

———. "Nietzschean Chronicle." In *Visions of Excess: Selected Writings, 1927-1939*. Translated by A. Stoekl. Minneapolis: University of Minnesota Press, 1985.

———. "Notes on the Publishing of 'Un Cadavre.'" In *The Absence of Myth: Writings on Surrealism*. Translated by M. Richardson. London: Verso, 2006.

———. "Notion of Expenditure." In *Visions of Excess: Selected Writings, 1927-1939*. Translated by A. Stoekl. Minneapolis: University of Minnesota Press, 1985.

———. "The Obelisk." In *Visions of Excess: Selected Writings, 1927-1939*. Translated by A. Stoekl. Minneapolis: University of Minnesota Press, 1985.

———. "The 'Old Mole' and the Prefix *Sur* in the Words *Surhomme* and *Surrealist*." In *Visions of Excess: Selected Writings, 1927-1939*. Translated by A. Stoekl. Minneapolis: University of Minnesota Press, 1985.

———. "The Problems of Surrealism." In *The Absence of Myth: Writings on Surrealism*. Translated by M. Richardson. London: Verso, 2006.

———. "Propositions." In *Visions of Excess: Selected Writings, 1927-1939*. Translated by A. Stoekl. Minneapolis: University of Minnesota Press, 1985.

———. "The Psychological Structure of Fascism." In *Visions of Excess: Selected Writings, 1927-1939*. Translated by A. Stoekl. Minneapolis: University of Minnesota Press, 1985.

———. "René Char and the Force of Poetry." In *The Absence of Myth: Writings on Surrealism*. Translated by M. Richardson. London: Verso, 2006.

———. "Rotten Sun." *Documents* 3 (1930): 173–4. In *Visions of Excess: Selected Writings, 1927-1939*. Translated by A. Stoekl. Minneapolis: University of Minnesota Press, 1985.

———. "The Sacred Conspiracy." In *Visions of Excess: Selected Writings, 1927-1939*. Translated by A. Stoekl. Minneapolis: University of Minnesota Press, 1985.

———. *The Sacred Conspiracy: The Internal Papers of the Secret Society of Acéphale and Lectures to the College of Sociology*, edited by M. Galletti and A. Brotchie. London: Altas Press, 2017.

———. "From the Stone Age to Jacques Prévert." In *The Absence of Myth: Writings on Surrealism*. Translated by M. Richardson. London: Verso, 2006.

———. *Story of the Eye*. Translated by J. Neugroschal. London: Penguin Books, 2001.

———. "On the Subject of Slumbers." In *The Absence of Myth: Writings on Surrealism*. Translated by M. Richardson. London: Verso, 2006.

———. "Surrealism." In *The Absence of Myth: Writings on Surrealism*. Translated by M. Richardson. London: Verso, 2006.

———. "Surrealism from Day to Day." In *The Absence of Myth: Writings on Surrealism*. Translated by M. Richardson. London: Verso, 2006.

———. "Surrealism and God." In *The Absence of Myth: Writings on Surrealism*. Translated by M. Richardson. London: Verso, 2006.

———. "Surrealism and How It Differs from Existentialism." In *The Absence of Myth: Writings on Surrealism*. Translated by M. Richardson. London: Verso, 2006.

———. "The Surrealist Religion." In *The Absence of Myth: Writings on Surrealism*. Translated by M. Richardson. London: Verso, 2006.

———. *The Tears of Eros*. Translated by P. Connor. San Francisco: City Lights, 1989.

———. *Theory of Religion*. Translated by R. Hurley. New York: Zone Books, 1992.

———. *The Unfinished System of Non-Knowledge*. Translated by M. Kendall and S. Kendall. Minneapolis: University of Minnesota Press, 2001.

———. "The Use Value of D.A.F. de Sade." In *Visions of Excess: Selected Writings, 1927-1939*. Translated by A. Stoekl. Minneapolis: University of Minnesota Press, 1985.

———. *Visions of Excess: Selected Writings, 1927-1939*. Translated by A. Stoekl. Minneapolis: University of Minnesota Press, 1985.

———. "W.C. Preface to *Story of the Eye* from *Le Petit* (1943)." In *Story of the Eye*. Translated by J. Neugroschal. London: Penguin Books, 2001.

Baudry, Jean-Louis. "Bataille and Science: Introduction to Inner Experience." In *On Bataille*, edited by L. A. Boldt-Irons. Albany: State University of New York Press, 1995.

Becker, Brian, John Manoussakis and David Goodman, eds., *Unconscious Incarnations: Psychoanalytic and Philosophical Perspectives on the Body*. Milton Park: Routledge, 2018.

Bishop, Paul. "Nietzsche's Anti-Christianity as a Return to (German) Classicism." In *Nietzsche and Antiquity: His Reaction and Response to the Classical Tradition*, edited by P. Bishop. Rochester: Camden House, 2004.

Blondel, Jacques. *Emily Brontë: Expérience Spirituelle et Création Poétique*. Paris: Presses Universitaires de France, 1955.

Boczkowski, Diana K. "Neither Loss nor Mourning, but Perversion." In *Perversion Now!*, edited by D. Caine and C. Wright. London: Palgrave-MacMillan, 2017.

Bois, Yve-Alain, and Rosalind Krauss. *Formless: A User's Guide*. New York: Zone Books, 1997.

Boothby, Richard. *Death and Desire: Psychoanalytic Theory in Lacan's Return to Freud.* New York: Routledge, 1991.

———. *Freud as Philosopher: Metapsychology after Lacan.* New York: Routledge, 2001.

Bou Ali, Nadia, and Rohit Goel, eds. *Lacan Contra Foucault: Subjectivity, Sex and Politics.* London: Bloomsbury, 2018.

Bower, Brady. "Story of the Eye: Fantasy of the Orgy and Its Limit." *American Imago* 59.1 (2002): 73–89.

Breton, André. *Manifestoes of Surrealism.* Translated by H. R. Lane. AnnArbor: Michigan, 1969.

Brobjer, Thomas H. "Nietzsche's Reading and Knowledge of Natural Science: An Overview." In *Nietzsche and Science*, edited by G. Moore and T. H. Brobjer. Aldershot: Ashgate, 2004.

———. "Nietzsche's View of the Value of Historical Studies and Methods." *Journal of the History of Ideas* 65 (2004): 301–22.

———. "The Origin and Early Context of the Revaluation Theme in Nietzsche's Thinking." *The Journal of Nietzsche Studies* 39 (2010): 12–29.

Buchanan, Brett. "Painting the Prehuman: Bataille, Merleau-Ponty, and the Aesthetic Origins of Humanity." *Journal for Critical Animal Studies* IX.1/2 (2011): 14–31.

Caillois, Roger. *Man and the Sacred.* Translated by M. Barash. Chicago: University of Illinois Press, 2001.

Calasso, Roberto. *The Marriage of Cadmus and Harmony.* Translated by T. Parks. New York: Vintage Books, 1994.

Camus, Albert. *The Rebel.* Translated by A. Bower. London: Penguin Books, 2000.

Cardew, Alan. "*The Dioscuri*: Nietzsche and Rohde." In *Nietzsche and Antiquity: His Reaction and Response to the Classical Tradition*, edited by P. Bishop. Rochester: Camden House, 2004.

Cavanagh, Sheila L. "Transsexuality as Sinthome: Bracha L. Ettinger and the Other (Feminine) Sexual Difference." *Studies in Gender and Sexuality* 17.1 (2016): 27–44.

Chasin, Noah. "Interview: Deborah Cullen." In *Bataille's Eye/ICI Filed Notes 4*, edited by D. Cullen. Santa Monica, CA: Institute of Cultural Inquiry, 1997.

Ciecko, Anne. "Notes on Desire: Bataille and Oshima." In *Bataille's Eye/ICI Filed Notes 4*, edited by D. Cullen. Santa Monica, CA: Institute of Cultural Inquiry, 1997.

Clark, Maudemarie. *Nietzsche on Truth and Philosophy.* Cambridge: Cambridge University Press, 1990.

Crane, Gregory R., ed. *Perseus Digital Library.* Medford: Tufts University, 2007. http://www.perseus.tufts.edu/hopper/ (accessed July 7, 2020).

Cullen, Deborah, ed. *Bataille's Eye/ICI Filed Notes 4.* Santa Monica, CA: Institute of Cultural Inquiry, 1997.

Daniels, Paul R. *Nietzsche and the Birth of Tragedy.* Durham: Acumen, 2013.

Davidson, Donald. "What Metaphors Mean." In *Inquiries into Truth and Interpretation.* New York: Clarendon Press, 1984.

Dean, Carolyn. *The Self and Its Pleasures: Bataille, Lacan, and the History of the Decentered Subject*. Ithaca: Cornell University Press, 1992.
De Kesel, Marc. *Eros and Ethics: Reading Jacques Lacan's Seminar VII*. Translated by S. Jöttkandt. Albany: State University of New York Press, 2009.
———. "The Real of Ethics: On a Widespread Misconception." In *Unconscious Incarnations: Psychoanalytic and Philosophical Perspectives on the Body*, edited by B. Becker, J. Manoussakis and D. Goodman. Milton Park: Routledge, 2018.
Deleuze, Gilles. *Nietzsche and Philosophy*. Translated by H. Tomlinson. New York: Columbia University Press, 1983.
Dodds, E. R. *The Greeks and the Irrational*. Berkeley: University of California Press, 1951.
Dragon, Jean. "The Work of Alterity: Bataille and Lacan." *Diacritics* 26.2 (1996): 31–48.
Dufresne, Todd. *Against Freud: Critics Talk Back*. Stanford: Stanford University Press, 2007.
Dumayet, Pierre, interviewer. "Georges Bataille: Literature and Evil." https://www.youtube.com/watch?v=5XCnGuK8CVc (accessed July 4, 2020).
Durkheim, Émile. *The Elementary Forms of Religious Life*. Translated by C. Cosman. Oxford: Oxford University Press, 2001.
Euripides. *Bacchae*. In *Bacchae and Other Plays*. Translated by J. Morwood. Oxford: Oxford University Press, 2000.
Evans, Dylan. *An Introductory Dictionary of Lacanian Psychoanalysis*. London: Routledge, 2005.
Falasca-Zamponi, Simonetta. *Rethinking the Political: The Sacred, Aesthetic Politics and the Collège de Sociologie*. Montréal: McGill-Queens, 2011.
Feldman, Alex J. "Review of Nadia Bou Ali, Rohit Goel, eds., *Lacan Contra Foucault: Subjectivity, Sex and Politics* (London: Bloomsbury, 2018)." *Notre Dame Philosophical Reviews: An Electronic Journal* (2019) https://ndpr.nd.edu/news/lacan-contra-foucault-subjectivity-sex-and-politics/ (accessed July 14, 2020).
Ffrench, Patrick. *After Bataille: Sacrifice, Exposure, Community*. London: Legenda, 2007.
———. "Bataille's Literary Writings." In *George Bataille: Key Concepts*, edited by M. Hewson and M. Coelen. London: Routledge, 2015.
———. *The Cut: Reading Bataille's Histoire de L'Oeil*. Oxford: Oxford University Press, 1999.
———. "Dirty Life." In *The Beast at Heaven's Gate: Georges Bataille and the Art of Transgression*, edited by A. Hussey. Amsterdam: Rodopi, 2006.
Foster, Hal. *Prosthetic Gods*. Cambridge, MA: The MIT Press, 2004.
Foucault, Michael. "A Preface to Transgression." Translated by D. Bouchard and S. Simon. In *Aesthetics, Method, and Epistemology, Essential Works of Foucault, 1954-1984, Volume Two*, edited by J. Faubion. London: Penguin, 1998.
———. "Return to History." Translated by R. Hurley. In *Aesthetics, Method, and Epistemology, Essential Works of Foucault, 1954-1984, Volume Two*, edited by J. Faubion. London: Penguin, 1998.

———. "Structuralism and Post-Structuralism." Translated by J. Harding. In *Aesthetics, Method, and Epistemology, Essential Works of Foucault, 1954-1984, Volume Two*, edited by J. Faubion. London: Penguin, 1998.

Franco, Paul. "Nietzsche's *Human, All Too Human* and the Problem of Culture." *The Review of Politics* 69 (2007): 215–43.

Freud, Sigmund. *The Standard Edition of the Complete Psychological Works of Sigmund Freud*. Translated by J. Strachey. London: Vintage, 2001.

———. (1900) *The Interpretation of Dreams*. In SE4 and SE5.

———. (1905) *Three Essays on the Theory of Sexuality*. In SE7, 125–245.

———. (1908) "Hysterical Phantasies and their Relation to Bisexuality." In SE9, 155–66.

———. (1908) "'Civilized' Sexual Morality and Modern Nervous Illness." In SE9, 177–204.

———. (1910) *Leonardo da Vinci and a Memory of his Childhood*. In SE11, 57–137.

———. (1910) "'Wild' Psychoanalysis." In SE11, 219–27.

———. (1911) "Psycho-Analytic Notes on an Autobiographical Account of a Case of Paranoia [*The Case of Schreber*]." In SE12, 3–82.

———. (1912) "On the Universal Tendency to Debasement in the Sphere of Love." In SE11, 177–90.

———. (1912) "The Dynamics of Transference." In SE12, 97–108.

———. (1913) *Totem and Taboo: Some Points of Agreement between the Mental Lives of Savages and Neurotics*. In SE13, 1–162.

———. (1913) "The Claims of Psycho-Analysis to Scientific Interest." In SE13, 163–90.

———. (1914) "Remembering, Repeating, and Working-Through." In SE12, 145–56.

———. (1914) "On the History of the Psychoanalytic Movement." In SE14, 1–66.

———. (1914) "On Narcissism: An Introduction." In SE14, 67–102.

———. (1915) "Instincts and Their Vicissitudes." In SE14, 109–40.

———. (1915) "Repression." In SE14, 141–58.

———. (1915–1917) *Introductory Lectures on Psychoanalysis*. In SE15 and SE16.

———. (1918[1914]) *From the History of an Infantile Neurosis* [*Wolf Man*]. In SE17, 1–123.

———. (1920) *Beyond the Pleasure Principle*. In SE18, 1–64.

———. (1921) *Group Psychology and the Analysis of the Ego*. In SE18, 65–143.

———. (1925) "An Autobiographical Study." In SE20, 1–74.

———. (1925) "The Resistances to Psychoanalysis." In SE19, 211–24.

———. (1925) "Letter to the Editor of the *Jewish Press Centre in Zurich*. In SE19, 291.

———. (1926) *Inhibitions, Symptoms and Anxiety*. In SE20, 77–172.

———. (1928) "Dostoevsky and Parricide." In SE21, 175–96.

———. (1930) *Civilization and Its Discontents*. In SE21, 57–145.

———. (1933) *New Introductory Lectures on Psychoanalysis*. In SE22, 1–182.

———. (1937) "Analysis Terminable and Interminable." In SE23, 209–53.

———. (1939) *Moses and Monotheism: Three Essays*. In SE23, 1–137.

Gavras, Costas-. *Adults in the Room*. Athens-Paris: KG Productions, with Odeon, France 2 Cinéma, Wild Bunch and Canal+, 2019.

Gherovici, Patricia. *Transgender Psychoanalysis: A Lacanian Perspective on Sexual Difference*. London: Routledge, 2017.

Gooding-Williams, Robert. "Nietzsche's Pursuit of Modernism." *New German Critique* 41, Special Issue on the Critiques of the Enlightenment (1987): 95–108.

Goux, Jean-Joseph. "General Economics and Postmodern Capitalism." Translated by K. Ascheim and R. Garelick. *Yale French Studies* 78 (1990): 206–24.

Greenberg, Clement. "Modernist Painting." In *The New Art: A Critical Anthology*, edited by G. Battcock. New York: Dutton, 1973.

Greenwood, Edward. "Literature: Freedom or Evil? The Debate between Sartre and Bataille." *Sartre Studies International* 4.1 (1998): 17–29.

Grigg, Russell. *Lacan, Language, and Philosophy*. Albany: State University of New York Press, 2008.

———. "Signifiers in the Real: from Schreber to Wolf Man." *Psychoanalysis Lacan* 4 (2020): 1–4.

Hacker, Frederick J. "Sublimation Revisited." *International Journal of Psychoanalysis* 53 (1972): 219–23.

Halley, Michael. "And a Truth for a Truth: Barthes on Bataille." In *On Bataille*, edited by L. A. Boldt-Irons. Albany: State University of New York Press, 1995.

Halwani, Raja. *Philosophy of Love, Sex, and Marriage*. New York: Routledge, 2010.

Hartmann, Nadine. "Eroticism." In *Georges Bataille: Key Concepts*, edited by M. Hewson and M. Coelen. London: Routledge, 2015.

Hecq, Dominique. "Uncanny Encounters: On Writing, Anxiety and jouissance." *Anatomy & Poetics* 6 (2005): http://www.doubledialogues.com/article/uncanny-encounters-on-writing-anxiety-and-jouissance/ (accessed July 7, 2020).

Heidegger, Martin. *Nietzsche: Volumes One and Two*. Translated by D. F. Krell. New York: HarperCollins, 1991.

———. "Logos (Heraclitus, Fragment B 50)." In *Early Greek Thinking*. Translated by D. F. Krell and F. A. Capuzzi. New York: Harper and Row, 1975.

———. "The Origin of the Work of Art." In *Poetry, Language, Thought*. Translated by A. Hofstadter. New York: Harper and Row, 1971.

Hewson, Mark. "Religion." In *Georges Bataille: Key Concepts*, edited by M. Hewson and M. Coelen. London: Routledge, 2015.

Hewson, Mark, and Marcus Coelen. "Introduction." In *Georges Bataille: Key Concepts*, edited by M. Hewson and M. Coelen. London: Routledge, 2015.

Hollier, Denis. *Against Architecture: The Writings of Georges Bataille*. Translated by B. Wing. Cambridge, MA: The MIT Press, 1992.

———. "The Dualist Materialism of Georges Bataille." Translated by H. Allred. *Yale French Studies* 78 (1990): 124–39.

Hollywood, Amy. *Sensible Ecstasy: Mysticism, Sexual Difference, and the Demands of History*. Chicago: The University of Chicago Press, 2012.

Horbury, Alison. "Digital Feminisms and the Split Subject: Short-circuits through Lacan's Four-Discourses." *CM: Communication and Media* XI.38 (2016): 135–66.

———. "What does Feminism Want?" *Continental Thought & Theory: A Journal of Intellectual Freedom* 1.3 (2017): 567–92.

———. *The Persephone Complex: Post-Feminist Impasses in Popular Heroine Television*. Basingstoke: Palgrave-MacMillan, 2015.

———. "A Psychoanalytic Ethics of the Pornographic Aesthetic." *Porn Studies* (2019): 1–13.

Hume, David. *A Treatise of Human Nature*. London: Penguin Books, 1986.

Hussey, Andrew. "Fascism and the Politics of 1930s France." In *Georges Bataille: Key Concepts*, edited by M. Hewson and M. Coelen. London: Routledge, 2015.

Johnston, Adrian. "The Freudian Thing, or the Meaning of the Return to Freud in Psychoanalysis." In *Reading Lacan's Écrits: From 'The Freudian Thing' to 'Remarks on Daniel Lagache,'* edited by D. Hook, C. Neil and S. Vanheule. New York: Routledge, 2020.

———. "The Vicious Circle of the Super-Ego: The Pathological Trap of Guilt and the Beginning of Ethics." *Psychoanalytic Studies* 3.3/4 (2001): 411–24.

Kant, Immanuel. *Critique of Judgement*. Translated by J. C. Meredith. Oxford: Clarendon Press, 1952.

Kendall, Stuart. *Georges Bataille*. London: Reaktion, 2007.

———. "Editor's Introduction." In Bataille, *The Cradle of Humanity: Pre-historic Art and Culture*. Translated by S. Kendall. New York: Zone Books, 2009.

Kennedy, Kevin. *Towards an Aesthetics of Sovereignty: Georges Bataille's Theory of Art and Literature*. Bethesda: Academica Press, 2014.

———. "Between Law and Transgression: Literature as a (Non-) Civilizing Strategy in the Early 20th Century." *Open Library of Humanities* 6/1 17 (2020): 1–20.

Lacan, Jacques. "Aggressiveness in Psychoanalysis." In *Écrits: The First Complete Edition in English*. Translated by B. Fink, H. Fink and R. Grigg. New York: W. W. Norton, 2006.

———. *Écrits: The First Complete Edition in English*. Translated by B. Fink, H. Fink and R. Grigg. New York: W. W. Norton, 2006.

———. "L'étourdit." Translated by C. Gallagher. *THE LETTER* 41 (2009): 31–80.

———. "The Freudian Thing, or the Meaning of the Return to Freud in Psychoanalysis." In *Écrits: The First Complete Edition in English*. Translated by B. Fink, H. Fink and R. Grigg. New York: W. W. Norton, 2006.

———. "The Function and Field of Speech and Language in Psychoanalysis." In *Écrits: The First Complete Edition in English*. Translated by B. Fink, H. Fink and R. Grigg. New York: W. W. Norton, 2006.

———. "The Instance of the Letter in the Unconscious, or Reason Since Freud." In *Écrits: The First Complete Edition in English*. Translated by B. Fink, H. Fink and R. Grigg. New York: W. W. Norton, 2006.

———. "Kant with Sade." In *Écrits: The First Complete Edition in English*. Translated by B. Fink, H. Fink and R. Grigg. New York: W. W. Norton, 2006.

———. "The Metaphor of the Subject." In *Écrits: The First Complete Edition in English*. Translated by B. Fink, H. Fink and R. Grigg. New York: W. W. Norton, 2006.

———. "The Mirror Stage as Formative of the *I* Function as Revealed in Psychoanalytic Experience." In *Écrits: The First Complete Edition in English*. Translated by B. Fink, H. Fink and R. Grigg. New York: W. W. Norton, 2006.

———. "On a Question Prior to Any Possible Treatment of Psychosis." In *Écrits: The First Complete Edition in English*. Translated by B. Fink, H. Fink and R. Grigg. New York: W. W. Norton, 2006.

———. "Some Reflections on the Ego." *International Journal of Psycho-Analysis* 34 (1953): 11–7.

———. "Response to Jean Hyppolite's Commentary on Freud's 'Verneinung.'" In *Écrits: The First Complete Edition in English*. Translated by B. Fink, H. Fink and R. Grigg. New York: W. W. Norton, 2006.

———. *The Seminar of Jacques Lacan Book I, Freud's Papers on Technique, 1953-1954*. Edited by J-A. Miller. Translated by J. Forrester. New York: W. W. Norton, 1991.

———. *The Seminar of Jacques Lacan Book III, The Psychoses, 1955–1956*. Edited by J-A. Miller. Translated by R. Grigg. New York: W. W. Norton, 1993.

———. *The Seminar of Jacques Lacan Book V, Formations of the Unconscious, 1957-1958*. Edited by J-A. Miller. Translated by R. Grigg. Cambridge: Polity Press, 2017.

———. *The Seminar of Jacques Lacan Book VI, Desire and Its Interpretation, 1958-1959*. Edited by J-A. Miller. Translated by B. Fink. Cambridge: Polity Press, 2019.

———. *The Seminar of Jacques Lacan Book VII, The Ethics of Psychoanalysis, 1959-1960*. Edited by J-A. Miller. Translated by D. Porter. New York: W. W Norton, 1991.

———. *The Seminar of Jacques Lacan Book VIII, Transference, 1960-1961*. Edited by J-A. Miller. Translated by B. Fink. Cambridge: Polity Press, 2015.

———. *The Seminar of Jacques Lacan Book X, Anxiety, 1962–1963*. Edited by J-A. Miller. Translated by A. R. Price. Cambridge: Polity Press, 2014.

———. *The Seminar of Jacques Lacan Book XI, The Four Fundamental Concepts of Psychoanalysis, 1964*. Edited by J-A. Miller. Translated by D. Sheridan. New York: W. W. Norton, 1998.

———. *Seminar XIII, The Object of Psychoanalysis*. Translated by C. Gallagher. In *Jacques Lacan in Ireland: Collected Translations and Papers by Cormac Gallagher.* http://www.lacaninireland.com/web/published-works/seminars/ (accessed July 7, 2020).

———. *The Seminar of Jacques Lacan Book XVII, The Other Side of Psychoanalysis, 1969-1970*. Edited by J-A. Miller. Translated by R. Grigg. New York: W. W. Norton, 2007.

———. *The Seminar of Jacques Lacan Book XIX, . . . Or Worse, 1971–1972*. Edited by J-A. Miller. Translated by A. R. Price. Cambridge: Polity Press, 2018.

———. *The Seminar of Jacques Lacan Book XX, On Feminine Sexuality: The Limits of Love and Knowledge, 1972–1973*. Edited by J-A. Miller. Translated by B. Fink. New York: W. W. Norton, 1999.

———. *The Seminar of Jacques Lacan Book XXIII, The Sinthome, 1975-1976*. Edited by J-A. Miller. Translated by A. R. Price. Cambridge: Polity Press, 2016.

———. *Talking to Brick Walls: A Series of Presentations in the Chapel at the Sainte-Anne Hospital (1971–1972)*. Translated by A. R. Price. Cambridge: Polity Press, 2017.

———. *Television: A Challenge to the Psychoanalytic Establishment*. Translated by J. Mehlman. New York: Norton, 1990.

———. "Trans. of *Logos*, by Martin Heidegger." *La Psychanalyse* 1 (1956): 57–79.

———. *Triumph of Religion, preceded by Discourse to Catholics*. Translated by B. Fink. Cambridge: Polity Press, 2013.

Leiris, Michel. "From Bataille the Impossible to the Impossible *Documents*." In Georges Bataille and Michel Leiris, *Correspondence*. Translated by L. Heron. London: Seagull Books, 2008.

Leiter, Brian. *Nietzsche on Morality*. New York: Routledge, 2002.

Lévi-Strauss, Claude. *Structures Elémentaires de la Parenté*. Paris: Presses Universitaires de France, 1949.

Liddell, Henry G., and Robert Scott. *A Greek-English Lexicon: With a Revised Supplement*. Oxford: Clarendon Press, 1996.

Marx, Karl, and Friedrich Engels. *The Communist Manifesto*. In *Karl Marx: Selected Writings*, edited by Lawrence H. Simon. Indianapolis: Hackett, 1994.

Mauss, Marcel. *The Gift: The Form and Reason for Exchange in Archaic Societies*. Translated by W. D. Halls. New York: W. W. Norton, 2000.

McGowan, Todd. "Looking for the Gaze: Lacanian Film Theory and Its Vicissitudes." *Cinema Journal* 42.3 (2003): 27–47.

———. *The Real Gaze: Film Theory after Lacan*. Albany: State University of New York Press, 2007.

Meltzer, Françoise. "On the Question of Aufhebung: Baudelaire, Bataille and Sartre." *RCCS Annual Review: A Selection from the Portuguese Journal Revista Crítica de Ciências Sociais* 0 (2009): 110–24.

Millot, Catherine. *Life with Lacan*. Translated by A. Brown. Cambridge: Polity Press, 2018.

Newman, Michael. "The Ball-Joint and the Anagram: Perversion and Jouissance in Hans Bellmer." In *Perversion Now!*, edited by D. Caine and C. Wright. London: Palgrave-MacMillan, 2017.

Nietzsche, Friedrich. *The Anti-Christ*. In *Twilight of the Idols /The Anti-Christ*. Translated by R. J. Hollingdale. London: Penguin Books, 1990.

———. *Beyond Good and Evil: Prelude to a Philosophy of the Future*. Translated by W. Kaufmann. New York: Vintage Books, 1989.

———. *The Birth of Tragedy*. In *The Birth of Tragedy and The Case of Wagner*. Translated by W. Kaufmann. New York: Vintage Books, 1967.

———. *The Case of Wagner*. In *The Birth of Tragedy and The Case of Wagner*. Translated by W. Kaufmann. New York: Vintage Books, 1967.

———. *Ecce Homo*. In *On the Genealogy of Morals /Ecce Homo*. Translated by W. Kaufmann and R. J. Hollingdale. New York: Vintage Books, 1989.

———. *The Gay Science: With a Prelude in Rhymes and an Appendix of Songs*. Translated by W. Kaufmann. New York: Vintage Books, 1974.

———. *On the Genealogy of Morals*. In *On the Genealogy of Morals/Ecce Homo*. Translated by W. Kaufmann and R. J. Hollingdale. New York: Vintage Books, 1989.

———. *Human, All Too Human: A Book for Free-Spirits*. Translated by R. J. Hollingdale. Cambridge: Cambridge University Press, 2004.

———. *Twilight of the Idols: Or How to Philosophize with a Hammer*. In *Twilight of the Idols /The Anti-Christ*. Translated by R. J. Hollingdale. London: Penguin Books, 1990.

———. *The Will to Power*. Edited by W. Kaufmann. Translated by W. Kaufmann and R. J. Hollingdale. New York: Vintage Books, 1968.

———. *Thus Spoke Zarathustra*. Translated by R. J. Hollingdale. London: Penguin Books, 1969.

Nobus, Danny. *The Law of Desire: On Lacan's 'Kant with Sade.'* London: Palgrave-MacMillan, 2017.

———. "Kant with Sade." In *Reading Lacan's Écrits: From 'Signification of the Phallus' to 'Metaphor of the Subject,'* edited by Stijn Vanheule, Derek Hook and Calum Neil. New York: Routledge, 2019.

Noys, Benjamin. *Georges Bataille: A Critical Introduction*. London: Pluto Press, 2000.

Nunberg, Herman, and Ernst Federn, eds. *Minutes of the Vienna Psychoanalytic Society, Vol. I & II*. New York: International Universities Press, 1962–1967.

Ons, Silvia. "Nietzsche, Freud, Lacan." In *Lacan: The Silent Partners*, edited by S. Žižek. New York: Verso, 2006.

Peignot, Laure (Colette). *Laure: The Collected Writings*. Translated by J. Herman. San Francisco: City Lights, 2001.

Perroux, François. *Le Plan Marshall ou l'Europe Nécessaire au Monde*. Paris: Librairie de Médicis, 1948.

Pétrement, Simone. *La Vie de Simone Weil*. Paris: Fayard, 1973.

Piel, Jean. "Bataille and the World from 'The Notion of Expenditure' to the Accursed Share." In *On Bataille: Critical Essays*, edited by L. Boldt-Irons. Albany: State University of New York Press, 1995.

Plato. *Gorgias*. Translated by W. D. Woodhead. In *The Collected Dialogues of Plato: Including the Letters*, edited by E. Hamilton and H. Cairns. Princeton: Princeton University Press, 1989.

———. *Phaedo*. In *Plato I*. Translated by H. N. Fowler. Loeb Classical Library. Cambridge, MA: Harvard University Press, 2005.

———. *Republic*. Translated by P. Shorey. In *The Collected Dialogues of Plato: Including the Letters*, edited by E. Hamilton and H. Cairns. Princeton: Princeton University Press, 1989.

———. *Symposium*. In *Plato III*. Translated by W. R. M. Lamb. Loeb Classical Library. Cambridge, MA: Harvard University Press, 2001.

Richardson, Michael. *Georges Bataille*. London: Routledge, 1994.

———. ed., *George Bataille: Essential Writings*. London: Sage Publications, 1998.

———. "Introduction." In Bataille, *The Absence of Myth: Writings on Surrealism*. Translated by M. Richardson. London: Verso, 2006.

Richardson, William J. "Heidegger and Psychoanalysis?" *Natureza Humana* 5.1 (2003): 9–38.
Richman, Michèle. "Art." In *Georges Bataille: Key Concepts*, edited by M. Hewson and M. Coelen. London: Routledge, 2015.
———. "Bataille Moralist?: *Critique* and the Postwar Writings." *Yale French Studies* 78 (1990): 143–68.
———. *Sacred Revolutions: Durkheim and the Collège de Sociologie*. Minneapolis: University of Minnesota Press, 2002.
———. "Spitting Images in Montaigne and Bataille for a Heterological Counterhistory of Sovereignty." *Diacritics* 35.3 (2005): 46–61.
Rohde, Erwin. *Psyche: The Cult of Souls and Belief in Immortality among the Greeks, Volume 1 and 2*. Translated by W. B. Hillis. Eugene: Wipf and Stock, 2006.
Rose, Louis. *The Freudian Calling: Early Viennese Psychoanalysis and the Pursuit of Cultural Science*. Detroit: WSU, 1998.
Roudinesco, Elisabeth. *Jacques Lacan: Outline of a Life, History of a System of Thought*. Translated by B. Bray. New York: Columbia University Press, 1997.
Russell, Jared. "*L'effet c'est toi*: Projective Identification from Nietzsche to Klein." *American Imago* 70.4 (2013): 563–83.
———. *Nietzsche and the Clinic: Psychoanalysis, Philosophy, Metaphysics*. London: Karnac, 2017.
———. *Psychoanalysis and Deconstruction: Freud's Psychic Apparatus*. London: Routledge, 2020.
Ruti, Mari. "The Ethics of the Real: A Response to De Kesel." In *Unconscious Incarnations: Psychoanalytic and Philosophical Perspectives on the Body*, edited by B. Becker, J. Manoussakis and D. Goodman. Milton Park: Routledge, 2018.
Sass, Louis. "Lacan: The Mind of the Modernist." *Continental Philosophy Review* 48 (2015): 409–43.
Scharff, David. "Psychoanalysis in China: An Essay on the Recent Literature in English." *The Psychoanalytic Quarterly* 85.4 (2016): 1037–67.
Shepherdson, Charles. *Lacan and the Limits of Language*. New York: Fordham University Press, 2008.
Shields, James M. "Eros and Transgression in an Age of Immanence: Georges Bataille's (Religious) Critique of Kinsey." *Journal of Religion and Culture* 13 (1999): 175–86.
Skelton, Ross. "Is the Unconscious Structured like a Language?" *International Forum of Psychoanalysis* 4.3 (1995): 168–78.
Smith, Paul. "Bataille's Erotic Writings and the Return of the Subject." In *On Bataille: Critical Essays*, edited by L. Boldt-Irons. Albany: State University of New York Press, 1995.
Soler, Colette. *Lacan: The Unconscious Reinvented*. Translated by E. Faye and S. Schwartz. London: Karnac, 2014.
Sontag, Susan. "The Pornographic Imagination." In Bataille, *Story of the Eye*. Translated by J. Neugroschal. London: Penguin, 2001.

Sophocles. *Antigone*. In *Sophocles II*. Edited and translated by H. Lloyd-Jones. Loeb Classical Library. Cambridge, MA: Harvard University Press, 1998.
Spiteri, Raymond. "Georges Bataille and the Limits of Modernism." *Emaj: Online Journal of Art* 4 (2009): 1–27.
———. "Surrealism and its Discontents: Georges Bataille, Georges Ribemont-Dessaignes, and the 1929 Crisis of Surrealism." *French History and Civilization* 4 (2011): 145–56.
Stein, Andrew. "The Use and Abuse of History: Habermas's Misreading of Bataille." *Symplokē* 1.1 (1993): 21–58.
Stoekl, Allan. "Introduction." In Bataille, *Visions of Excess: Selected Writings, 1927-1939*. Translated by A. Stoekl. Minneapolis: University of Minnesota Press, 1985.
Suleiman, Susan. "Transgression and the Avant-Garde." In *On Bataille*, edited by L. A. Boldt-Irons. Albany: State University of New York Press, 1995.
Surya, Michael. *Georges Bataille: An Intellectual Biography*. Translated by K. Fijalkowski and M. Richardson. London: Verso, 2002.
Tawney, Richard H. *Religion and the Rise of Capitalism: A Historical Study*. New York: Penguin Books, 1947.
Taylor, Chloë. *The Culture of Confession from Augustine to Foucault: A Genealogy of the 'Confessing Animal.'* New York: Routledge, 2009.
Themi, Tim. "Bataille and the Erotics of the Real." *Parrhesia: A Journal of Critical Philosophy* 24 (2015): 312–35.
———. "Bataille, Literature, Happiness, and Evil." *Continental Thought and Theory: A Journal of Intellectual Freedom* 2.3 (2019): 180–201.
———. "Lacan, Barthes, Bataille, and the Meaning of the Eye—or Gaze." *The Undecidable Unconscious: A Journal of Deconstruction and Psychoanalysis* 3 (2016): 93–123 (Lincoln: University of Nebraska Press).
———. *Lacan's Ethics and Nietzsche's Critique of Platonism*. Albany: State University of New York Press, 2014.
———. "Nietzsche's Relation with Psychoanalysis: From Freud to Surrealist Modernism, Bataille and Lacan." In *Understanding Nietzsche, Understanding Modernism*, edited by B. Pines and D. Burnham. New York: Bloomsbury, 2019.
Thucydides. *History of the Peloponnesian War, Volume I: Books 1-2*. Translated by C. F. Smith. Loeb Classical Library 108. Cambridge, MA: Harvard University Press, 1919.
Timofeeva, Oxana. "'The Only Real Outlaws': Animal Freedom in Bataille." In *Georges Bataille and Contemporary Thought*, edited by W. Stronge. London: Bloomsbury, 2019.
Vanderwees, Chris. "Talking to Brick Walls: A Series of Presentations in the Chapel at the Sainte-Anne Hospital, by Jacques Lacan (Translated by A.R. Price)." *Psychoanalytic Discourse* 4.1 (2019): 104–8.
Varoufakis, Yanis. *Adults in the Room: My Battle with Europe's Deep Establishment*. London: The Bodley Head, 2017.
———. *And the Weak Suffer what they Must? Europe's Crisis and America's Economic Future*. New York: Nation Books, 2016.

Weber, Max. *The Protestant Ethic and the Spirit of Capitalism*. Translated by T. Parsons. New York: Scribner, 1958.
Weiss, Allen S. *Perverse Desire and the Ambiguous Icon*. Albany: State University of New York Press, 1994.
Welldon, Estela V. "No Longer a Taboo: Understanding Female Perversion in Motherhood." In *Perversion Now!*, edited by D. Caine and C. Wright. London: Palgrave-MacMillan, 2017.
Winkiel, Laura. *Modernism: The Basics*. New York: Routledge, 2017.
Wohl, Victoria. "The Eros of Alcibiades." *Classical Antiquity* 18 (1999): 349–85.
Zafiropoulos, Marcos. *Lacan and Lévi-Strauss or The Return to Freud (1951–1957)*. Translated by J. Holland. London: Karnac Books, 2010.
Žižek, Slavoj. "Ideology III: To Read Too Many Books is Harmful." In *Lacan.com* (2007), 4, http://www.lacan.com/zizchemicalbeats.html (accessed July 4, 2020).
———. *The Parallax View*. Cambridge, MA: The MIT Press, 2006.
———. *The Puppet and the Dwarf: The Perverse Core of Christianity*. Cambridge, MA: The MIT Press, 2003.
Zupančič, Alenka. *Ethics of the Real: Kant, Lacan*. London: Verso, 2000.
———. *The Shortest Shadow: Nietzsche's Philosophy of the Two*. Cambridge, MA: The MIT Press, 2003.

Index

abundance, 9, 78, 87–88, 126, 138, 178; lack and, 7, 76, 80, 122n32, 146n19, 178. *See also* lack
accumulation, 65, 91, 112, 116, 153, 183; Calvinist, 35–36, 38, 109–10, 175; capitalist and communist, 90, 163–65, 167; happiness and, 127–28, 132, 180
Acéphale, 2, 97, 108, 112, 123, 149, 183
Adler, Alfred, 105
aesthetics, 81, 83, 88, 94n13, 117, 125, 131, 154, 173–74; Bataille on, 6–9, 76–77, 93n1, 161; criterion of, 91–92, 97; ethics and, 4–5, 66; Kant's, 126, 137; Nietzsche's, 78, 80; sublimation and, 139–40, 177–78; surrealist modernism and, 114, 179–80. *See also* art
affect, 6, 18–19, 22, 50, 82, 165; *Acéphale* and, 183; fascist, 112, 155
affirmation, 8, 16, 31, 37–38, 92, 105–8, 114, 118, 126; of animality, 83, 85, 88; Dionysian, 1, 22, 89, 100, 115, 120, 145n2; sublimation as, 139, 142, 178
aggression, 15, 26, 100, 119n11, 177
Alcibiades, 25–26, 41n23
Ambrosino, Georges, 171n30
anal, 30, 52, 68n14, 108, 143–44

animality, 43n39, 94n14, 127, 129, 144, 177–78, 183; affirmation of, 31, 38; denial of, 18, 20–21, 89, 153, 163; divine, 28, 108–10; latent, 130, 175; Palaeolithic, 6–7, 76, 81–87, 146n14; transgressive, 92, 112–14, 117, 135–36
anthropology, 2, 4, 26, 61, 70n25, 122; ethnography-ethnology, 11n11, 29, 161; Mauss's, 17–18, 40n8, 109, 175
Antigone, 78, 93n8, 128, 134, 137, 145n2, 146n9, 170n18
anxiety, 18, 43, 55–58, 71, 114, 129, 174
Aphrodite, 85, 87, 152–53, 184n3
Apollo, 10n2, 64, 77, 117; Dionysos and, 21–23, 25, 44n49, 56, 116, 178
Aristophanes, 110
Aristotle, 11, 30, 35, 57, 67, 89, 120, 136, 146, 174–75; catharsis in, 115, 123n45
art, 12n16, 105–6, 118, 137–38, 140, 178–79, 185n4; Bataille on, 4, 7–8, 75–76, 97, 125; *Documents* and, 6, 41n19; neurotic, 84, 153; Nietzsche and, 78–80, 88, 90, 120n18; Palaeolithic, 81–83, 85, 87, 94n13; and politics, 124n47, 141–44, 149, 173–74, 177, 182–84; and science,

203

103, 181; sublimation as, 86, 116; surrealist, 108, 114; tragic, 19, 24–25, 115, 123n45. *See also* aesthetics
asceticism, 35, 44–45, 59, 100–1, 122–23, 126, 162–66; Christian, 31, 39n1, 42n29, 61, 66, 144, 161; Lazare's, 152, 157, 160; Nietzsche on, 32, 119n11, 131, 146; Plato's, 24, 46n54, 135–36
Assoun, Paul-Laurent, 7, 98, 100, 105, 119
Athens, 22, 25, 102, 120n22
automatic writing, 107, 143

bad conscience, 28, 59, 66, 90, 163–65; super-egoic, 48, 100, 119n11
Badiou, Alain, 120n19
Barthes, Roland, 5, 49–54, 64–65, 71n29, 73, 176; in *Critique*, 3, 48, 67n4, 71n26
Bass, Alan, 72n38, 73n4, 81, 99
Bataille, Georges, works of: *L'Abbé C*, 143–44; "Absence of Myth," 7, 113–14; *Accursed Share*, 3, 5–6, 9, 16, 19, 23, 28, 35, 44n45, 45n51, 47, 88, 90, 92, 93n11, 109, 138, 147n23, 149, 153–54, 156, 163, 168, 168n1, 171n30, 182–84; *Acéphale*, 2, 12n15, 97, 108, 112, 123n41, 149, 183; "Age of Revolt," 12n17; "André Masson," 8; "Autobiographical Note," 1, 97, 150; "Base Materialism and Gnosticism," 6, 24, 80, 122n35; "Big Toe," 6, 65, 76–77; *Blue of Noon*, 9, 145n9, 147n23, 149–54, 156–63, 168, 168n2, 168n4, 169n6, 174, 182–83; "Cadavre Maternal," 169n7; "Castrated Lion," 92n1; *Cradle of Humanity*, 6, 82–87, 94n13, 146n14; *Critique*, 3, 8, 32, 48, 60, 125, 137; "Critique of Hegelian Dialectic," 185n5; *Documents*, 6, 24, 41n19, 65, 70n23, 75–76, 80–81, 92n1, 94n13, 110–12, 122n35, 161, 174, 177; *Eroticism*, 1, 3–6, 10n1, 15–19, 23–35, 39, 41n18, 42n32, 43n35, 47–48, 55–56, 59–60, 62–63, 66, 83, 89, 94n13, 108, 122n37, 124n47, 139, 145n5, 153–54, 161, 174, 184n3; "Formless," 6, 76, 80, 122n35; *Guilty*, 12, 39n4, 43n35; "Happiness, Eroticism, and Literature," 8, 125, 127–30, 143; *Inner Experience*, 7, 113, 150, 168n2; "Language of Flowers," 6, 76, 77; *Lascaux; or, Birth of Art*, 6, 82, 87, 94n13, 108; "Letter to René Char," 147n26; *Literature and Evil*, 8, 72n34, 125–27, 130–34, 139, 144, 174; "Little One [Le Petit]," 67n1; *Madame Edwarda*, 12, 69n18, 69nn20–21, 111, 122n36, 141, 143; "Materialism," 80, 122n35; "Method of Meditation," 13n19; "Nietzschean Chronicle," 123n41; "Notes on 'Un Cadavre,'" 7, 13n18, 110; "Notion of Expenditure," 18, 22, 151; "Obelisk," 93n7, 93n10; "'Old Mole' and Prefix *Sur*," 81; *On Nietzsche*, 3, 6, 75; "Problems of Surrealism," 46n52; "Propositions," 123n41; "Psychological Structure of Fascism," 9, 151, 155; "René Char and Force of Poetry," 8, 137; "Rotten Sun," 6, 70n23, 76–77, 111; "Sacred Conspiracy," 13n22, 123n41; "Stone Age to Jacques Prévert," 8, 135; *Story of Eye*, 5, 38, 47–50, 52, 54, 64, 66–66, 75, 95n19, 97, 111, 122n37, 124n47, 141, 150–51, 154, 176; "Subject of Slumbers," 7, 13n18, 113–14; "Surrealism," 7, 107; "Surrealism and God," 7, 114; "Surrealism and How It Differs from Existentialism," 7, 107, 109; "Surrealism from Day to Day," 7, 13n18, 110, 122n34; "Surrealist Religion," 7, 107–8, 114; *Tears of Eros*, 5, 66, 73n42, 83, 94n13, 124n47, 130, 174; *Theory of*

Religion, 5, 23–25, 35–37, 41n22, 70n21, 107–8; *Unfinished System of Non-Knowledge*, 113; "Use Value of Sade," 118n3, 122n35; "W.C. Preface to *Story*," 5, 67n1, 154, 169n7; *Writings on Surrealism*, 110, 113
Bataille, Sylvia, 3, 117, 151, 169n7
Baudry, Jean-Louis, 43n42
beauty, 24, 26, 62, 75–80, 115, 126, 131, 138, 164; aesthetic, 6–7, 93n8, 128; animal, 31, 82, 87; Apollo's, 21, 64; Dirty's, 150, 152; *Story of Eye*'s, 50, 60
binary thought, 50, 75, 85, 122n32, 178; in dualist religion, 23–24, 38
biology, 32, 38, 40n7, 99, 133, 142, 147
Blake, William, 8, 131–34, 138, 143, 146
Blanchot, Maurice, 67n4
Boczkowski, Diana K, 169n7
body, 16, 30, 46, 58, 70n25, 77, 129, 133, 143; aesthetics in, 4, 88, 137, 177; ascetics in, 136, 173; despisers of, 89, 95n21, 105, 108, 141, 179; drive-instinct in, 142, 179; heterology of, 34, 70n22; as profane, 135, 153; real of, 21, 105, 138, 160–61; Simone's, 50, 63; taboos on, 122n32, 181
Bois, Yve-Alain, and Rosalind Krauss, 93
Boothby, Richard, 10n2, 71n25, 115
Borel, Adrien, 2, 65, 93n12, 150, 168n3, 174; *Story of Eye* and, 5, 47, 51, 53, 176
Breton, André, 2, 6–7, 92n1, 107, 110, 123n43, 150, 161; idealism of, 47, 66, 75–77, 111–13
Brontë, Emily, 8, 131–32, 139
Butler, Judith, 72n36

Caillois, Roger, 41, 42, 69, 71, 109, 112
Calasso, Roberto, 21, 42n31
Camus, Albert, 12n17, 71n29

capitalism, 35–38, 45n51, 101, 116, 164, 166–67, 171, 182; communism and, 9, 45, 149; transgression and, 32, 44n49
castration, 11n12, 26–27, 41n23, 72n38, 105, 145n3; as language, 70n25, 85; morality as, 38, 108; as phallic function, 73n40, 158; as separation, 57, 129; Wolf Man's, 68n14, 147n27
catharsis, 20, 115, 123n45
Cavanagh, Sheila L, 147n27
Char, René, 8, 125, 134–39, 147n26, 181
Christianity, 26, 31–32, 43n37, 44n49, 62, 64, 103, 124n47, 136, 153; ascetic, 39n1, 131, 163; as curse, 16, 56, 102, 109, 118, 133, 138; as denaturing, 69n21, 116; enjoyment in, 42n29, 100; as feudal, 44n43, 90, 182; Jesus, 27, 36, 104, 158; as Plato for masses, 23, 99, 146n10; sin and, 28–29, 89, 175; taboo in, 6, 48, 60, 111. *See also* God
civilization, 22, 27, 37, 102, 105, 119n11, 153; sublimations of, 34, 86, 142, 181
Clark, Maudemarie, 136
class, 33, 35, 63, 102, 155, 159; working, 81, 167, 185n5
College of Sociology, 41n19, 42n30, 69n20, 97, 109, 112, 135; Lacan and, 108
communism, 12n17, 90, 149, 151, 163–66, 170n25; Bataille on, 9, 45n52, 161, 182; revolution in, 112, 156; socialism, 141, 150–51, 156–58, 164–65
consumption, 23, 35, 65, 127, 166, 168, 171n30; as consumerism, 45n51, 100, 116; as expenditure, 18, 36–37
continuity, 1, 61–62, 66; dis-, 31
Contre-Attaque, 108, 112
creativity, 4, 86, 93n12, 102, 137, 140, 146n21; imaginary as, 181, 183; Nietzsche's, 75, 79–80, 88; in

psychoanalysis, 6, 117; transgression as, 7, 141; of writing, 72n34, 125
crime, 60, 64, 87, 93n8, 130, 145n2
Critique Sociale, La, 151, 161, 185n5
cruelty, 21–22, 42, 85, 154, 164–67, 174

Darwinism, 104
Davidson, Donald, 72n40
Dean, Carolyn, 2
death, 29, 31, 34, 62, 66, 73n42, 109, 169n7, 170n18; Bataille's, 8, 48, 60, 71n26, 137, 167, 174; in *Blue of Noon*, 150, 153–62, 182; drive, 3, 10n2, 69, 85, 99–100, 110–12; erotics of, 1–2, 9, 15–16, 63, 68n16, 69n20, 73n40, 83, 98, 139, 181, 183; God's, 81, 106, 113; Plato and, 108, 120n22, 135; in *Story of Eye*, 54, 59, 71n29; as taboo, 28, 55, 87–88, 91, 127; tragic, 23, 78, 115
de Beauvoir, Simone, 42n32
de Chazal, Malcom, 125, 143
de Kesel, Marc, 39n2, 69n17
Deleuze, Gilles, 94n18, 122, 185n5
Democratic Communist Circle, 151, 161
Democritus, 103
denaturalizing, 116, 123n39, 137, 153, 179; Judaeo-Christian-Platonic, 26, 69n19, 89, 99–104, 133–35; Nietzsche on, 95n21, 119n10, 146n16
Derrida, Jacques, 11n9, 94n18
desire, 10n6, 19, 39n2, 41n20, 57, 64, 70n25, 86, 122n32, 145n3, 163; aesthetics and, 125–26, 146n19; analyst's, 90–91; animality in, 38, 87–88, 182; Antigone's, 137, 146n10; Christian, 28–31, 109, 141, 152–53; communist, 164; Dionysian, 100, 105, 179; ethics of, 46n54, 95n19, 115, 134–35, 173; feminine, 69n21, 94n14; Hamlet's, 84–85; happiness in, 127, 129–30, 143; hysteric's, 26–27, 165; in *jouissance*, 114, 116, 123n39; Kinsey and,

33–34; Law and, 15, 41n26, 60–62; Marxist, 161–62; object of, 43n40; passive, 68n14, 133, 144, 158; perverse, 4, 16, 169n7; in poetry, 136, 140; real of, 71n28; in *Story of Eye*, 48, 58; taboo on, 18, 43n42, 56, 175; transgressive, 23, 154; unconscious, 5, 183
Devil, 3, 125, 130, 153; snare of, 31
Dionysos, 5, 26, 83, 89, 100, 152; Apollo and, 21–23, 25, 44n49, 56, 64, 116, 178; devil and, 3, 130, 153; Nietzsche and, 10n2, 69n20, 108, 112, 180
discontents, 85, 105, 123n40, 163
Dodds, E. R., 41n20, 135
Dostoyevsky, Fyodor, 2, 141
dreams, 2, 87, 99, 107, 155
drives, the, 2, 10n1, 45n52, 65, 81, 134, 137–38, 145n8; aesthetics and, 26, 76, 139, 179; affirmation of, 105–10, 112, 118; desire and, 34, 123n50; erotics of, 166, 173; in ethics, 1, 46n54, 115–16; gaze and, 57, 77, 177; partial, 43n40, 52, 68n12, 175; perverse, 4–5, 69n17, 159–61; repression of, 37–38, 42n32, 48, 55–56, 62, 99, 130; satisfaction of, 15–16, 127, 152; sovereignty of, 19–20, 156; sublimation of, 21–22, 85–86, 91–92, 132, 142–44, 147n25, 181–85
dualism, 41n19, 107–8, 117, 135, 158; Christian-Platonic, 23–25, 38, 70n21
Dufresne, Todd, 119n9
Durkheim, Émile, 17, 41n19, 61, 135

economy, 22, 36–38, 45n52, 80, 149, 156, 184; general, 44–45, 171n30; libidinal, 157, 175; political, 164, 167, 173
ecstasy, 19, 69n20, 70n25, 79, 110, 112–13, 131, 136; Dionysian, 22, 115, 130
ego, 10n2, 57, 86, 115, 121n28, 137, 155, 165. *See also* superego

Eleusinian mysteries, 135
Ellis, Havelock, 33
emotion, 34, 56, 85, 103, 131, 136, 159
empiricism, 32, 38, 43n41, 91, 120n19, 121n27, 122n32, 146n21, 180
England, 38, 70, 94, 121, 132, 156, 164
Enlightenment, 7, 44, 90, 106, 150, 170
epistemology, 16, 43, 103, 139–40, 146
eroticizing, 29, 48, 139, 174, 180
eternal return, 77, 80, 86, 112, 178
ethics of the real, 5, 15, 16, 38–39, 46
ethnography and ethnology. *See under* anthropology
Euripides, 20–22, 24–26, 110, 130
evil, 28, 61, 69n17, 75, 80, 167; dualism as, 24–25, 41n19, 70n21, 108; as eye, 64, 89, 111, 158; literature as, 8, 117, 125–27, 130–34, 144, 180–81
existentialism, 7, 113, 179. *See also* Sartre
expenditure, 35, 37, 71n29, 116, 166, 182; as happiness, 127–28, 132, 180; non-productive, 18–19, 45n51, 92, 109–10, 164; as outlet, 153, 168, 183

Falasca-Zamponi, Simonetta, 77, 93n1
fantasy, 50, 53, 72n34, 120n18, 135–36, 165, 170n21; of castration, 68n14, 72n38; Christ as, 101, 139; defensive, 46n54, 123n39; Father as, 27, 41n26, 104; hysteric's, 41n24, 69n21, 145n8; of metaphysics, 43n41, 92, 121n27
fascism, 112, 167, 170n21; as backwards, 90, 154; communism and, 9, 45n52, 147n23, 149–50, 161; as group, 155–56, 159–60; return of, 171n30, 182
father, 17, 31, 41n24, 68n14, 99, 155, 158; Antigone's, 93n8, 129, 145n2; Bataille's, 52–54, 64–65, 176; as Good, 38, 140–41; primal, 26–27, 104
femininity, 27, 31–32, 53, 84–85, 126, 144; in *Blue of Noon*, 150–52, 154, 156–57; feminism on, 41nn23–24, 68n10, 70n21, 70n25, 94n14, 145n8, 165; as Woman, 58, 60, 69n21, 99, 133, 137
festival, 5, 19, 23, 56, 61, 78, 176
feudalism, 23, 44, 156, 164–65, 182
Ffrench, Patrick, 2, 47–48, 50, 54, 71n28, 147n23, 150, 158, 162
foreclosure, 9, 42n32, 69n21, 87, 142, 147n23, 175–76, 181; Christian-Platonic, 44n49, 45n52, 72n36, 116, 141; of the symbolic, 147n27, 178
formalism, 6, 12n15, 43, 48, 50, 71, 133
Foster, Hal, 118n4
Foucault, 11, 51, 70n25, 72n36, 121n28; *Critique* and, 3, 57, 67n4, 71n26
free-association, 7, 107
Freud, Sigmund, works of: "Analysis Terminable and Interminable," 119n11, 124n50; "Autobiographical Study," 98; *Beyond the Pleasure Principle*, 2, 20, 44n45; *Civilization and Its Discontents*, 64, 79, 119n11; "'Civilized' Sexual Morality," 86, 102; "Claims of Psycho-Analysis," 147n25; "Dostoevsky and Parricide," 2; "Dynamics of Transference," 107; *Group Psychology*, 2–3, 9, 61, 104, 155, 159; *History of Infantile Neurosis* [*Wolf Man*], 68n14, 144, 147n27; "History of Psychoanalytic Movement," 11n7, 119n6; "Hysterical Phantasies and Bisexuality," 42n26, 58; *Inhibitions, Symptoms and Anxiety*, 119n7; "Instincts and their Vicissitudes," 179; *Interpretation of Dreams*, 2, 84, 99, 107; *Introductory Lectures*, 2; *Leonardo da Vinci*, 40n7, 78, 102, 130, 178; "Letter to *Jewish Press Centre*, 103; *Moses and Monotheism*, 26, 41n24, 104; *New Introductory Lectures*, 119n7; "On Narcissism," 183; "Remembering, Repeating, Working-Through,"

151; "Repression," 78, 121n30; "Resistances to Psychoanalysis," 9, 103, 165; *Schreber Case*, 72n36, 139; "Tendency to Debasement in Love," 9, 42n33, 43n39, 152–53; *Three Essays on Sexuality*, 42n26, 46n54, 178, 183; *Totem and Taboo*, 2, 26–27, 61; "'Wild' Psychoanalysis," 67n8

gaze, the, 5, 20, 57–60, 64, 71n29, 77; feminist, 41, 70; metaphorized, 48, 65–66, 73, 176–77; as object, 58, 68n12
genealogy, 119n11; of economics, 9, 149, 168; of erotics, 4, 10n6, 16, 38, 44, 55, 65, 173; of morality, 5, 25–26, 28, 42, 61, 99–100, 133; of sacred, 152, 161, 182; of taboo–transgression, 175–77
genital, 18, 30, 49, 52–53, 80, 108, 133, 147n27; worship of, 42–43, 130–31
Gherovici, Patricia, 147n27
gift, 22–23, 35, 109–10, 114, 160, 167, 182, 184n3; Nietzsche as, 70n25, 76, 90; transgression as, 18, 116–17
God, 63, 66, 83, 101, 104–6, 123n39; Calvinist, 36–38, 166; death of, 81, 88, 113; of the Good, 35, 89, 140–41; as whore, 12n15, 69nn20–21, 72n36, 111
gods, 31; and goddesses, 5, 28; as the real, 25–26, 41n20; as sovereign animality, 82, 87, 108; as transgression, 29, 39, 56
Goethe, 104, 120n21, 138
Good, the, 25, 29, 35, 57, 70n21, 137, 145; as capitalist profit, 109, 175; as Icarian, 117, 174; as imaginary, 20, 80, 101, 111, 124n48; Nietzsche on, 5, 16, 112
Gooding-Williams, Robert, 106
goods, service of, 35, 65, 116, 175
Goux, Jean-Joseph, 45n51

Greeks, the, 5, 23, 28, 100, 104–5, 135, 169n15; Dionysianism of, 21–22, 44n49; eroticism of, 42n29, 56, 130, 160; gods of, 24, 31, 83, 87; pre-Platonic, 1, 152, 175, 182; Renaissance and, 107, 121n27; tragic art of, 16, 19, 78, 131, 136, 180. *See also* Hellenism
Greenberg, Clement, 117
Grigg, Russell, 50, 72n40, 138–39, 147n27
Gross, Otto, 105
guilt, 17, 83, 104, 134, 159, 163; Christian, 31, 56; eroticism as, 130, 160

Habermas, Jürgen, 106, 170n21
Halley, Michael, 68n14, 71n29, 72n40, 73
Hamlet, 84–85
happiness, 79, 139–40; evil and, 132–34, 181; literature and, 8, 117, 125–26; two forms of, 127–30, 144, 180
Hecq, Dominique, 129, 145n3
Hegel, 45n52, 94n16, 151, 185n5
Heidegger, 6, 11n9, 12, 34, 50, 67, 93, 147
Hellenism, 28, 32, 42n31, 81, 99, 102–5, 119n8, 124n46, 135; religion of, 3, 24, 39. *See also* the Greeks
Heraclitus, 67n6, 81, 103, 120n19
heterogeneous, 8, 10n6, 111, 155, 157, 184; heterology of, 34, 94n12, 97, 118; the real as, 3–4, 9, 70n25, 126, 173–77
Hewson, Mark, 10n6, 11n11, 70, 73n42
Hollier, Denis, 2–3, 24, 41n19, 47, 65, 68
Hollywood, Amy, 42n32
Homer, 21, 46n54, 105, 142
homogeneity, 70n22, 118n3, 175
Horbury, Alison, 41n23, 73n42, 94n14, 165; on censorious feminism, 69n21, 145n8; on hysteric, 41n24, 68n10
Hume, David, 101, 120n16

Hussey, Andrew, 155
hysteric's discourse, 26–27, 41n24, 68n10, 165; bisexuality of, 42n26, 58; in Lacan's four-discourses, 44n43, 170n26

Icarian complex, 79, 81, 111, 117, 162, 179; Rotten Sun of, 70n23, 77
id, the (*das Es*), 86, 110
idealism, 11n12, 24, 30, 44n49, 102, 122n32, 133, 175–79; in aesthetics, 75–84; atheology and, 112–13; Breton's, 4, 47, 65–66, 92n1, 111; German, 39n1, 185n5; Nietzsche on, 120n18
identification, 59, 66, 68n14, 69, 141, 155
ideology, 24, 38, 43, 61, 68, 70, 75–76, 101, 117, 163; Freud and, 99, 119
imaginary, the, 4, 10n2, 31, 37, 68n10, 101, 116, 137, 161; as aesthetics, 91–92, 141–44, 178, 181–83; castration and, 130, 147n27; ethics and, 16, 69n17; of the Good, 20, 124n48, 170n21, 174; as phallus, 145n3; as religious, 18–19, 42n32, 82; symbolic and real with, 5, 8, 117, 126, 140, 180
incest, 43n39, 78, 84, 128, 131, 137, 143–44, 152; taboos on, 17, 27–28
inner experience, 7, 33, 42, 113, 150, 168, 175; Schreber with Bataille's, 12, 72
instinct, 3, 46, 69, 99–100, 103, 106, 116, 133, 145, 151, 178, 182; as abundance, 80, 138; difference to drive, 142, 147, 179, 181, 185; perversity of, 20–21, 43, 97; Sadean, 59; taboos on, 18, 127, 166
internalization, 59, 66, 100, 119, 155, 165

Johnston, Adrian, 43n41, 119n11
jouissance, 10n6, 38, 72n34, 92, 100, 113, 143, 160; aesthetics as, 114–18, 177; animal roots of, 87, 127, 144; in death, 83, 98, 109–10; erotics of, 166, 173, 183; Marxism and, 9, 147n23; the real and, 76, 118n3, 179, 181–82; taboo and, 47, 66; of transgression, 1–2, 4, 7–8, 15–16, 39n3, 60, 129–30
Joyce, James, 8, 118n3, 129, 140–41
Judaism, 99–104, 135; Moses, 26–27, 41; Yahweh, 28, 37, 45n49, 141, 175
Jung, Carl, 105

Kant, 38–39, 44n49, 117, 120n21, 121, 139; in aesthetics, 8, 125–26, 129, 137–38, 146n15, 180; with Sade, 60–62
Kendall, Stuart, 2, 32, 94n13, 113, 123n43, 145n9, 161, 168n3, 169n10; on *Blue of Noon*, 150–51, 157, 169nn6–7
Kennedy, Kevin, 93n1, 124, 147, 177, 185
Klossowski, Pierre, 4
knowledge, 11n2, 27, 34–35, 59, 72, 103, 126, 173; Dionysian, 21, 108, 116; of drives, 37, 56, 161; heterological, 97, 118; psychoanalytic, 3, 10n6, 139, 144, 165; self-, 59, 173; sexual, 26, 32, 66, 141–42, 175; symbolic as, 17, 180–82

Lacan, Jacques, works of:
"Aggressiveness in Psychoanalysis," 40n10; "L'étourdit," 42n28; "Freudian Thing," 43n41; "Function and Field of Speech and Language," 6, 17, 34; "Instance of the Letter," 5, 50, 51, 64, 73n40; "Kant with Sade," 60–61, 72n34, 137; "Metaphor of the Subject," 73n40; "Mirror Stage as Formative," 40n10, 70n24; "Question Prior to Any Possible Treatment," 72n36; "Reflections on the Ego," 123n44; "Response

to Jean Hyppolite's Commentary," 139; *Seminar I*, 91, 99, 109, 146n10; *Seminar III*, 18, 51, 73; *Seminar V*, 87, 110; *Seminar VI*, 84–85; *Seminar VII*, 1, 15–16, 19, 29–30, 35, 37, 39n3, 46n54, 57, 61, 67, 85, 93n8, 95n19, 108, 118n3, 127, 131, 137, 174; *Seminar VIII*, 19–20, 23, 25–26, 36–37, 41n23, 102, 115, 141, 166, 175; *Seminar X*, 18, 55, 114, 116, 129, 174; *Seminar XI*, 23, 25, 52, 57, 64, 77, 85–87, 91; *Seminar XIII*, 52, 55; *Seminar XVII*, 18, 26–28, 30, 34–35, 41n21, 41n26, 52, 57, 66, 76, 85, 103–4, 118, 128, 133, 141; *Seminar XIX*, 158; *Seminar XX*, 47, 68n10, 69n21, 94n14, 103–4, 133; *Seminar XXIII*, 114, 118n3, 129, 140; *Talking to Brick Walls*, 3, 11n12; *Television*, 68n14; "Trans. of *Logos*," 67n6; *Triumph of Religion*, 31, 42n34, 72n34, 145nn6–8

laceration, 28, 31, 70, 85

lack, 38, 58, 64, 70n25, 85, 103, 176–79, 184n3; abundance and, 7, 75–76, 78, 80, 146n19; animality as, 87, 139, 175; castration as, 57, 145n3; Christian, 35, 104; happiness and, 128, 132; Kant's, 61, 138; real as, 101, 117; *ressentiment* as, 122n32, 146n21; sexual relation as, 68n10. *See also* abundance

Lamarckism, 104

language, 67n6, 86, 99, 110, 136; as castration, 70n25, 85; eroticism and, 48–50, 129, 143; the symbolic as, 17, 91; taboo and transgression and, 15, 61

Lascaux, 4, 82–83, 86–87, 94, 108, 178

laughter, 128, 157

Laure, 150–51, 168n2

Leiris, Michel, 41n19, 42n30, 67n4, 69n20, 123n43, 150, 168n4, 169n6

Leiter, Brian, 104

Leonardo da Vinci, 102, 178

Lévi-Strauss, Claude, 17, 27–28, 41n25

libido, 26, 46n54, 87, 132, 179–80, 184; Christianity and, 102–3, 153, 160–61; polymorphous drives of, 52, 108, 173, 183; in *Story of Eye*, 59, 66

linguistics, 5, 48–54, 65, 94, 99, 136, 176

literature, 8, 23, 51, 111, 117, 143–44, 165, 181; evil in, 72n34, 130–34; happiness in, 125–29, 180; poetry and, 135–40; Sartre on, 12n17, 142

Luther, Martin, 35–36, 106

Maquet, Jean, 141

Marshall Plan, the, 167

Marx, 11, 45, 85, 99, 141; in *Blue of Noon*, 151, 156–66; *jouissance* and, 9, 147

masochism, 38, 44n45, 62, 114, 118n3, 129, 132, 158

Masson, André, 112, 143, 181

materialism, 24, 80, 111, 175

math, 43n41, 70n23, 77, 80, 85, 91, 103

Mauss, Marcel, 17–18, 22–23, 40, 41, 61, 175; transgression and, 71n27, 109, 135

McGowan, Todd, 57, 70n25

memory, 33, 52, 54, 65, 85, 169, 176, 182

metaphor, 25, 28, 72, 94, 136, 177; *Blue of Noon* and, 153–54, 160; return of repressed as, 4, 19, 162, 176; in *Story of Eye*, 5–6, 38, 47–66, 75, 95, 111, 122

metonymy, 5, 57, 64–65, 70, 71n26, 80, 94n16; in *Story of Eye*, 48–51

Métraux, Alfred, 67n4

Miller, Jacques-Alain, 3, 12n15

Millot, Catherine, 12n15

modernism, 105–6, 111, 117; Nietzsche-Freud influence on, 7–8, 97–98; *post-*, 110, 122n32; surrealist, 113, 125, 180

Molinier, Pierre, 169n7

moralism, 16, 22, 39, 61, 106, 133, 146, 174; Lazare's, 160, 182–83; slave, 44, 90; Western, 91, 109, 173–74
mother, 56–57, 68n14, 85, 145n3, 151–52, 156–57; Bataille's, 53–54, 65, 68n16, 169n7, 176; taboos on, 26, 145n8
mysticism, 4, 6, 42n32, 103, 120n19, 155, 170n16, 185n5; *Accursed Share* and, 183–84; atheology and, 112–13, 168n1
myth, 25, 46n54, 47, 108–10, 113–14, 125, 152; belief in, 123n39, 184; father as, 27, 41n24, 42n26; Hades-Persephone, 41n23, 73n42, 135; metaphysical, 39n1, 146n21; pre-Platonic, 16, 175

nature, 3, 9, 22, 46n54, 69n21, 114, 118, 122n37, 161, 176, 179, 185n5; beauty and ugly in, 77–78; Christianity and, 28, 89–90, 123n39; moralism and, 16, 26, 30, 67n6, 68n14, 108, 123n39, 138, 173; Palaeolithic transition from, 17–20, 27, 40n5, 42n27, 70n25; in post-modernism, 121n32; the real of, 62; sexual relation in, 33, 43n39, 80, 133
neurosis, 25, 40n9, 99, 102, 128, 144, 153, 155, 159; art as, 84, 129, 142; inner catastrophes, of, 29, 81, 134; moralizing as, 39n1, 112, 116–17, 174; sublimation and, 86, 161, 177–78
Newman, Michael, 14
Nietzsche, Friedrich, works of: *Anti-Christ*, 26, 28, 44n49, 89, 99, 103, 105–6, 119n10, 121n27, 133, 138, 146n21; *Beyond Good and Evil*, 16, 23, 35, 41n23, 99, 102, 120n18, 178; *Birth of Tragedy*, 5, 20–22, 24–25, 56, 76, 115–16, 130, 136, 175; *Case of Wagner*, 93n2; *Ecce Homo*, 95n20, 99, 108, 173; *Gay Science*, 76, 102, 105, 120n18, 122n32, 138,

184n3; *Genealogy of Morals*, 5, 8, 31, 35, 46, 61, 90, 93n2, 100–102, 105, 111, 119n11, 121n27, 126, 131, 142, 163, 166, 170n22; *Thus Spoke Zarathustra*, 141; *Twilight of the Idols*, 1, 19–20, 22–23, 26, 35, 93n2, 101, 103, 106, 108, 111–12, 115–16, 120nn18–21, 121n27, 129, 146n21, 173; *Will to Power*, 6, 20, 25, 78–80, 88, 90, 93n2, 102–3, 105, 119n10, 129, 138, 184n3
nihilism, 45n52, 89, 106, 116; aesthetics and, 80, 92, 179; ascetic as, 35, 119n11; Schopenhauer's, 39n1, 112, 122n39
Nobus, Danny, 60–61, 71–72nn30–34, 137
Noys, Benjamin, 2, 10n6, 11n12, 57, 69n20, 70n25, 94n12, 121n32, 123n43; on Dworkin, 67n10; on Goux, 45n51

object, 18, 25, 62, 64, 69n21, 137, 145n3, 146n15; as object *a*, 34, 43n40, 86, 116; in science, 90; in *Story of Eye*, 52; in sublimation, 39n2, 147n25; time as, 112
obsessional, 69n16, 111, 144, 150, 152, 154, 160, 182
Oedipus, 52–53, 84, 93n8, 145n3, 170n26; Bataille's, 68n14, 71n28; as Christian, 26–28, 64, 104; Nietzsche on, 16, 129
Ons, Silvia, 100
oral, 18, 52, 68n12, 108, 109
Orphism, 135

Palaeolithic era, 104; birth of art in, 6–7, 75, 81–82, 85–86, 97, 177–79; transition in, 4, 16, 42n29, 89, 175, 184
Pericles, 103, 105, 120n22
Perroux, François, 167, 171nn29–30
perversion, 25, 31, 61, 63, 64, 72n36, 85, 158–59; Bataille's inscription

of, 4, 47, 66n1, 69n21, 75, 111–12; capitalist, 100, 116–17; fascism as, 156, 162–63; libido as, 18, 46n54, 69n17; sexual relation as, 52, 134; sublimation and, 5, 177–78, 183; as transgression, 128, 137
phallus, 68n10, 68n14, 73n40, 87, 136, 145n3, 158, 162; in *Story of Eye*, 48–54
Picasso, Pablo, 77
Piel, Jean, 44n45
Plato, works of: *Gorgias*, 19; *Phaedo*, 135–36; *Republic*, 57, 135, 142, 147; *Symposium*, 25, 146n16
Platonism, 12n16, 35, 44n43, 82, 122n32, 175, 180; as ascetic, 46n54, 166; Christian, 99, 107; as denaturalizing, 116, 153; inflationary of, 94n16, 124n48, 146; Nietzsche on, 2, 23–24
pleasure, 1–2, 16, 20, 39n3, 57, 78, 83; Christianity and, 44n45, 100; literature and, 125, 127–29, 143; sexual, 69, 166
poetry, 65–66, 132, 137–40, 147n24, 136; prose and, 8, 125, 134, 142–43
politics, 38, 91, 147n23, 164–67, 181–84; art and, 8–9, 117, 124, 141, 144, 173–74, 177; in *Blue of Noon*, 149, 154–55
pornography, 48, 58, 67n10, 68n16, 71n28
positivism, 32–33, 101–2, 119, 120, 175
post-structuralism. *See under* structuralism
potlatch, 22–23, 35, 109, 116
Prévert, Jacques, 8, 125, 134–36, 140, 181
profane, 24, 36, 41n19, 114, 135, 153
prohibition. *See under* taboo
psychoanalysis, 7, 43n41, 67n8, 123, 132, 145n8, 155, 161, 170n25; Bataille and, 1–4, 45n52, 151; ethics and, 15, 29, 173–74; Lacan and, 121n28, 133; Nietzsche and, 8, 76, 81, 88, 92, 97–100, 105, 114, 116, 119n11, 125, 179–80; resistances to, 103, 165–66; in *Story of Eye*, 47–48, 51
psychosis, 72n36, 135, 174
puritan structure, 24, 38, 42n29, 108, 158, 182; Christian, 46n54, 100, 111, 175; feminist, 68n10, 69n21, 94n14
Pythagoras, 43n41, 135

real, the, 3, 21, 33, 40n9, 44n49, 124n48, 147n27, 157; aesthetics and, 8, 76–78, 81, 86, 88, 90–92, 126, 177–80; affirmation of, 105, 107–8, 110–12; in Bataille-Lacan, 11n12, 24, 31, 94n12, 97; as erotic, 5–6, 15–19, 62, 173–75; ethics of, 7, 38, 39nn1–2, 45n52, 46n54, 181–82; feminism and, 68, 69, 70, 145; gods as, 25–26, 72n36, 153; as *jouissance*, 114–16, 118n3, 129–30; in poetry, 134, 136–37, 144; in *Story of Eye*, 48, 55–60, 64–66, 68n14, 71n26, 71nn28–29, 73n40; sublimation of, 123n39, 138–41; symbolic-imaginary and, 101, 117; transgression and, 4, 28
reason, 32–34, 84, 101, 107, 133–34, 166, 168n1; animality in, 85, 87; in *Blue of Noon*, 150, 167; Enlightenment, 7, 97; fascism and, 9, 155; Kant and, 120n21, 121n27, 139; moralism and, 70n21, 89, 129–30; poetry and, 136, 143–44; politics as, 178, 181–83; the symbolic as, 17, 91; taboo as, 25, 56, 141
Reich, Wilhelm, 105
religion, 11n11, 43n38, 101, 103, 121n24, 136, 140; *Acéphale* as, 183–84; animal in, 82, 83, 178; Christian, 29, 31; as denaturalizing, 69n19, 131; dualist, 23–24, 117; in Durkheim-Mauss, 71n27, 135; erotic in, 5, 45, 55, 72n36; surrealist, 92n1, 107–8, 114; taboo–transgression in, 17, 28, 47

Renaissance, 102, 106–8, 120n21, 121n27
repetition, 2, 45n52, 57; as eternal return, 112, 122n38; as parricide, 26–27, 103–4; as taboo–transgression, 20, 95n19
repression, 20, 39n1, 40n9, 103–4, 146, 155; in aesthetics, 4, 78, 82, 84–86, 179; in *Blue of Noon*, 151, 153, 158–62; Lacan on, 109, 121n30; in literature, 125, 130, 135–38, 144; Nietzsche on, 81, 100, 102, 105, 112, 116; in *Story of Eye*, 47–48, 57–59, 64; in sublimation, 45, 183; in taboo–transgression, 10n6, 18, 21, 25–29, 31, 38, 61, 175–76, 178
ressentiment, 28, 80, 121, 122, 146
revaluation: of all values, 5, 16, 99, 103, 106, 118, 173; *Birth of Tragedy* as, 116; Hellenism as, 119n8; Orphism and, 135
revolution, 44, 114, 134, 181; bourgeois, fascist, communist, 37, 112, 154–58, 161, 164–66; Lazare's, 145n9, 151, 159; Nietzsche's, 39n1, 44n49, 173
Richardson, Michael, 10n1, 37, 40n8, 41, 41n22, 45n52, 72n35, 93n11, 145n1, 156, 175; on postmodern, 11n11, 121, 122; on surrealism, 92n1, 110, 113, 123
Richardson, William, 67n6
Rimbaud, Arthur, 141, 143, 169n6
Ritschl, Friedrich, 40n14
Rohde, Erwin, 21, 40n14, 135
romanticism, 131
Roudinesco, Elisabeth, 3, 11n10, 15n12, 42n29, 93n12, 108, 118nn2–4, 121n24
Russell, Jared, 11n9, 81, 94n18, 122n38
Ruti, Mari, 39n2

sacred, the, 19, 41n19, 45n52, 56, 62–63, 69n20, 112; aesthetics as, 66, 77, 83, 87, 92; animal, 38, 69n21; *Blue of Noon* and, 152–53, 156, 159–61; genealogy of, 37, 107–8, 124n46, 175–76, 182, 184n3; literature and, 130, 135, 137, 139–40; transgressive, 16, 23–24, 28, 31–32, 35, 47, 61, 118n3
sacrifice, 20, 28, 42n35, 53, 62, 71n25, 87, 98, 140, 176; as expenditure, 22, 35
Sade, 5–6, 69n20, 71n29, 72n34, 118n3, 131, 176; *Story of Eye* and, 47–48, 59–62, 65–66; in surrealism, 77, 122, 157
Sartre, 7, 12n17, 42n32, 113, 123n43, 142, 147n26, 179. *See also* existentialism
Sass, Louis, 117
Saussure, Ferdinand de, 51
Schiller, Friedrich von, 107
Schopenhauer, 30, 39n1, 93n9, 98, 105, 112, 122n39
science, 5, 16, 49, 57, 90, 141–42, 166; Bataille and, 10n6, 168n1; Freud and, 98–102, 119, 147n25; heterology and, 3, 94n12, 97, 118n3; Kinsey and, 32–34, 39; Lacan and, 35–36, 43n41, 117; Nietzsche and, 103, 106, 120n18, 123n39; symbolic as, 180–81, 183; taboo and, 43n42, 175
senses, 4, 16, 25, 46, 120n19, 133, 136–37
sexuality, 32, 60, 68n10, 79, 84, 105, 153, 158; Bataille and, 1–2, 117, 174; bi-, 42nn26–27, 58, 147n27; Christian, 30, 124n47; death and, 98, 161; Freud and, 46n54, 130; homo-, 31, 101; taboo on, 16–17, 88, 91; trans-, 147n27
sexual relation, 66, 68n10, 69n21, 80, 133; castration and, 27, 30, 52, 85
sinthome, 140–41, 144, 147n27
Skelton, Ross, 94n16
socialism. *See under* communism
sociology, 11n11, 27, 45n52; College of, 41n19, 42n30, 69n20, 97, 108–9,

112; of Mauss-Durkheim, 17, 135, 151
Socrates, 102–5, 110, 175; dualism in, 89, 108, 146; incompetence in, 5, 16, 19–20, 22–26, 28, 44n49, 130, 141; transference to, 115–16, 123n45
Soler, Colette, 11n12, 141
Sollers, Philippe, 3, 67n4
Sontag, Susan, 71n28
Sophists, 102–3, 105
Sophocles, 84, 93, 128, 134, 136, 145, 170
Souvarine, Boris, 151
sovereignty, 20, 26, 29, 70, 92, 109, 137–38, 168, 173; aesthetic, 76, 177–78, 185; bourgeois, 38, 163; feudal, 9, 44, 156, 182; Nietzschean, 3, 6–7, 88–90, 107, 179; of the real, 128–29, 160, 183
Spiteri, Raymond, 111, 123n40
split-subject, 32, 149, 163
Stalin, Joseph, 151, 164, 167
Stein, Andrew, 69n20, 162, 168n1, 170n21
Stoekl, Allan, 77, 81, 92n1, 150, 168n3
structuralism, 3, 5, 42n27, 51, 54, 94n18; Lacan's, 43n41, 50; post-, 11n11, 110
sublimation, 111, 142, 161–62, 170n26, 173, 181; aesthetics as, 76, 81, 85–86, 139, 177–80; drive-instinct in, 147n25, 185n6; in ethics, 7, 38, 39nn1–2, 45n52, 46n54, 100; repression in, 102, 183; transgression in, 56, 137–38; weak-strong, 94n17, 123n39, 146n19
Suleiman, Susan, 67n10, 68n14, 71
superego, 37, 39n1, 69n21, 155, 158–59; Nietzsche and, 61, 100, 119n11; in *Story of Eye*, 48, 66, 111. *See also* ego
surrealism, 41n19, 93n11, 169n7, 177; Bataille's, 4, 6, 75–76, 81, 92n1, 121n32, 123n40, 123n43; Breton's, 150, 157, 161; Lacan's, 117, 118n4;

modernist, 7–8, 92, 97–98, 105–14, 125, 179–80; poetic, 134, 141–43; *Story of Eye* and, 47–48, 65–66, 176
Surya, Michel, 39n4
symbolic, the, 17–18, 61, 117–18, 144; foreclosure of, 147n27, 178; Good and, 21, 25, 40n9, 124n48, 170n21; with real and imaginary, 8, 91–92, 138–41, 180
symptom, 21–23, 31, 44n49, 91, 130, 144, 160, 165, 179, 182; Father as, 27, 104; idealist, 4, 39n1; Joycean, 129, 140; as metaphor, 58, 65; repressed as, 18, 85, 105, 112, 178; *ressentiment* in, 122n32

taboo, 10n6, 70n25, 71n27, 109–10, 122, 135; aesthetics and, 75–76, 114; animality and, 81–83, 91, 93n11, 112; in *Blue of Noon*, 153, 156–57, 161–62; Christian, 6, 95n19, 124n47; Dionysos and, 44n49, 89, 108, 116–17; erotic, 1, 4–5, 173–84; in literature, 125, 127–30, 132, 134, 139–41, 144; as prohibition, 1, 28, 43n40, 61, 88, 92; in *Story of Eye*, 47–48, 55–63, 66, 111; and transgression, 7–8, 11n11, 15–39; as work, 40n5, 43n42, 45n52, 145n5
Tawney, Richard H, 36, 44n46, 166
theology, 37, 101–3, 121n27, 124n48, 133; atheology, 113, 168n1, 183
Thing, the, 81, 86, 105, 116, 121n27; in ethics, 35, 69n17; structuralist, 43n41, 64–65, 176; in sublimation, 39n2, 86, 137–38, 142, 177–78, 181
Thucydides, 103, 105, 111, 120n22
Timofeeva, Oxana, 11n6
totality, 19, 28, 31, 92, 132, 139–40, 179
tragedy, 128, 131, 136, 149; Dionysos in, 56, 145n2, 180; Nietzsche and, 69n20, 70n25, 76, 78, 89, 115–17; Socrates on, 5, 19–24, 44n49, 105, 130, 141, 175

transcendence, 19, 30–31, 69n17, 133, 137, 153, 155; dualist, 24, 41, 70, 135
transference, 23, 84, 115, 151
transgression, 69n21, 70n25, 175–82; in aesthetics, 75, 83, 87, 91–92; Capitalist, 32, 35, 124n46; Christian, 26–31, 42n29, 95n19, 153; *jouissance* of, 1, 4, 15, 39n3, 98, 118n3; in literature, 127–41, 144; Mauss and, 71n27, 145n5; Nietzsche and, 88–89, 93n11; in (post)modernism, 11n11, 108–10, 112, 114, 116–17, 122; science and, 33, 43n42; in *Story of Eye*, 47–50, 54–58, 60–63, 66; with taboo, 5, 7–8, 10n6, 16, 18, 20, 38–39, 173–74; in tragedy, 21–25, 93n8; Žižek and, 44n49, 45n52
trauma, 2, 20, 33, 65

Übermensch (Overman), 104
unconscious, the, 39, 51, 68, 76, 94, 145, 155, 161, 175, 183; aesthetics and, 91–92, 141–42, 178; Christian-Platonic, 27, 40, 119n10, 120n19; debasement and, 153, 159–60; ethics and, 5, 15, 23, 134, 146; happiness and, 128, 130; as language, 67, 86; primitivity and, 108, 115; science and, 33–34, 57, 99; *Story of Eye* and, 54, 65, 176–77
utility, 23, 36, 45n52, 50, 86, 88–90, 109–10, 181; aesthetics and, 76, 91, 117; economy and, 44n45, 164

Vanderwees, Chris, 11n12
violence, 9, 28, 35, 92n1, 97, 154, 177; Capitalist, 37–38, 44n49, 175–76;
dualist, 22, 25; literature and, 127, 131–32, 134, 181; nature as, 16–17; Sade's, 72n34; sex and, 2, 159, 161; *Story of Eye* and, 5–6, 48, 55–60, 63, 66, 67n10, 71n29, 95n19; superego as, 100; in *W.C.*, 150; Yahweh as, 26–27

Wagner, Robert, 93
war, 18, 105, 109, 120, 149, 154, 162, 166
waste, 37, 45n51, 109, 117, 166, 175
Weber, Max, 35, 37, 44n48, 124n46, 175
Weil, Simone, 145n9, 151, 170n16
Weiss, Allen S, 93n1
will to power, 70n25, 99, 100, 122n38, 138; as art, 6, 78; as Dionysos, 112
work, 27, 87, 90, 109–10, 178; Christian God as, 83–84; happiness and, 127–29; as politics, 141, 183; Protestant, 35–37, 101, 166, 175; sex, 62, 184n3; symbolic as, 91, 117–18, 144, 180–81; taboo as, 17, 19, 23–25, 33, 43, 57, 112, 140
Wuthering Heights, 131–32. *See also* Brontë, Emily

Yahweh. *See under* Judaism

Zafiropoulos, Marcos, 17
Žižek, Slavoj, 39n2, 44n49, 45n52
Zupančič, Alenka, 43n43, 106, 121n27, 123n39, 138; ascetic ideal and, 44n45, 45n52; on Calvinism, 44n48, 101; ethics in, 39nn1–2, 46n54; Lacan-Nietzsche in, 38, 42n29, 46n53, 100

About the Author

Dr Tim Themi
PhD (Philosophy & Psychoanalysis), Deakin University
BA Hons (Philosophy), La Trobe University
BENG Hons (Chemical), University of Melbourne

Tim Themi is a PhD in Philosophy and Psychoanalysis from Deakin who also holds honours degrees in Philosophy from La Trobe and in the Engineering Sciences from Melbourne. His doctoral dissertation bringing together Lacan and Nietzsche was supervised by leading Lacan scholar, translator, and psychoanalyst Russell Grigg, and presented at the seminar of the Lacan Circle of Australia. He is the author of *Lacan's Ethics and Nietzsche's Critique of Platonism* (SUNY, 2014), along with numerous refereed articles, and teaches in the School of Culture and Communication at The University of Melbourne.

www.ingramcontent.com/pod-product-compliance
Lightning Source LLC
Chambersburg PA
CBHW062220300426
44115CB00012BA/2157